Thomas Hardy

THE MAYOR OF CASTERBRIDGE

Thomas Hardy

THE MAYOR OF CASTERBRIDGE

[Edited with Complete Introduction, Biography, Author's Background, Complete Text, Study Questions, Select Criticism and Bibliography]

Misha Kandhari
M.A., M. Phil. English,
Delhi University

ANMOL PUBLICATIONS PVT. LTD.
NEW DELHI - 110 002 (INDIA)

ANMOL PUBLICATIONS PVT. LTD.

H.O.: 4374/4B, Ansari Road, Darya Ganj,
New Delhi-110 002 (India)
Ph.: 23278000, 23261597

B.O.: No. 1015, Ist Main Road, BSK IIIrd Stage
IIIrd Phase, IIIrd Block
Bangalore - 560 085 (India)
Visit us at: www.anmolpublications.com

The Mayor of Casterbridge

First Published, 2009

PRINTED IN INDIA

Printed at Mehra Offset Press, Delhi.

Contents

Preface

Thomas Hardy, (June 2, 1840 – January 11, 1928) was an English novelist, short story writer, and poet of the naturalist movement, though he saw himself as a poet and wrote novels mainly for financial gain only. The bulk of his work, set mainly in the semi-imaginary county of Wessex, delineates characters struggling against their passions and circumstances. Hardy's poetry, first published in his fifties, has come to be as well regarded as his novels, especially after The Movement of the 1950s and 1960s.

The Mayor of Casterbridge (1886) is a tragic novel by English author Thomas Hardy subtitled, "The Life and Death of a Man of Character". It is set in the fictional town of Casterbridge (based on the town of Dorchester in Dorset). The book is one of Hardy's Wessex novels, all set in a fictional rustic England.

Author

Chapter 1

Introduction

Thomas Hardy was born on June 2, 1840, in Higher Bockhampton in Dorset, a rural region of southwestern England that was to become the focus of his fiction. The child of a builder, Hardy was apprenticed at the age of sixteen to John Hicks, an architect who lived in the city of Dorchester. The location would later serve as the model for Hardy's fictional Casterbridge.

Although he gave serious thought to attending university and entering the church, a struggle he would dramatize in his novel Jude the Obscure, declining religious faith and lack of money led Hardy to pursue a career in writing instead. He spent nearly a dozen years toiling in obscurity and producing unsuccessful novels and poetry. Far from the Madding Crowd, published in 1874, was the author's first critical and financial success. Finally able to support himself as a writer, Hardy married Emma Lavinia Gifford later that year.

Although he built a reputation as a successful novelist, Hardy considered himself first and foremost a poet. To him, novels were primarily a means of earning a living. Like many of his contemporaries, he first published his novels in periodic installments in magazines or serial journals, and his work reflects the conventions of serialization. To ensure that readers would buy a serialized novel, writers often structured each installment to be something of a cliffhanger, which explained the convoluted, often incredible plots of many such Victorian novels. But Hardy cannot solely be labeled a Victorian novelist. Nor can he be categorized simply as a Modernist, in the tradition of writers like Virginia Woolf or D. H. Lawrence, who were determined to explode the conventions of nineteenth-century literature and build a new kind of novel in its place. In many respects, Hardy was trapped in the middle ground between the nineteenth and twentieth centuries, between Victorian sensibilities and more modern ones, and between tradition and innovation.

In June of 1883, Thomas Hardy and his wife Emma settled into their new home in Dorchester. The Hardys had spent the last few years traveling about England, although they wanted to settle down and perhaps begin a family. Finally, Hardy and Emma decided to return to Dorchester. This town, located only a few miles from his birthplace of Upper Bockhampton, was long important to Hardy—he attended school there in his youth, and later he was apprenticed as a young architect there.

Now Hardy had returned home, and he was there to stay, as he proved through his attempts to become part of the town. He quickly built his home, Max Gate, in town. He also became interested in the issues important to the townspeople, such as the status of the labourers. He eagerly read historical records from the area, savoring the "really valuable and curious" Records of the Town of Weymouth. Despite his efforts to return to the community, however, Hardy's first love was his writing. Although he had written various short stories, he had not written a new novel in three years.

Hardy had long wanted to write a novel that combined his love of history with his love of Dorsetshire. In addition, he wanted to capitalize on the success of the Wessex setting from his earlier novels. His desire to immerse himself in the history of the region led him to examine the files of the Dorsetshire County Chronicle in the spring of 1884. In these files, he found an article describing the sale of a wife by an auction. The article about the wife-sale provided him with a spectacular situation for his characters.

After spending several weeks immersed in research, Hardy began to write the novel that would become The Mayor of Casterbridge in the summer of 1884. He wrote it in bursts, constantly writing and putting it aside until he finally completed the novel on April 17, 1885. The literary magazine Graphic agreed to publish the novel serially, although with misgivings. The publishers wanted to see everything before it was published, since Hardy was known for his ability to offend everyone, even atheists. Hardy felt so constrained by the Graphic's demands that he alluded to their heavy-handed treatment in the courtroom scene: Stubberd substitutes all the curse words with letters, to the annoyance of the court. Nevertheless, Hardy's novel eventually began its serialization on January 2, 1886. On May 10 of the same year, The Mayor of Casterbridge was published in two volumes. Although the critics loved Hardy's realism and poetic style, most agreed that the novel was too improbable and too shocking—opinions that would only increase as Hardy continued to write novels.

The Mayor of Castrbridge is set in the county of Wessex, a land that has relied on the beliefs of the farming folk for centuries. Because the farmers are more connected to the land, they follow a more primal religion, based on the changing of the seasons and the forces of Nature. One of the forces of nature is cruel Fate, that "sinister intelligence bent upon punishing" which stops at nothing to keep things from being "as you wish it." This fate usually works through two channels: chance and irony. Chance often brings chraracters:

Farfrae and Lucetta are brought to Casterbridge quite unexpectedly, but their arrivals ruin the lives of the Henchards. Irony works upon the people who are already there, making the best laid plans go awry. Just as Michael convinces Elizabeth-Jane that she is his daughter, he finds the note from Susan that tells the truth. Nature also serves to assist Fate—the harvest weather is bad until Michael buys all the ruined grain at high prices and cannot sell it back. With the actions of a primal and unchanging world working against the weak human, life becomes a series of pains, punctuated only by flashes of happiness.

Yet it is not completely the whims of fate that bring the characters to their downfall. When The Mayor of Casterbridge was first published in serial form, Hardy wrote, "It is not improbabilities of incident but improbabilities of character that matter." This is the basic theme of the novel, which has the additional title, "The Story of a Man of Character." Fate may create the situations for the characters, but in the end their personalities determine how they will react. Michael gains a true confidant in Farfrae, but his quick temper and mercurial ways only serve to push the young man away. Michael's pride keeps him from confessing whatever secret he has at the time. Lucetta's reckless nature causes her to do dangerous things for love. The gossiping nature of the townspeople is responsible for the skimmity ride that kills Lucetta, and the gossip that ruins Michael's career. Even Elizabeth-Jane's prudishness pushes Michael away for the first and last time. Character is just as responsible for the foibles of mankind as Fate is.

The Mayor of Casterbridge is a tragedy, in the tradition of the Greek tragedies and the plays Othello and King Lear. However, the novel still ends with a hope for humanity. The belief that fate is to blame is a tool of the past, of the superstitious farmers such as the townspeople. When Michael believes that fate is destroying him, his problems continue. Only when Michael looks into the future by casting off old beliefs is he able to change. When he sacrifices duty for love of Elizabeth-Jane, he becomes more aware of his feelings as an individual. That is humaity's only way to escape the pain of life: by relying on present instead of past, character instead of fate, the individual instead of the multitude.

Chapter 2

Historical Context

The Victorian Era when Hardy lived was a time of great change. Queen Victoria ruled England from1837 until her death in 1901. During her 63-year reign, England became the most powerful and wealthiest country in the world through its colonial acquisition and by harnessing the power of the Industrial Revolution. The population in England doubled during Victoria's reign, and the economy of the country changed from agriculture-based to industry-based. More people were enfranchised (that is, given the right to vote) and, through this, gained influence in government. The Parliament passed labour laws that improved labour conditions, established universal schooling for all children, and reformed the civil service system. Britain ended restrictions on foreign trade, opening the way for the island to become a source for both raw materials and finished goods to an ever-increasing international market.

Victoria, interested in the welfare of her people, worked hard to pass meaningful reforms, and she earned the respect of her subjects. Her prime ministers were her greatest assets, and with them, Queen Victoria decreased the powers of the monarchy to empower the members of the prime minister's cabinet. As a result, the British monarchy has been able to endure, unlike the monarchies in most other countries.

The changes that occurred during the Victorian era affected the lives of every person living in England in both great and small ways. As England quickly moved from an agriculture-based society to one that would produce many of the world's goods, factories replaced individual workshops, and people moved from small towns to large cities in search of work. Mobility and the transport of goods were increased with the invention of steamships and the development of a railway system. The balance of traditional class distinctions shifted as more people prospered, amassing wealth and power that had been unthinkable in the years prior to this era. These tumultuous changes resulted in an examination of the traditional ways of thinking and acting, and the foundations of English society—family, religion, class divisions, and so on—came under increasing scrutiny.

One area that was particularly affected by the changes in England was religion. The Church of England was traditionally conservative and offered a literal interpretation of the Bible. During the Victorian period, however, as people began to see the church as an agent for social change as well as an agent for personal salvation, the question became how—and even whether—the church should best fulfill these missions. The result was a schism in the church that fostered three movements: the High Church movement, the Middle Church movement, and the Low Church movement.

The High Church movement was designed to align the Church of England with the "Catholic" side of Anglicanism. The thinking here was that traditional practices were the standard by which faith could be expressed and that supreme authority resided in the Church. The Middle Church movement cared less for tradition and believed that faith could be expressed in various ways, including through social action. The Low Church Movement believed that evangelicals were a force that could reform the church from within and without. Individual and biblical bases of faith were hallmarks of this movement. Evangelicals tackled serious issues of the day: housing and welfare of the poor, as well as social reform. They also believed in spreading the gospel around the world by any means necessary.

The growing reliance on science to explain the nature of man and his relationship with his world opened the doors for further examination of traditionally held beliefs. The publication of Darwin's Origin of Species (1859), which suggested that species evolved from common ancestors that could be found through scientific research, challenged the belief that God created each species individually and separately from every other species. The agnostic movement, which relied on scientific evidence and reason to find universal truths and which held that the existence of God could not be empirically proven, took hold and gained momentum.

From these ideological splits, religious liberals and conservatives battled over fundamental questions of faith and religious practice. In Hardy's work, we can see that this debate was one that he entered into. In Tess of the d'Urbervilles, Hardy's protagonist finds herself in a world where she questions religion, questions faith, looks for meaning in life, and searches for the truths that mankind has sought for centuries.

Chapter 3

Biography

About the Author

Formative Years

Thomas Hardy was born in Higher Bockhampton, Dorset, England on June 2, 1840, the eldest son of Thomas Hardy and Jemima (Hand) Hardy. His father was a stonemason and builder; his mother passed on her love of reading and books to her son. Hardy had somewhat of an isolated life on the open fields of the region. He grew up living and examining rural life, which figures prominently in many of his novels. His primary school education lasted until he was sixteen, at which time he was sent to an apprenticeship with John Hicks, a local architect.

Early Career

By 1862, when he was 22, Hardy left for London to work as a draftsman in the office of Arthur Blomfield. While in London, Hardy was influenced by the works of Charles Swinburne, Robert Browning, and Charles Darwin (the author of Origin of Species, 1856). Poor health forced Hardy to return to his native region in 1867, where he worked for Hicks again and for another architect, G.R. Crickmay.

Hardy's education was interrupted by his work as an architect. He had wanted to attend the university and become an Anglican minister, but lack of funds and his declining interest in religion swayed Hardy away from that avocation and more toward a self-study of poetry and writing. Hardy tried his hand at writing when he was 17 and wrote for years while he was a practicing architect. His first novel manuscript, The Poor Man and the Lady, was rejected by several publishers, but one editor, George Meredith encouraged him, and so Hardy set out to refine his style. A second story, Desperate Remedies (1871), was accepted and published. His next novel, Under the Greenwood Tree (1872), demonstrates a more polished Hardy now coming into his own style.

By 1870, Hardy was sent by his employer to begin a restoration project of the St. Juliot Church in Cornwall. Here he met his first wife, Emma Lavinia Gifford, whom Hardy married in 1874. Emma encouraged Hardy to write, and by 1872, Hardy left architecture to devote his time to his literary career.

Literary Work

When Hardy left his career as architect, he did so with a contract for 11 monthly installments of a tale, A Pair of Blue Eyes, in the Cornhill Magazine. His reputation as one of England's newer novelists sustained the Hardy family from that time on. The next novel, Far from the Maddening Crowd (1874), introduced the Wessex area setting, which also is the setting for Tess. The next two novels, The Return of the Native (1878) and The Mayor of Casterbridge (1886), established Hardy as a formidable writer.

Hardy published two more novels, Tess of the d'Urbervilles (1891) and Jude the Obscure (1895), which were his last long fiction works. The last novels challenged the sensibilities of Victorian readers with situations that ruffled many a Victorian feather: immoral sex, murder, illegitimate children, and the unmarried living together. Heated debate and criticism over these two books helped Hardy decide that he would rather write poetry. In fact, so stung was he by the criticism of his works that Hardy did not write another novel.

Hardy wrote short stories, poems, and plays for the rest of his life. Two further volumes of poetry and short stories appeared, The Dynasts: A Drama of the Napoleonic Wars and Winter Words (1928), a volume of verse. Hardy was quite prolific during this period, writing some 900 poems on a variety of subjects. In 1912, Hardy's wife, Emma, died, ending 20 years of "domestic estrangement." In 1914, Hardy married Florence Emily Dugdale, with whom he lived until his death on January 11, 1928.

Hardy's body was buried at Westminster Abbey in Poet's Corner, while his heart was buried in Stinson, England, near the graves of his ancestors and his first wife, Emma. His second wife was later buried near her husband

Chapter 4

Chronology of Thomas Hardy

Titles of Stories as they are best known are used Throughout. Some Dates of Composition are Approximate

1840 In the third year of Victoria's reign, Thomas Hardy is born on the 2nd of June in a large cottage bordering the heath at Higher Bockhampton, three miles outside Dorchester, Dorset. The eldest son of a violin-playing builder and an ambitious mother, Thomas Hardy received from the former parent a love of music, and from the latter a love of books.

1848 Hardy could read before he entered the new school at Lower Bockhampton.

1849 Hardy was transferred to a private school in Dorchester.

1856 Hardy articled with Dorchester architect John Hicks.

1862 Hardy moved to London to take up more advanced architectural work with Arthur Blomfield. At this time, he wrote many poems, but failed to get any published.

1865 March: "How I Built My House" [Hardy's first published work and first short story] appears in Chamber's Journal, 18 March.

1867 Returning to Dorset, depressed and disappointed by publishers' rejection of his early verse, Hardy assisted Hicks in church restorations.

1868 January: Hardy finished his first novel, The Poor Man and the Lady, and submitted to both Macmillan and Chapman and Hall, but it was never published.

1870 7 Match: Hardy travelled to St. Juliot, northern Cornwall, to plan the restoration of the local parish church; here he met the rector's sister-in-law, Emma Lavinia Gifford

1871 March: Hardy published the sensation novel Desperate Remedies in three volumes with William Tinsley, but its sales were mediocre.

1872 June: Under the Greenwood Tree is published in two volumes by Tinsley, London. Instantly, critics compared it favourably to the work of George Eliot.

1872 Sept: A Pair of Blue Eyes, illustrated by J. A. Pasquier, is published in Tinsley's Magazine in eleven parts, until July, 1873.

1874 Jan-Dec: Far From the Madding Crowd is published in serial in the Cornhill Magazine in twelve numbers, illustrated by H. P. Allingham. February: Hardy agrees to have" Destiny and a Blue Cloak" published in the New York Times. F. B. Pinion describes this as" Hardy's first short story" in New Wessex edition of Thomas Hardy: Collected Short Stories (1988): p. 929. September: Hardy sends off finished draft of" Destiny and a Blue Cloak" to the New York Times; Thomas Hardy marries Emma Gifford on 17 September. October 4: "Destiny and a Blue Cloak" published in the New York Times.

1875 July: The Hand of Ethelberta is published in serial in the Cornhill Magazine in eleven numbers, illustrated by George Du Maurier.

1876 April: The Hand of Ethelberta is published in volume form; Hardy and his wife have moved to Yeovil. May: Last instalment of The Hand of Ethelberta.

1877 "The Thieves Who Couldn't Help Sneezing" published in a children's annual. While living at Sturminster Newton, Hardy writes The Return of the Native.

1878 January: The Return of the Native begins in serial in Belgravia, il. Arthur Hopkins. March 22: Hardy moves to Hardy and his wife move to Upper Tooting, near Wandsworth Common. April 6: "The Duchess of Hamptonshire" (as "The Impulsive Lady of Croome Castle") published on 6 and 13 April in Light (11 and 18 May in Harpers Weekly). July: An Indiscretion in the Life of an Heiress published in The New Quarterly Magazine, and the first of its five instalments appears in Harper's Weekly.

1879 April 19: "The Distracted Preacher" published in the

New Quarterly Magazine and in five parts in Harper's Weekly. Hardy at work on The Trumpet Major.

1880 January: The Trumpet-Major begins in serial in Good Words, il. John Collier. April 15: "Fellow-Townsmen" published in the New Quarterly Magazine, pp. 335-83 (17 April-15 May, in 5 parts in Harpers Weekly). October: Hardy is seriously ill for next six months. December: A Laodicean begins in serial in Harper's New Monthly Magazine (Dec., 1880-Dec., 1881) in 13 numbers, il. George Du Maurier.

1881 June: Hardy moves to Wimborne. December 5: "What the Shepherd Saw" published in the Illustrated London News, pp. 19, 22-3. December 10: "The Honourable Laura" published as "Benighted Travellers" in Harper's Weekly, pp. 826-7, and 17 Dec., pp. 858-9; and on 17 December in Bolton Weekly Journal.

1882 May: Two on a Tower begins in serial in Atlantic Monthly in eight monthly nos. July: "A Tradition of Eighteen Hundred and Four" sent off. November 25:" A Tradition of Eighteen Hundred and Four" published in Harper's Christmas, pp. 26-7. December: last instalment of Two on a Tower in Atlantic Monthly.

1883 February: "The Romantic Adventures of a Milkmaid" sent off to the Graphic, beginning a nine-year relationship with this large-format weekly illustrated journal. March 1:" The Three Strangers" published in Longman's Magazine, pp. 569-88; in Harper's Weekly 3 March and 10. June: the Hardys move to Dorchester, deciding to build a house there. June 25:"

The Romantic Adventures of a Milkmaid" is published in the Graphic, pp. 4-25, with four full-page illustrations by C. S. Reinhart; and in Harper's Weekly from 23 June to 4 August (with only three of Reinhart's illustrations). Hardy's essay "The Dorsetshire Labourer" is published in Longman's Magazine for July. By the end of the summer, Hardy has completed the children's adventure story Our Exploits at West Poley.

1884 Hardy is working on The Mayor of Casterbridge in this year. February 7: "The Duchess of Hamptonshire" is published as" The Impulsive Lady of Croome Castle" in Light:

7-8, 51-2; in Harper's Weekly: 370-1, and 394; as" Emmeline; or, Passion versus Principle" in the Independent 7 Feb., 1884.

1885 February: "A Tryst at an Ancient Earthwork" written. March 15: "A Tryst at an Ancient Earthwork" published in The Detroit Post. April: The Mayor of Casterbridge finished. June 29: The Hardys move from ShireHall Place to Max Gate, a great house that he himself has designed and built on the outskirts of Dorchester. October 17 and 24: "A Mere Interlude" published in Bolton Weekly Journal.

1886 January 2: The Mayor of Casterbridge begins in weekly serial in The Graphic, illustrated by Robert Barnes. May: Last instalment of MoC; first instalment of The Woodlanders in Macmillan's Magazine. May 10: The Mayor of Casterbridge is published in two volumes by Smith, Elder..

1887 February: Hardy finishes writing The Woodlanders; visits Italy. April: Last (12th) instalment of The Woodlanders in Macmillan's Magazine. August: "Alicia's Diary" written. September: "The Withered Arm" written. October 15: "Alicia's Diary" published in Manchester Weekly Times Supplement. December 31: "The Waiting Supper" published in Harper's Weekly, pp. 965-7.

1888 January 7: "The Waiting Supper" published in Harper's Weekly, pp. 17-19. January: "The Waiting Supper" published in Murray's Magazine, pp. 42-67, and February, pp. 199-218. "The Withered Arm" published in Blackwood's Edinburgh Magazine, pp. 30-48. May: Wessex Tales published by Macmillan. August: "A Tragedy of Two Ambitions" written. September:" The First Countess of Wessex" written. December: "A Tragedy of Two Ambitions" published in The Universal Review, with six illustrations by George Lambert.

1889 September: About half of Tess of the D'Urbervilles sent off. December: "The First Countess of Wessex" published in Harper's New Monthly 80, il. A. Parsons and C. S. Reinhart.

1890 January: "The Lady Penelope" published in Longman's Magazine, pp. 279-287. May: A Group of Noble Dames sent off. July: Hardy revised A Group of Noble Dames and sent off. July, second half: Most of stories in Life's Little Ironies written. November-December 1: A Group of Noble

Dames published in The Graphic, Christmas: No. 1: "Barbara of the House of Grebe," p. 4-5; Harper's Weekly 29 Nov. No. 2: "The Marchioness of Stonehenge" (originally, "The Lady Caroline ") p. 9-12; Harper's Weekly 6 Dec., p. 959-62. No. 3: "Anna, Lady Baxby," p. 12-13; Harper's Weekly6 Dec., p. 962, 964. No. 4:" The Lady Icenway," p. 13; Harper's Weekly 13 Dec., p. 981, 984. No. 5:" Squire Petrick's Lady," p. 16; Harper's Weekly 13 Dec., p. 984. No. 6:" Lady Mottisfont," p. 16-20; Harper's Weekly 20 Dec., p. 994-5.

1891 March: "For Conscience' Sake" published in the Fortnightly Review 49: 370-382." The Doctor's Legend" in the New York Independent. March-June:" A Few Crusted Characters" published in Harper's New Monthly, illustrated by C. Green. april: "The Son's Veto" written. May: A Group of Noble Dames published by Osgood, McIlvaine June 27: "To Please His Wife" published in Black and White, 678-82, il. W. Hennessy. July 4: Tess of the D'Urbervilles begins its serial run in The Graphic, illustrated by Hubert Herkomer et al. November-December:" On the Western Circuit" published in The English Illustrated Magazine, il. W. Paget, and Harper's Weekly 28 Nov., il. W. T. Smedley. December 1: "The Son's Veto" published in The Illustrated London News: 20-21, 25. December 5: "What The Shepherd Saw" published in The Illustrated London News. December 26: Tess ends in weekly serial in The Graphic.

1892 July: Death of Hardy's father. October 1: The Well-Beloved begins in serial in The Illustrated London News December 17: Last instalment of The Well-Beloved, il. Walter Paget.

1893 January: "The Fiddler of the Reels" sent off. March:" Master John Horseleigh, Knight" sent off. May: "The Fiddler of the Reels" published in Scribner's Magazine 13: 597-609, il. W. Hatherell. Hardy meets Florence Henniker. June 12: "Master John Horseleigh, Knight" published in The Illustrated London News, il. W. B. Wollen. September: "An Imaginative Woman" finished; "A Tryst at an Ancient Earthwork" revised. October: Life's Little Ironies assembled. December: "A Tryst at an Ancient Earthwork" published in The English Illustrated

Magazine, with four photographs by W. Pouncy. Hardy is working on Jude the Obscure

1894 February: Life's Little Ironies published by Osgood, McIlvaine. April: "An Imaginative Woman" published in The Pall Mall Magazine, 951-69, il. A. J. Goodman. December: Jude the Obscure begins in serial as The Simpletons, and then as Hearts Insurgent for remaining eleven parts, and in Harper's New Monthly Magazine (Dec., 1894-Nov., 1895), illustrated by William Hatherell.

1895 March: Hardy finishes writing Jude. November: Jude is published in book form.

1896 August: "A Committee-Man of 'The Terror'" sent off. November 22:" A Committee-Man of 'The Terror'" is published in The Illustrated London News, illustrated by H. Burgess. December 14: "The Duke's Reappearance" is published in Saturday Review: 14-16. Throughout the year, the critics' hostile reception to Jude dispirits Hardy. His growing financial independence leads Hardy to return to his first love, poetry.

1897 March: The Well-Beloved published in book form. July: "The Grave by the Handpost" finished. November 30: "The Grave by the Handpost" is published in St. James's Budget, illustrated by G. H. Patterson.

1898 December: Hardy publishes his first book of verse, Wessex Poems; many of the poems contained therein date well back to the 1860s.

1900 January: "A Changed Man" written; on April 21 and 28, it is published in The Sphere, illustrated by A. S. Hartrick. December: "Enter a Dragoon" is published in Harper's Monthly, illustrated by A. Hayman.

1902 The Dynasts, in dramatic blank verse, is published in three parts, one of the longest poems in the English language.

1910 Hardy receives the Order of Merit.

1912 April: Hardy responds to the sinking of the Titanic with the elegy "The Convergence of the Twain (Lines on the Loss of the ''Titanic')." November: Life's Little Ironies published (Wessex edition; Preface dated "May, 1912").

Wessex Tales published (Wessex edition; Preface dated "May, 1912"). A Group of Noble Dames published. The death of Emma Hardy sets off a wave of self-recrimination and regret in Hardy that prompts him to write many poems about their relationship, since termed "The Emma Poems."

1913 October: "A Changed Man" and Other Tales published by Macmillan. Poems of 1912-13 published.

1914 "A Changed Man" and Other Tales published. Shortly after his marriage to young Florence Dugdale, the First World War breaks out.

1928 11 January: Hardy dies at Max Gate. His eighth and last book of verse appears posthumously. In addition to his short stories and novels 'of character and environment' he has left us 1093 poems, both lyric and narrative, and numerous essays.

1929 February: "Old Mrs. Chundle" published posthumously in The Ladies' Home Journal at the instigation of Florence Hardy. Hardy recollected having written the story between 1888-1890.

Chapter 5

Character List

Michael Henchard

He is the mercurial main character, the "man of character" that the novel follows. Like his wife Susan, he believes that an evil fate is responsible for his misfortunes. However, unlike his wife, he tries to fight back against this fate with his bullish nature. He does have a kind spirit, wanting to make amends to Susan and Elizabeth-Jane, happily taking Farfrae under his wing, caring for the poor of the village. He also lives with high morals, confessing in several instances when he could easily lie. Yet when he believes he is crossed, he becomes extremely angry and will stop at nothing to ruin his rival. Unfortunately, he always comes to regret his anger, usually when it is too late to make amends. The whole novel tries to determine whether his character works against him, or if a heartless fate has brought him down.

Susan Henchard Newson

She believes that everything that happens to her is controlled by a menacing fate, and the events of the novel seem to support her view. She accompanies Michael Henchard to Weydon-Priors, and seems to be a dutiful wife to him. However, upon being sold for five guineas, she becomes angry and willingly leaves with Newson the sailor, effectively dissolving the marriage with Michael. After Newson's death, she returns to Wessex to find her husband. Although she eventually has a normal marriage with Michael, she carries the secret of Elizabeth-Jane's birth with her to her grave, revealing it in a letter that should be opened on Elizabeth-Jane's wedding day.

Elizabeth-Jane Henchard

She is the first Elizabeth-Jane introduced in the novel. As a small girl, she is sold with her mother for five guineas to Newson the sailor. Three months later after the auction, she dies. She has black hair, one trait that Michael remembers about her.

The Furmity-seller

She is the owner of the furmity tent in Weydon-Priors, where Susan and Elizabeth-Jane Henchard were sold. She is the one who adds liquor to Michael's furmity, which in turn makes him angry enough to sell his wife. She only remembers the auction when Susan mentions it eighteen years later. Later, she again leads Michael into despair by disclosing the whole story of the auction at her trial.

The Townspeople of Weydon-Priors

These are the witnesses to the sale of Susan Henchard. Unlike the people of Casterbridge, they make no attempt to get involved in the lives of others. Although they do not approve of the sale of a wife, they make no attempt to stop the auction or to show him the error of his ways.

Richard Newson

He is the kind sailor who offers to buy Susan and Elizabeth-Jane Henchard, but not before asking Susan if she is willing to go with him. After Elizabeth-Jane Henchard dies, he becomes the father of Elizabeth-Jane Newson. Later he fakes his death at sea, planning to return after a few months for Elizabeth-Jane. Even though he discovers that Michael has lied about Elizabeth-Jane's death, he asks Elizabeth-Jane to forgive him.

Elizabeth-Jane Newson

She is the daughter of Susan Henchard and Newson the

sailor, and from her parents she inherited her fair hair. She is overly concerned with manners and respectability. Although she has a melancholy air, Elizabeth-Jane has a great ability to love, giving it to her mother, her father, her stepfather, and later her husband.

The Townspeople of Casterbridge

Unlike the people of Weydon-Priors, the people of Casterbridge make it a point to remark and get involved in the affairs of the other townspeople. They are the ones who point out that Michael's crops don't sell, that Farfrae is a charming and wise young man, that Lucetta needs a comeuppance. Through these remarks, they serve as a Greek chorus.

Donald Farfrae

He is a young Scotsman who passes through Casterbridge on his way to America. However, Michael quickly realizes Farfrae's great head for business, and makes him general manager. Farfrae is well-rounded: he knows business, and he also understands society's desires for courtly manners and entertainment. Michael greatly respects Farfrae and asks him for advice on several occasions. However, Farfrae has everything that Michael doesn't: the love of Lucetta, the support of the townspeople, and eventually the mayorship of Casterbridge. At the end of the novel, Farfrae finds happiness in his marriage to Elizabeth-Jane.

Joshua Jopp

He is the first applicant for the position of Michael Henchard's general manager. Because Farfrae was chosen, Jopp hates him and will do anything to ruin him. From this point, Jopp behaves as the typical villain. He hates Lucetta because she refuses to help him, and he plays upon the hatred of the townspeople and the weaknesses of Michael to ruin her.

Abel Whittle

Abel works in Henchard's company, but he is always a

bit tardy. Michael becomes so angry one day that he punishes Abel by making him come to work without pants. Nevertheless, Abel remains a faithful employee. Because Michael was kind to his mother, Abel willingly cares for Michael in his final days and delivers his last will to Elizabeth-Jane.

Lucetta Templeman

She is a flighty and indiscreet woman who follows her emotions. In her youth, she met Michael Henchard in her native Jersey. She wishes to marry him, but is stopped when Susan returns. After Susan's death, she moves to High-Place Hall in Casterbridge to keep an eye on Michael. However, she falls in love with Michael's rival Farfrae and marries him. She constantly fears that Michael will reveal their past connections through her scandalous love letters. Eventually the letters are read by the townspeople of Casterbridge, and they hold a skimmity-ride to mock the relationship between Lucetta and Michael. The shock of seeing the skimmity-ride kills Lucetta.

Chapter 6

Brief Synopsis

The novel opens on a dirt road near the village of Weydon-Priors, in the English county of Wessex. Michael Henchard, a hay-trusser, is traveling with his wife, Susan, and young daughter, Elizabeth-Jane. However, a passing farmer tells the Henchards that there is no chance of finding employment or housing in the village. Discouraged, Michael takes his family to a furmity seller's tent in Weydon-Priors. The furmity seller adds liquor to Michael's meal, and after several servings Michael becomes an angry drunk. Because he believes his marriage at a young age ruined all his chances for success, he offers to sell his wife and daughter to the highest bidder. After several unanswered calls for bids, Susan says that someone should buy her, since her present owner isn't to her liking. Most of the other customers in the tent treat the auction as a joke, but soon a passing sailor hears the announcements and enters the tent. He offers to buy Susan and Elizabeth-Jane for five guineas, first making sure that Susan is willing to go. When Michael takes the money, Susan and Elizabeth-Jane leave with the sailor. Before leaving, Susan hurls her wedding-ring at Michael. Michael merely falls into a drunken slumber as the rest of the shocked customers leave.

The next morning, Michael awakens. Seeing the wedding ring and the money brings the events of the previous evening back to him. He realizes that he was partly to blame for his actions, but he also blames Susan for actually thinking that the auction would be binding. Nevertheless, because his excessive drinking caused the whole situation, he makes an oath: he will abstain from all liquor for twenty-one years. Then he sets out to search for his wife and daughter. At first the search is unsuccessful because Michael refuses to explain the circumstances of their parting. Finally he learns that three people matching the descriptions of the sailor, Susan, and Elizabeth-Jane have just emigrated. Resigned, Michael gives up the search and goes to another town in Wessex, the town of Casterbridge.

Eighteen years later, Susan and Elizabeth-Jane return to Weydon-Priors searching for Michael. Elizabeth-Jane believes that Michael is just a relative, since Susan has kept her previous marriage a secret. Susan seeks Michael because she believes that he can help them now that the sailor, named Newson, has died. The women stop in the furmity seller's tent, which is still there. They learn that Michael stopped in the tent a year after the auction and left word that he lived in Casterbridge. Susan and Elizabeth-Jane leave for Casterbridge right away.

When the women arrive in Casterbridge, they learn that Michael has become extremely influential as a prosperous merchant and as the mayor of the town. The night they arrive, the townspeople are discussing Michael's bad business deals in selling sprouted grain. A young Scotsman, Donald Farfrae, overhears the discussion and gives Michael some suggestions for making the grain usable. Farfrae also engages in a light flirtation with Elizabeth-Jane.

Eventually Michael and Susan meet secretly. They decide to keep their past relationship a secret from Elizabeth-Jane. In fact, Michael suggests that they begin their relationship again. Susan should rent a cottage and allow Michael to court her in a respectable manner. Susan complies, and soon after they marry. Michael hopes that someday he can openly acknowledge Elizabeth-Jane as his daughter. At the same time, Michael has success in business as well by choosing Farfrae as his general manager and confidant. Farfrae's charm impresses all the townspeople and gains the attentions of Elizabeth-Jane once again. Michael has taken the young man under his wing and regards him almost as a brother. The only enemy Farfrae has is Joshua Jopp, a man who wanted the position of general manager.

When Susan and Michael remarry, Michael has another period of prosperity thanks to Farfrae's skills. The new wealth to which Elizabeth-Jane has been introduced produces a new beauty in her. Michael becomes fond of her and wants her to take his name legally. Susan, however, is reluctant to agree. Farfrae also takes an interest in Elizabeth-Jane. However, Elizabeth-Jane's shyness and discord between Farfrae and Michael have stopped any hope of a romance. Farfrae and Michael first have a disagreement over the punishment for an habitually late worker, Abel Whittle. Next, during a public celebration, Farfrae's diversions are a success while Michael's are a complete failure. The townspeople openly praise Farfrae, which leads Michael to remark that Farfrae's term as general manger is ending. Farfrae resigns and opens up his own corn and hay store.

Susan dies, leaving a letter for Michael that is not to be opened until Elizabeth-Jane's wedding-day. Michael is lonely from the arguments with Farfrae and the lack of any tie with Elizabeth-Jane, so he tells the girl that he is her father. After thinking it over, Elizabeth-Jane is convinced. Meanwhile, Michael finds Susan's letter and reads it. The letter reveals that Michael's own daughter died, and this Elizabeth-Jane is the child of the sailor Newson. The discovery shocks and angers Michael, and he becomes cold to Elizabeth-Jane without telling her the truth.

Elizabeth-Jane is confused, but tries to win the love of Michael by immersing herself in her studies. She also visits her mother's grave. One day she meets a wealthy and charming young woman at Susan's grave, and she pours out her story to the woman. The lady, Miss Lucetta Templeman, says she will soon be a resident of Casterbridge, and she would like it if Elizabeth-Jane can be her companion. Michael allows it despite his misgivings, and Elizabeth-Jane leaves that day.

Lucetta invites Michael to her home, even going so far as to send Elizabeth-Jane away on errands just to convince him to visit. Michael and Lucetta had an agreement long ago when he was in Jersey, but it had been put on hold because of his marriage. Now that Susan is dead, Lucetta wishes to renew the agreement. To her joy, a caller comes—but it is Farfrae coming to call on Elizabeth-Jane. Lucetta and Farfrae are instantly attracted to each other, and she begins to ignore Michael completely. While Michael tries to propose to Lucetta despite the presence of an unknown rival, Elizabeth-Jane realizes that Farfrae and Michael are in love with Lucetta, and she renounces any interest she may have had in Farfrae.

The competition between Farfrae and Michael extends into business, complicating the situation. Michael hires Joshua Jopp as his general manager, and orders Jopp to do all he can to force Farfrae out of business. Michael tries to base his grain purchase on the predictions of a weather-prophet, but the prediction is incorrect, and the bad investment drives Michael into debt. Farfrae buys wisely and gains money.

Despite his losses, Michael is still determined to marry Lucetta. After learning that Farfrae is the secret suitor, Michael forces Lucetta to agree to marrying him—or he will reveal their past connection by using her earlier love letters. Lucetta reluctantly agrees. The next day, Michael hears the trial of an old woman. The old woman is the furmity seller from long ago, and she tells the story of the wife auction. Lucetta is so horrified that she runs away to Port-Bredy. There she marries Farfrae secretly, and she tells Michael a few days later.

Meanwhile, Michael has terrible luck in business. One of his debtors fails; his men make bad decisions about corn to bring about Michael's bankruptcy. Farfrae takes the opportunity to buy Michael's headquarters and offer a job to Michael. Michael accepts, but feels real hatred at Farfrae's success. After all, Farfrae is the popular choice for mayor, and he has Lucetta. Michael looks forward to the ending of his oath not to drink liquor.

Elizabeth fears that Michael will hurt Farfrae, and the townspeople know all about Michael's hatred of Farfrae. Although Farfrae gives up the idea of giving Michael his own shop, he cannot leave Casterbridge because he is offered the position of mayor. Lucetta begs Michael to return her letters, and a combination of pity and contempt makes him agree.

Joshua Jopp meets Lucetta after her meeting with Michael.

He asks her to help him get a position with Farfrae. Lucetta refuses. Michael gives Jopp a package to deliver to Lucetta, and Jopp reasons that they are love letters. He shares the letters with some poor townswomen who hate Lucetta. They plan to have a skimmity-ride through town the next night. When the effigies of Michael and Lucetta ride through town, Lucetta sees and is so shocked that she has a seizure that kills her.

The whole world has crashed around Michael, yet he still has the love of Elizabeth-Jane. Even this reconciliation is threatened by a surprise visit from Newson, whom everyone thought dead. Michael tells him that Elizabeth-Jane is dead, and the sailor accepts this, then leaves. Although Michael and Elizabeth-Jane soon settle into a peaceful life, Michael constantly worries about Newson's return.

Meanwhile, Farfrae returns to court Elizabeth-Jane. Michael is nervous about their courtship, and he becomes even more nervous when Elizabeth-Jane says she must meet someone. She meets Newson, who tells her the truth about her birth. At the wedding of Elizabeth-Jane and Farfrae, Michael comes to reconcile with his step-daughter, but he sees Newson and decides to never trouble Elizabeth-Jane again. Later, Elizabeth-Jane realizes that Michael wanted to make peace with her, and she sets out to find him. Abel Whittle, the man whom Michael wanted to fire once, cared for Michael in his last days. He tells Elizabeth-Jane that Michael is dead. Michael's last will states that no man should remember him. Elizabeth-Jane resolves to do as she is told, preferring to concentrate all her love on her husband and family.

Chatper 7

Chapter Wise Summary and Analysis

SUMMARY AND ANALYSIS OF CHAPTERS 1-5

Chapter 1: Summary

The novel opens in the early part of the nineteenth century. One summer evening, a young family is walking towards the village of Weydon-Priors, in the region of England known as Wessex. From the beginning, it is obvious that something is strange about this family. Although the man, woman, and child are not poorly dressed, the dirt that has collected on them during their journey makes them look shabby. In addition, the man and woman do not regard each other at all, even though they are clearly traveling together.

Eventually the family stops to rest. While they rest, a turnip-hoer speaks to them. From him, the family learns that there is no work and no housing available in Weydon-Priors; however, since it is Fair Day, there is some excitement in the village. The family goes to the fair-field, but ignores all the goings-on in favour of finding food. They decided to stop in a furmity tent, a place where they can buy some pudding. The man demands some liquor for his furmity, and drinks it lustily, ignoring his wife's pleas for lodging. Soon the man, who has been called Michael, complains loudly about his marriage and his poverty.

Outside, Michael hears an auction of horses, and he wonders why men can't sell their wives at auction. Some people inside the tent actually respond favorably to this question, and Michael openly offers his wife for sale (with the child as a bonus). Although the wife, named Susan, begs her husband not to do such a thing, Michael ignores her. A sailor soon speaks from the doorway. He will take Susan and Elizabeth-Jane for five pounds and five shillings—though he will not if Susan is unwilling. Susan sweeps out of the tent with Elizabeth-Jane and the sailor, cursing her husband.

As Michael drinks, the villagers wonder about the sailor and the woman's spirit. Michael says that he will never take his wife back, and begins to fall asleep in the tent. Eventually, the other villagers depart, leaving Michael there to sleep off his drunken state.

Analysis

The setting of the novel reflects the emotions of the characters. On the way to Weydon-Priors, nature is in a state of decay. The road is surrounded by clouds of dirt; the dirt obscures any radiance that the grass might have; the leaves and the trees are rotting. Thus nature adequately reinforces the feelings that both Michael and Susan have about their marriage—Michael feels that his marriage at a young age rotted any chance he had of living decently, while Susan is soiled by the fact that her husband would sell her as he would sell a horse.

Indeed, the natural world frequently identifies with the characters and mirrors their actions. This extends not only to trees, but to animals as well. For instance, while Michael announces the auction for the first time, a sparrow flies into the tent, and everyone watches until the sparrow is able to fly away. The sparrow serves as a metaphor for Susan's plight. She is seen as a sparrow: her husband frequently dismisses her complaints as "bird-like chirpings," and everyone in the furmity tent is forced to watch until Susan can escape the tent with the sailor.

Michael, the drunken husband, is not seen as an animal, but his physical appearance hints at his inner nature. He is a tall man "of fine figure." This outward goodness is reflected in his haste to get food for his family and his asking about employment and lodging. Yet he will frequently show his darker side as a sharp contrast to his goodness. Just as he is dark and "swarthy" while he is of a fine figure, he does harsh things while he behaves admirably. He searches for food for the family, then wants to drink himself into a state and actually sells his wife and child. The alternate title for the novel is "A Story of a Man of Character," and the contrasts such as these in the character of Michael will be what drives the novel.

Hardy wrote a number of novels set in the fictional shire of England known as "Wessex." Readers followed the novels that Hardy set in this region because of Hardy's skill in bringing life to the Wessex natives. The Weydon-Priors characters are examples of this skill. Although we don't see the turnip-hoer for more than a few lines, we have already learned that he is a morose man, intent on finding the negative in every situation (even the happy events such as the village fair). In a novel dealing with the character of one man, Hardy also tries to explore how one character touches others—another theme that one should trace through the story.

Chapter 2: Summary

The next morning, the hay-trusser awakens, confused about his surroundings and about the events of the previous evenings. Upon discovering his wife's wedding-ring and the five guineas the sailor gave as payment, the man suddenly remembers the auction. He decides that he must find his wife and Elizabeth-Jane, and he leaves the furmity tent. As he walks from the deserted fair-field, he realizes that no one ever learned his name. Then he becomes angry that his simple-minded wife actually thought the auction was binding. Soon he returns to blaming himself and searching for his family.

Before he begins his investigation, the hay-trusser resolves to swear an oath: he will not drink any strong liquors for twenty-one years. He enters a nearby church, places his head upon the bible, and makes the oath. Then he begins looking for the woman and girl. Days, then weeks pass, and he gets no clues from anyone. Because he cannot explain why he is searching for his family (he is ashamed of his actions), his search is hampered. Eventually, he stops at a seaport. Three people that match his descriptions have left the country some time before. Discouraged, he gives up his search and heads for Casterbridge, a town in the southwestern part of Wessex.

Analysis

In the last chapter, we saw the dark side of Michael Henchard through his drunkenness, greed, and temper. In this chapter, we realise that Michael does have positive attributes. He shows great determination in tirelessly searching for his wife and daughter, and he takes responsibility for his actions in accepting the blame for the sale. However, his negative qualities also return in this chapter. He blindly blames Susan for being simple enough to believe that such a sale is lawful. He also shows his excessive pride when he refuses to tell anyone why he has lost his family. The tension between Michael's good and bad qualities will be one major theme of the book that concerns itself with "a man of character."

This chapter also concludes the development of the primary dramatic conflict within the novel. Although there will be other conflicts arising later in the novel, the wife auction will come back to haunt all the characters involved. It will shape the later decisions of Michael, Susan, Newson, and Elizabeth-Jane.

Chapter 3: Summary

Eighteen years later, a mother and daughter travel on the road to Weydon-Priors. They are the cast-off wife and daughter of long ago, Susan Henchard and Elizabeth-Jane. Susan remembers that this is where she met Newson the sailor, and the women mourn the man who is now lost at sea. Now they have returned to Weydon-Priors to find their lost "relative," Michael Henchard. Elizabeth-Jane does not know the real connection between Susan and Michael, and Susan wants to keep it that way.

The mother and daughter stop at the old furmity tent. Elizabeth-Jane tells her mother that it is not respectable to stop there, but Susan ignores her and goes inside. She is greeted by the old furmity seller, who says that she has seen better days in her business. Susan asks if she remembers the wife auction, and after a few moments of thought, the woman does remember. In fact, the husband returned to the tent a year later and said he lived in Casterbridge. Susan leaves the tent. She tells Elizabeth-Jane that they will go to Casterbridge, even though a lot of time has passed since Michael's last visit to Weydon-Priors.

Analysis

This chapter begins with a recreation of the walk to Weydon-Priors that occurred in the opening of the novel. However, the scene is different. This time there are two women who obviously have connections to each other. They both dress in similar black gowns (emphasizing their connection through their mourning for the dead Newson), and they walk hand in hand. We can infer that Susan's marriage to Newson has made her more able to connect with people, as well as bringing Elizabeth-Jane to a more loving lifestyle.

Elizabeth-Jane does seem to be a very nice girl. She loves her mother, as we can see from her willingness to walk hand in hand with her mother and her unquestioning belief in her mother's story. However, Hardy injects a bit of irony into her character in making her concerned with what is proper and what is not. She tries to keep her mother away from the furmity tent by saying, "It isn't respectable"—despite our belief that Elizabeth-Jane came from the same improper conditions within the tent, with her working-class parents.

Hardy also includes a few elements of suspense into the story. We wonder why Susan is so determined to find Michael, and why Susan has never told Elizabeth-Jane about her former marriage. Then the question arises: What will happen when she finds Michael? Will he take his family back, or has he made another engagement in the years since his marriage? We must also remember the furmity seller, who is now desperate for any sort of business. Now that she remembers the auction, can she ruin the Henchards by announcing it? Hardy brings all these questions to mind to keep the reader engaged and eager to see how the story will unfold.

Chapter 4: Summary

The chapter begins by recounting the eighteen previous years for Susan and Elizabeth-Jane. Elizabeth-Jane grew up believing that Newson and Susan were legally married, because Susan believed it. The new family traveled to Canada and stayed a while before returning to England. When Susan told Newson that she could no longer live with him, he left on a trade ship and was lost at sea. While Susan gained peace of mind from her "husband's" death, she wanted to make a better life for Elizabeth-Jane. Returning to Michael might give the women a better life, and Susan planned the trip specifically to find Michael.

The women arrive in Casterbridge, and Elizabeth-Jane finds it an "old-fashioned place." As they walk, they hear two men arguing. The men drop Henchard's name in their argument, and the women hear it. However, Susan stops Elizabeth-Jane from talking to the men, since their relative could be a criminal. They continue through the town, passing shops and churches. They ask a group of women where they can find good bread. The women explain the town's latest crisis. There is no good bread because the cornfactor has been selling grown wheat. The grown wheat has made the bread flat. Susan and Elizabeth-Jane buy a couple of biscuits at a nearby shop, then go towards a place that has music playing.

Analysis

Hardy hastens the present action of the novel in his flashback. By relating the events of the past eighteen years quickly instead of relating them, he forces us to focus on the events of the present and on the characters who will be directly influenced by those events. In addition, he heightens suspense in the events of the present by mentioning

We learn much more about Susan's temperament and beliefs in this chapter. We know that she is naive: she blindly believes that the auction makes marriage to Newson binding.

She is also swayed by public opinion. After sharing the events of her marriage with a friend who ridiculed her position, she instantly changes her mind and decides she cannot live with Newson anymore. Yet she is intensely devoted to Elizabeth-Jane and will do anything for her. Returning to find her former husband is a sign of this devotion: although she fears him, she will return to him if her can provide Elizabeth-Jane with a future.

Casterbridge is described in great detail. Hardy's gift for description brings the town to life. From his description, we can learn a lot about the people here. They have a connection with the land, as we can see from their stores selling "scythes, reaphooks, sheep-shears...plough-harness..." and other agricultural needs. However, the people are all concerned with the gathering places. They gather at the church, the bar, the streets. They also share gossip, as shown in the willingness of the townswomen to share the town gossip with the strangers. The public opinions will be a force in Casterbridge, as we shall see through the novel.

Chapter 5: Summary

The music is coming from Casterbridge's main hotel, the King's Arms, where people are having fun and drinking. Susan is nervous, but she sends Elizabeth-Jane inside to ask about Michael. An old man, Christopher Coney, tells the young woman that a public dinner has brought everyone to the inn, including the mayor—Michael Henchard! Susan overhears this and hurries to her daughter's side. They get a glimpse of Michael in his finery. Susan becomes agitated and says she wants to die. Elizabeth-Jane is confused: in her eyes, their relative seems very grand, although no one fills his wineglass. The old man says that the mayor never drinks because he swore an oath. Another old man, Solomon Longways, says that the mayor punishes any worker who is drunk in his presence. He also tells the women that he is a powerful man in the wheat, oats, and barley business.

Inside the tavern, Michael is telling stories of his business exploits when a group of minor tradesmen mock his sales of grown wheat. The poor people watching outside take up the jeers. Michael grows angry, and tells them that businesses have accidents. However, he is looking for a general manager who can help him. When a baker asks how the mayor will repay their losses, Henchard says he cannot change the grown wheat, then sits down stiffly.

Analysis

As we can see, the events of eighteen years ago still haunt the personalities of Susan and Michael. Susan continues to be swayed by the power that men have over her. She is awed at the power and splendor of her husband even as she fears that her husband can actually overpower her. Meanwhile, Michael remains true to his oath, even to the extent of forcing others to follow his example (though no one knows why he has made such an oath, a very important omission). He still has the paradoxes inherent in his character. He reveals his caring side in his concern for the wheat that is unhealthy to his citizens. Yet again Hardy proves that Michael also has a darker and angrier side, subtly shown in both his "coarse build" and his sharp retort at the end of the chapter.

Like Dickens, Hardy is very skilled in bringing his minor characters to life, a talent that is revealed in portrayal of the townspeople of Casterbridge. These villagers actually comment upon the action, taking more of a role in the story than the people of Weydon-Priors were willing to take. Because of their running commentary on all the events, the Casterbridgians serve as a Greek chorus. As such, they all carry a dark and pessimistic tone, as befits the chorus in a tragedy. However, Hardy tries to give each villager a distinct personality that can sometimes be determined in his or her name. For instance, Solomon Longways frequently behaves as his Biblical counterpart, giving a rational perspective on the events.

Summary and Analysis of Chapters 6-10

Chapter 6: Summary

The crowd of poor people watching outside has grown

during the conversation in the inn. One young man, ruddy and bright-eyed with a Scotch accent, stands out of the crowd. He quickly writes a note and orders someone to give it to the Mayor. He then asks for lodgings, and the waiter points him toward the Three Mariners Inn. Meanwhile, the note is delivered to the Mayor, who reacts with shock and surprise.

Elizabeth-Jane, who watched the young man with interest, now suggests that she and her mother spend the night at the Three Mariners as well. After the women leave, Michael asks about the note writer. When the mayor learns that the young Scotsman is staying at the Three Mariners, he walks there. Before entering the inn, Michael tries to "tone himself down to his ordinary everyday appearance."

Analysis

The chapter opens with a description of the young Scotsman, who is "ruddy and of a fair countenance, bright-eyed, and slight in build." Compare this description to that of Michael from Chapter 5: "a man... of heavy frame, large features... his general build being rather coarse than compact." The two men are complete opposites in physical appearance. Here their appearances serve as a sort of foreshadowing of their personalities. We know that Michael behaves as he looks: coarse and bullish, relying upon his strength. We can assume that the young Scotsman will act as his appearance indicates: weak but relying more on his intellect than his strength.

Through his use of metaphorical place names, Hardy shows that his characters are motivated by a power stronger than their free will. Relying first upon the Bible, Hardy sends Michael away from the King's Arms Hotel. The "King's Arms" could represent the control exerted by God's force (the weapons that the King of Heaven uses to guide men). The Henchards are drawn to the Three Mariners in because they act as three mariners, adrift on the tumultuous sea of Chance.

Indeed, chance dominates this chapter. By chance the Scotsman hears the conversation about the corn and happens to have the solution. By chance Elizabeth-Jane notices the young man, and by chance all three stay at the Three Mariners.

Michael just misses his family on the way to find the man. Coincidence plays a major role in Hardy's novels. The coincidences in this chapter are just a few examples of the work of a greater power that seems to constantly work against mankind—at least in Hardy's view.

Chapter 7: Summary

Elizabeth-Jane and Susan arrive twenty minutes before the mayor arrives. They are shown to a room, which is so marvelous that the women fear that they cannot afford such a fine room. Elizabeth-Jane decides to go downstairs and offer her services as a helper, in the hope that the landlord will give them a discount. As she works, the Scotsman calls for supper, and Elizabeth-Jane is ordered to carry his meal. The landlady follows her, and kindly tells her to see to her own dinner. Elizabeth-Jane finds her mother listening to the conversation that is taking place in the room next door—the Scotsman's room.

Michael is there to see the note writer, believing that he is an applicant for the position of general manager, someone named Joshua. The Scotsman introduces himself as Donald Farfrae, a young man leaving for America. He has a method for turning the bad grain into usable grain, and he gives it to Michael freely. Michael is so pleased that he offers Farfrae the position of general manager, but Farfrae declines. Michael says the young man reminds him of his brother, and Farfrae seems to have a wonderful head for figures. Farfrae is touched, and offers to drink with Michael, but Michael tells him about the oath. Farfrae is moved by Michael's honesty, but says he cannot stay because he wants to see the world.

Analysis

Hardy applies a bit of irony to Elizabeth-Jane's character here. The girl desperately wants to stay at a fancy inn because "we must be respectable." Yet she offers her services in the disreputable job of serving-maid. While Hardy tries to put a noble spin on it, saying that Elizabeth-Jane sacrifices her dignity to save money for her mother, we must remember that the townspeople can still see Elizabeth-Jane acting as a maid, a fact that will return later to haunt the girl.

The inn itself serves as a metaphor for Michael (and Casterbridge as a whole). The inn has so many instances of "awkwardness, crookedness, and obscurity" that it attempts to cover up with "quantities of clean linen." Likewise, Casterbridge is covered up with "clean linen," the false fronts of the villagers, that will eventually be swept away to reveal the crookedness of the gossipy villagers. Michael stands at the centre of this, dressed in mayor's clothing that covers the obscurity of his past.

Yet Hardy prevents us from seeing Michael as a completely wicked man. We learn that he regards his previous mistake as a cross to continually bear. Michael seems to be a lonely man, wanting someone to help him run the business and give him advice. Although Farfrae is different in mindset from Henchard (freely giving the solution and wanting to travel to different lands), it seems that he will be a worthy candidate for friendship and partnership. Nevertheless, Hardy gives another hint that Michael is a fickle man—he cannot remember the previous applicant's Jopp's name.

Chapter 8: Summary

The women hear the whole conversation. Susan is especially affected by the confession of the oath. Elizabeth-Jane collects Farfrae's tray, then hangs back to watch the events in the sitting-room. Farfrae has joined the townspeople gathered there, and at the request of the tradesmen, he sings a beautiful Scottish song, full of pathos. The listeners are moved, and they convince him to sing two more songs. By the end of his songs, the townspeople are charmed by Farfrae, and they try to convince him to stay. Elizabeth-Jane has watched the whole scene, scoffing at the comments of the lower classes and marveling at the beauty of Farfrae's voice and ideals. The landlady tells her to turn down Farfrae's bed, and she hurries off to do so. On her way downstairs, she passes Farfrae on the staircase. Although she is a plain girl, he smiles at her and softly hums a love song to her. The girl flees in embarrassment.

When Elizabeth-Jane returns to her room, Susan scolds her for helping out in the inn. Her conduct could bring shame to the Mayor. Elizabeth-Jane believes her mother speaks of Farfrae, and says that he seemed to a charming and refined man. Meanwhile, Michael, who has heard the singing, believes that he would give anything to make the young man stay as a cure for his own loneliness.

Analysis

Chance appears to play another vital role in this chapter. Farfrae just happens to be able to entertain the guests with his songs, and the villagers happen to be in the mood for his sad, sweet songs. Elizabeth-Jane, who has been eyeing the young man all evening, passes him on the staircase, and seems to have won his heart. Is it all really based upon chance, though?

First, the townspeople take to Farfrae not because they were manipulated, but because the young man has charm. He willingly answers their questions, shows kindness, and sings like an angel. In addition, the fact that he has other talents apart from business and work appeals to the townspeople, who have no time to waste upon creative exploits. Finally, the townspeople love Farfrae's sad songs because they reflect their own lost ideals—love of country, a longing for freedom and home. The townspeople, who have a sour and ill-tempered tone through the chapter, find a symbol of hope and longing simultaneously in Farfrae, just as Michael does.

As for Elizabeth-Jane, she is obviously attracted to the sobre and idealistic Farfrae as well. While their meeting on the staircase was an accident, his song to her was teasing. Thus Hardy introduces foreshadowing to the plot. Elizabeth-Jane misinterprets both Donald's song (as a sign of affection) and her mother's "he" (as referring to Donald). These mistakes foreshadow the larger, more damaging miscommunications that will occur later in the story.

Chapter 9: Summary

The next morning, Elizabeth-Jane sees the Mayor calling up to Farfrae from the street. Farfrae meets the mayor to walk through town before his coach comes. Elizabeth-Jane feels regret at Farfrae's departure. Susan thinks that Michael will accept them, since he accepts the strange young man so easily. As they talk, they see five of Michael's haywagons pass. The sign of such wealth convinces Susan to send a note to Michael. Elizabeth-Jane carries the note through the bustling town. When she finally arrives to meet Michael, she is shocked to find Farfrae there. On the walk to the coach, the mayor begged Farfrae to stay, and Farfrae agreed. The mayor happily makes arrangements in his office, leaving Farfrae to meet Elizabeth-Jane.

Analysis

This chapter begins the process of furthering the plot by using parallel scenes. Both Susan and Michael have to save themselves with the help of the younger and more idealistic people. Susan decides to salvage her marriage to Michael by sending Elizabeth-Jane with the note. Michael decides to salvage his stumbling business by persuading Farfrae to stay as general manager.

The event that links these reunions of marriage and business is the walk through the city. Elizabeth-Jane's walk not only gives Hardy a chance to show his careful attention to the details of the Wessex town. It also serves to create suspense for the reader, both delaying the meeting between Michael and Elizabeth and shrouding the conversation of Michael and Farfrae in secrecy. More importantly, it reinforces the social standing of Michael as the most powerful man in the community. As we continue through the novel, we will slowly watch that standing fall.

Chapter 10: Summary

As Elizabeth-Jane waits, someone new is presented—Joshua Jopp, the previous applicant for general manager. Michael coldly sends the man away, saying the post has been filled. He then turns to Elizabeth-Jane, who announces that Susan is in town. Michael is visibly shaken, but he invites Elizabeth-Jane to his dining-room, where he asks about her life. The girl tells her story, saying that her father left them "not very well off." Michael writes a letter to Susan, enclosing a five-pound note. After Elizabeth-Jane leaves, Michael thinks the women could be impostors, but calms down. Still, Farfrae wonders at his new friend's now-cold demeanor.

Elizabeth-Jane delivers the note to Susan. The note says that Susan should meet him at the Ring amphitheater that evening. Susan waits impatiently for the close of the day.

Analysis

Once again, the two sides of Michael's personality are revealed. At first, he behaves kindly towards Elizabeth-Jane, treating her with tenderness when he learns who she is and who sent her. In addition, he shows great tact in inquiring after Susan's finances, foreshadowing other times when he will care for those in financial need. He even appears to buy Susan back by enclosing the five guineas, showing a great chivalry in the symbolism. From all outward appearances he is a very respectable man, even owning the three books that every respectable household of Hardy's time owned—the Bible, a copy of Josephus (who chronicled Biblical times), and Whole Duty of Man (a book of devotions).

Yet his dark side now begins to manifest itself more openly. He coldly turns Joshua Jopp away, ignoring the promised interview and thus creating a new enemy. Although he is kind to Elizabeth when she is present, later he explodes into a rage, convinced that the women are impostors, and is barely able to calm himself down. Most importantly, his own pride leads him to meet Susan in a secret place—he is too ashamed to meet her openly, lest some villagers learn the truth and mock him. Over time, pride, anger, and tactlessness will continue to bring him down.

SUMMARY AND ANALYSIS OF CHAPTERS 11-15

Chapter 11: Summary

Hardy describes the Ring as a Roman amphitheater in Casterbridge, a city that was built in the spirit of old Rome.

Although the Ring was the Casterbridgian equivalent of Rome's Coliseum, it was now a meeting place for any other groups needing secrecy—but never for lovers. Henchard chose this place because it would be improper to invite her to his house.

Michael and Susan meet in the middle of the arena. He beings by saying that he no longer drinks; then he asks why she has never contacted him. Susan says she was moved by faithfulness to Newson. Michael says she is innocent because of her faith. They agree that Elizabeth-Jane must not know the truth of their relationship. Michael suggests that Susan take the name Mrs. Newson and live in a cottage with Elizabeth-Jane. Michael will meet, court and marry her. This will save his reputation and bring his child back to her proper home. Susan meekly agrees. Michael promises to provide them with money to keep a wealthy lifestyle. Susan is pleased to repeat her marriage. She runs away, leaving Michael to run to his home a few moments later.

Analysis

Hardy describes the Ring in gruesome detail at the beginning of the chapter. It is a marvelous example of Hardy using his life experience. The description of the Ring's shape and dimensions reflects his many years as an architect, and his comparison of the Ring to the Coliseum as well as noting the other Roman features shows his lifelong interest in the classical world.

Yet the place, despite its architectural glory and reflection of cultures past, has a sinister aura. A spot such as the Ring is a common setting in Hardy's works—an outdoor place, steeped in pagan superstition, with a grotesque past. Nothing positive can take place within the Ring: the boys cannot make the Ring a good cricket arena, lovers cannot meet there, and no one can meet there without having a hidden secret.

The one thing keeping the positive experiences away are the ghosts of the past: the gladiator killed in battle or in a sporting contest, and the woman who was strangled and burned. These past ghosts serve as "metaphors" for Michael and Susan, who have their own past problems haunting them. Although the meeting seems to bring the couple together, they are actually being led to their destruction as those in the past were. Michael will fall in a "battle" for his pride, while Susan is being strangled by Michael's control.

Chapter 12: Summary

Farfrae has been busily working in the office while Michael had his meeting. Michael enters and orders the young man to join him for supper. After dinner, Michael wants to tell the young man about his family matter. Farfrae listens intently as Michael tells him about his early marriage, his sale of his wife, and how his family has returned. Michael says that another woman is wronged by the return of his family. A young, well-bred woman in Jersey nursed the young Henchard to health, and during his recovery they fell in love. The young woman was careless of appearances; through her carelessness a scandal arose. She wrote many letters to Michael describing the severity of the scandal. Finally Michael promised to marry her if his wife never returned. Now that Susan is alive, Michael must honour his promise to her. Farfrae agrees that a letter must be written to the young lady to tell her of the situation, and to let her go. He also thinks that Elizabeth-Jane should know the truth, but Michael refuses to tell her. Farfrae writes the letter to the young lady in Jersey, and Michael sends it.

Analysis

Hardy now combines foreshadowing and the previous implications in this chapter. In Chapter 3, we speculated that Michael may have an attachment to another woman, and here we learn that there was, in the form of the young lady from Jersey. Having learned that Hardy never introduces anyone who does not affect the plot, we know that the young woman from Jersey will not be forgotten that easily.

Michael remains true to his mercurial character, and Hardy presents these traits in equal portions, both good and bad. Here he shows real remorse for all his actions against the women in his life, and a determined willingness to make everything right again. He wants to relieve his loneliness, so he confesses to the man whom he regards as his best friend. Yet he shows recklessness and impulsiveness in revealing his past to a man he has known for only a day.

Farfrae also has the ability to handle sticky situations with people. Although he planned to eat alone, he changes his plans to accommodate Michael's whim. He also gives Michael good advice in handling the woman from Jersey. However, there is a sign of discord between the friends. Michael disregards Farfrae's advice on telling Elizabeth-Jane the truth. This foreshadows future disagreements for the men.

Chapter 13: Summary

Michael begins calling upon the women in the cottage near the Roman ruins. The conversation is so skillfully made that Elizabeth-Jane has no idea of the plot her parents have created. Susan worries that this is taking up too much of Michael's time, but Michael says he will have free time now that he has a new manager. Soon the town begins to gossip openly about the relation between the mayor and the widow. Most of the townspeople are confused by his choice because Mrs. Newson is so pale and fragile. Still, no one can tell that Michael courts only out of a sense of duty to Susan and as a punishment to himself. The townspeople agree that the couple will eventually grow tired of each other.

Analysis

Michael finally lives up to his promise, making amends to Susan by openly courting and marrying her. Despite this, the whole chapter carries a tone of ill will and melancholy that is revealed in the natural world and within the townspeople of Casterbridge. Hardy uses pathetic fallacy—the act of having nature reflect the feelings the characters—to show the couple's true feelings about the wedding. The wind and rain that fall as they enter the church foreshadow the darkness, oppressiveness, and futility of their relationship, as well as showing the turbulent feelings of the man and woman who have no feelings for each other.

The townspeople also give a sense of uneasiness about the wedding. Although they don't know the secrets behind the proceedings, they understand that something is not quite right with the marriage. Ironically, they feel that Susan is of lower birth than Michael, a strange judgment since Susan exhibits more restraint and delicacy than Michael should as a gentleman.

At the centre of the turbulence Michael and Susan stand. Again Michael is willing to lower himself to make amends to Susan—going so far as to abase himself in the eyes of the community. Susan is in a difficult position: she secretly fears him and feels that their deception is wrong, but again she succumbs to her meekness and allows Michael to have his way.

Chapter 14: Summary

Susan and Elizabeth-Jane settle into their new household happily. Elizabeth-Jane in particular flourishes in her new environment, becoming more beautiful over time. However, her change in status does not change her mindset in any way. She is still respectable and sobre in tastes.

One day, Michael looks at Elizabeth-Jane's brown hair and asks Susan if the girl's hair was black when she was a baby. An astonished Susan jerks Michael's foot, and he saves himself from giving away their secret. However, after Elizabeth-Jane leaves, Michael continues to press for a deeper connection to his daughter. He wants her to take the name Henchard. Susan is hesitant, but agrees only if Elizabeth-Jane will accept it. Later, the mother goes to her daughter and convinces her not to take the name Henchard.

Elizabeth-Jane watches her stepfather's business and relationship from her new position as well. Under Farfrae's guidance, the corn business runs more smoothly. Michael also regards the younger man as a best friend, and he refuses to be separated from him for any reason. Elizabeth-Jane wants the attentions of the handsome Farfrae, but notices sadly that he never looks at her.

One day, Elizabeth-Jane finds a note from someone who wants to meet her at the granary on Durnover Hill. As she waits there, Farfrae arrives, looking for someone as well. Elizabeth-Jane hides, but a machine covers her in wheat husks and the noise catches the attentions of Farfrae. They realise that someone has sent them the same letter. Farfrae thinks someone has played a trick on them. He tells Elizabeth-Jane not to mention the incident to anyone. Before she leaves, Farfrae helps dust the embarrassed young woman off. He looks at her thoughtfully, affected by her beauty.

Analysis

Hardy introduces more elements of suspense in this chapter. Obviously something about Elizabeth-Jane's birth is amiss. We can see this in Michael's insistence on her hair colour and in Susan's reluctance to give her Michael's name. In addition, Hardy hints that the relationship between Michael and Farfrae may not be as rosy as it seems. Farfrae tries to separate from Michael and do his job, but Michael dismisses his feelings by saying, "don't take too much thought about things." Finally, we wonder who wants to bring Elizabeth-Jane and Farfrae together—is it really an act of fate, or has someone like Michael planned to bring them together?

Elizabeth-Jane begins to grow in this new environment, gaining beauty and more freedom. However, she still retains the lessons that her previous lifestyle has taught her. She retains her mother's mistrust of destiny, believing that Providence will ruin her if she shows too much happiness and gaiety. She also retains her sensitivity, offering to change her name if Michael really wishes it.

Chapter 15: Summary

Hardy begins by describing Elizabeth-Jane's rise in stature as the town beauty. Michael gives her some tinted gloves one day, and she slowly purchases articles that match the gloves. When she finally completes the ensemble, she wears it into town, delighting everyone with her beauty. At home, she expresses wonder at her new status, but then feels sadness because she hasn't received a good education.

Downstairs, Michael and Farfrae are watching the workers

leave for the day. Michael stops one worker, Abel Whittle, and says that Abel should show up on time for work the next day. Abel has a history of oversleeping and being late for work. The next morning, Abel is late, and Michael is so angry that he threatens to get Abel out of bed himself if he is late again.

Again, the next day Abel is late. Michael marches to Abel's home on Black Street, yanks him out of bed, and orders him to work—without his breeches. Farfrae sees the man arriving without pants, and is shocked. In front of all the workers, Farfrae orders Abel back home to get his pants. When Michael objects, Farfrae threatens to leave. Michael bends to his wishes, but not without feeling embarrassment. Later in the day, Farfrae learns that Michael cared for Abel's mother last winter. Michael continues to behave coldly towards the young man.

One day a young messenger asks for Farfrae to look at a haystack. The messenger says that the townspeople have more respect for Farfrae. When Michael meets Farfrae later in the day, Michael explodes in anger. He accuses Farfrae of trying to hurt his feelings. When the confused Farfrae apologizes, Michael quickly forgives him, but begins to regret confiding in him.

Analysis

This chapter has a bit of allegorical progression. Elizabeth-Jane and Michael serve as opposing forces (youth and old age, respectively) that open and close the chapter. Both use Farfrae as a measure of how far they have come or fallen, with Farfrae and the townspeople acting as catalysts for change. Through the characters of father and stepdaughter, Hardy seems to imply that youth has more freedom to fight fate, simply because young people are not as set in their ways as their elders are.

Elizabeth-Jane, the embodiment of gentle youth and beauty, is appreciated by Farfrae alone at first. As she begins to wear finer clothing to impress him, the Casterbridgians become more aware of her and begin to regard her as a good person. While she does feel a little prideful, however, she chooses to find ways to improve herself, so that she can properly meet the high regard of the townspeople. Michael, however, closes the chapter with a more negative view. Because the wiser Farfrae is present, the townspeople are not as fond of the older and bullish Michael. His outdated morals (severe punishment for a tardy but overworked man) and headstrong nature make him seem foolish. Rather than attempt to change himself for the public, Michael places all the blame on his young friend, becoming cold and moody.

In the character of Abel, Hardy utilizes several levels of Biblical allegory. Abel represents his namesake in the Cain and Abel story, who in turn has been taken to be a metaphor for Christ. Here Michael acts as a Cain figure, slaying his brother (that is, fellow worker's) with a weapon (the embarrassment of going to work without pants). After that, Abel becomes a Christ figure, crucified by the "mortification" of losing his pants. His fear that the townswomen are "laughing me to scorn" cites a Biblical passage, "All they that see him laugh him to scorn", often used to foretell the Crucifixion scene.

Summary and Analysis of Chapters 16-20

Chapter 16: Summary

Michael becomes more reserved towards Farfrae since the incidents of the last chapter. While the men are still close business partners, Michael no longer invites the young man to dinner with his family.

To celebrate a public holiday, Farfrae borrows some rick-cloths from Michael for some sort of entertainment. Michael lets him have the cloths, but then wonders why he (in his role as Mayor) has not found a way to celebrate the holiday. With the blessing of the city council, he plans a large outdoor entertainment with games. To ensure that everyone will come, he even announces that the festivities will be free of charge (unlike Farfrae's entertainment, which have an admission charge).

On the holiday, the stormy weather completely ruins Michael's fair. Gloomily he closes his own festivities and goes into Casterbridge, where all the townspeople are going to Farfrae's dance. Farfrae has used the cloths to form a tent, using some nearby trees for poles. Now the whole company dances wildly in the warm surroundings. Even Susan and Elizabeth-Jane have arrived, and later Farfrae has a dance with Elizabeth-Jane. The evening is a great success for Farfrae, as Michael jealously sees. After overhearing the remarks of the townspeople and the taunts of the councilmen, Michael says that Farfrae's time as manager is coming to a close. Farfrae quietly agrees. That night, Michael goes home, pleased that his reputation will be protected by firing Farfrae. The next morning, with his jealous rage spent, he regrets his mistake.

Analysis

Although Hardy adopts the omniscient narrator's voice through the novel, he manipulates the viewpoint throughout the novel to get inside a character's head. It is a way of understanding the character's motivations and a means of creating sympathy for the characters. In this chapter, Hardy writes so we see the events unfolding from Michael's view. This is an ironic choice, since we are looking at the events of a public holiday from the viewpoint of a private person who is nearly disconnected from the community. Yet we can experience Michael's frustrations by hearing only the jibes of the townspeople and the councilmen, and we can feel the jealousy that Michael feels upon seeing Farfrae's successful dance.

Even nature sides with Farfrae. The rain that ruined Michael's entertainment magically disappears in the evening, when Farfrae's dance is about to begin. The natural world appears to work for the success of the dance: the trees provide convenient, living poles for the tent cloths. Of course, Farfrae is the one who had the idea to use this spot in the first place. Like the townspeople, he is able to understand and adapt to nature. Perhaps the fate that is working against the business-oriented Michael works so well for the nature-loving Farfrae.

Chapter 17: Summary

Elizabeth-Jane feels ashamed when a friend tells her that she should have considered her position as the Mayor's stepdaughter before dancing. Susan has already left the ball, so Elizabeth-Jane leaves alone. Farfrae runs into her and offers to walk her home. As they walk, he says that he must leave Casterbridge because he has offended her stepfather. He also reveals that he would "ask her something" if he were richer. Elizabeth-Jane shyly hopes that he will not leave, then rushes home. She spends the following days waiting to hear any news about Farfrae.

Farfrae is not leaving Casterbridge; in fact, he plans to open his own hay and corn business. Upon hearing this, Michael openly calls Farfrae his enemy in front of the city council. The councilmen, however, practically ignore Michael's hurtful words, since Michael is rapidly falling out of favour in the town. Undaunted, Michael forbids Elizabeth-Jane to have any relationship with Farfrae. Next, he writes Farfrae to say that Elizabeth-Jane has promised to obey her stepfather and stay away.

Farfrae's business grows quickly, but he avoids any competition with Farfrae's company as a gesture of goodwill. He even sends away a customer who had dealt with Michael's company three months ago. Nevertheless, eventually the two men meet at the weekly market. When Farfrae receives an official stall at the marketplace, Michael considers the action to be a new attack. Michael becomes so bitter that he cannot stand it when Susan and Elizabeth-Jane mention the Scotsman's name at home.

Analysis

The chapter gives the upright Elizabeth-Jane more of a human character. Although her reckless dancing makes her blush, she indulges herself with fantasies of Farfrae's love letters. In addition, she also voices the same concerns that we as readers have. What will happen to their courtship now that Michael and Farfrae are on bad terms? While Susan seems to encourage the suit by conveniently leaving the dance early and by talking about Farfrae, Michael simply silences her.

Once again, Michael quickly changes his mind about his friends. He drags his hatred into the business arena by encouraging competition. Despite this, Farfrae continues to act friendly, even refusing business from customers to keep his friendship. It is worth noting that the city councilmen don't seem to share the belief that Michael can take Farfrae in competition.

"Character is Fate, said Novalis." This is one of the most debated comments in Hardy's novels. At first it seems to run against all of Hardy's insistence that man is ruined by an impersonal fate. Is Michael's fate determined by the gods, his own flaws, or a combination of the two? A case can be made for each response, since the novel seems to change opinions in several places.

Chapter 18: Summary

To Elizabeth-Jane's shock, Susan becomes too ill to leave her room. Michael sends for the richest and busiest doctor in town. Elizabeth-Jane spends the time at her mother's bedside.

One morning, Michael receives a letter from his former lover, the young lady in Jersey named Lucetta. She writes that she understands the situation of his remarriage, and that he is not to blame for her misfortunes. She only hopes that he can return the letters that she wrote to him early in their relationship. She plans to get them next Wednesday as she passes through town. Michael sighs and wishes that he could have married Lucetta. On the appointed day, he waits for her, but she does not appear, to his relief.

Meanwhile, Susan grows weaker. One day she asks to write something. After pen and paper are brought to her, she writes for a short while, then seals the letter, addressing it to "Michael Henchard. Not to be opened till Elizabeth-Jane's wedding day." Then she locks the letter in her desk.

Elizabeth-Jane, who has been lovingly watching over her mother, awakens at Susan's call. Susan confesses that she was the one who wrote the notes to the girl and Farfrae asking them to meet each other. She says that she wanted Farfrae to marry the girl, and laments that she will never see them wed.

One Sunday morning, Farfrae passes the house only to notice that all the blinds are down. When he rings the bell, he is informed that Susan has died. The townspeople discuss her death around the water pump.

Analysis

As usual, Hardy introduces more elements of suspense as he furthers the plot. Susan dies, but not before writing a cryptic letter that cannot be opened until a certain time. To replace Susan's role in more ways than one, Lucetta appears once more through her letters, though she does not appear when she is expected.

Susan leaves the novel with no real change in her outlook on life. Fate continued to treat her cruelly until the very end. As she says, "Nothing is as you wish it." In a sense nothing in her life has been as she wished it. Her "first" marriage ended horribly both times, and her "second" marriage was loving but eventually unlawful in her eyes. Her plan to bring Farfrae and Elizabeth-Jane together failed miserably. Through it all, she has remained meek, moved by the whims of her men. She cannot control the amount of happiness that Elizabeth-Jane gets after she is gone, though she lived for the girl's happiness. The poor woman does not even have the power to die in our presence—we only learn that she has died from Farfrae's questioning. Is the writing of this letter her last attempt to manipulate fate and take some sort of control? Mrs. Cuxsom foreshadows that the secret of the letter will be harmful: "Little things a' didn't wish seen, anybody will see."

Both Michael and the townspeople have little regard for Susan's death. Michael wishes that he had married Lucetta as Susan is dying. Mrs. Cuxsom shares the details of Susan's death with the eager listeners over the water pump. Coney even digs up the pennies that Susan had placed on her dead eyes and buried in the garden. These actions continue the disregard that everyone in Casterbridge has for Susan's feelings. They also emphasize the gruesome touch that Hardy brings to every novel.

Chapter 19: Summary

Three weeks after Susan's funeral, Michael and Elizabeth-

Jane speak of the old times. Elizabeth-Jane repeatedly refers to Newson as her father. This annoys Michael: after his wife's death and Farfrae's forced estrangement, the mayor feels a deep loneliness again. After a few moments, he confesses that he is her real father, and tells her an abbreviated version of their first marriage (carefully omitting the auction). Elizabeth-Jane bursts into tears as Michael says he will do anything to be a real father to her. He then asks if she is willing to change her last name to Henchard, and she helps him write up an announcement for the Casterbridge Chronicle. With that, he sends the girl to bed, telling her that he will have proof for her in the morning.

As he searches for the proof in Susan's desk, he thinks joyfully of his daughter and her good sense. Soon he comes across the letter that Susan wrote on her deathbed. The letter was not sealed very well, and as a result, the letter was already opened. Believing that the note on the front was just a whim of Susan's, Michael opens the letter and reads it. In the letter, Susan confesses that Elizabeth-Jane is actually Newson's daughter. The Elizabeth-Jane that was sold with Susan died three months after the sale. At first, Michael doesn't believe the letter, but the sleeping Elizabeth-Jane's features are definitely like Newson's features.

Michael spends the rest of the night cursing his fate. He walks past the jail and the gallows in the northeastern side of town, the most barren part of Casterbridge. When he returns, he is convinced that he must continue the lie rather than tell the truth and face humiliation. He experiences a deep blow to his emotions when Elizabeth-Jane admits that she believes Michael's confession from the night before, and she resolves to call him Father.

Analysis

Hardy delivers the most painful bit of irony yet in this chapter, revealing that Elizabeth-Jane is actually the sailor's daughter just as Michael convinces her of his claim to her. Mrs. Cuxsom's words from the last chapter were prophetic: "Little things a' didn't wish seen, anybody will see." Michael is forced to see everything that Susan didn't want him to see, both the letter that reveals the secret and the resemblance to Newson evident in Elizabeth-Jane's face.

Hardy has again shifted the viewpoint of the chapter back to Michael. We feel sympathy for him because we experience the joy of making her his daughter, followed quickly by the defeat the letter symbolizes, all through his eyes. We even see Nature mocking the fact that he does not have a child, as he walks through the section of Casterbridge that is the most barren, where "frost lingered" in springtime. As before, however, "Character is Fate." If Michael had not been so insistent on making Elizabeth-Jane his daughter, he would not have felt such a crushing blow when he learned the truth. If he had not blindly ignored the note on the front of the letter, he could have saved himself the pain. The bullish nature that he cannot shake has brought all of this upon him.

Chapter 20: Summary

Elizabeth-Jane is extremely shocked to feel Michael's cold demeanor so soon after his announcement. Soon he begins mocking the girl in the open, critical of her country dialect, her bold handwriting, and her consideration of the servants. Another fact brings him great shame. One day, when Elizabeth-Jane brings Nance Mockridge some bread and cider, Michael scolds her for helping the commoners. Nance indignantly tells Michael that Elizabeth-Jane once worked as a waitress in the Three Mariners. Elizabeth-Jane tries to explain, but Michael is convinced that her actions have cast him into the deepest shame. His beliefs seem to be confirmed when he is informed that he is not in the running for the position of alderman when his term as mayor ends. In addition, he becomes even angrier when her realizes that Farfrae will be given a position on the council. Wishing to rid himself of the girl who seems to have brought all of his misfortune, he invites Farfrae to continues his courtship of Elizabeth-Jane.

Now that her "father" avoids her, the miserable Elizabeth-Jane tries to win him back by devoting herself to her studies, teaching herself Latin with books and from the relics of Casterbridge's past. On the nice winter days, she spends some time at her mother's grave. One day, she goes to the graveyard to find a pretty young lady reading her mother's gravestone. The young lady is not from Casterbridge, but Elizabeth-Jane cannot catch up to speak to her. On another visit, the young lady finally speaks to Elizabeth-Jane after overhearing her lamentations. She is so sympathetic that Elizabeth-Jane pours out her heart to the young woman. The young lady is so moved that she offers the girl a position as companion. Elizabeth-Jane joyfully accepts, but the young woman promises to return for her final answer in a week.

Analysis

The suspense continues in this chapter. Who is the mysterious young lady that Elizabeth-Jane meets in the graveyard? Why is she so concerned about Elizabeth-Jane's problems? What will happen when Farfrae gets the letter about courting Elizabeth-Jane?

Now the viewpoint of the chapter shifts to Elizabeth-Jane. We automatically feel for the young lady who is being treated so cruelly by her "father." Hardy is so skilled at evoking pathos for her that we can easily turn on Michael, the man whom we sympathized with in the last chapter. Yet Hardy avoids making the girl into a saint and tries to make her behaviour more human. Elizabeth-Jane works hard at being the perfect girl for Michael, but she does it with tears streaming down her face and while wishing that she would die. Fortunately, the chapter also hints that good things are in store for the girl. She has a position with a charming young lady, and she has the promise of a courtship from Farfrae. In addition, she attempts to grow closer to the townspeople, giving them food and trying to learn more about the town.

Michael behaves very ironically in this chapter. He asks his stepdaughter, "Why do you lower yourself so confoundedly?" when in fact he seems to lower himself. He also shows that he prefers to believe both factions of public opinion. He is concerned with what the upper classes think, as in his concern for the girl's handwriting and her speech. Yet he also easily believes the lower classes, listening to Nance's words rather than Elizabeth-Jane's explanation. The ultimate irony is that the townspeople don't even like Michael anymore, choosing Farfrae over Michael for the city council.

SUMMARY AND ANALYSIS OF CHAPTERS 21-25

Chapter 21: Summary

Elizabeth-Jane concentrates on High-Place Hall and the lovely new stranger who has offered her a position there. The town is talking about the new lady who is coming to live there. One evening she sneaks away to have a look at the outside of the Hall. Because of its location directly over the marketplace, many of the previous owners have not spent very long at the hall. However, the lights upstairs and the movers have signaled that the new owner is here to stay for a while. As she turns to run home, she hears footsteps and runs to hide. She does not see that the footsteps belong to Michael, and he does not see her because she is so well hidden.

When Michael returns home, Elizabeth-Jane asks if she may leave home to go somewhere where she can gain some education. Michael quickly agrees, eager to have the girl out of his sight. Elizabeth-Jane later meets the lady, Miss Templeman, at the churchyard again. Together the women decide that Elizabeth-Jane will move into High-Place Hall that evening. Michael is surprised to see her leave so quickly, and tries to make her stay. Elizabeth-Jane assures him that she won't be far away—just at High-Place Hall. Michael is shocked to learn her destination.

Analysis

Hardy draws upon his architectural experience again. He describes the facades, parapets, and other sections with the eye of an architect. His talent for architectural detail also benefits the story. High-Place Hall has many little gruesome features that act as metaphors for the corruption within its walls. There are "damp nooks where fungi grew" and a mask over an archway that has been so beaten that it seems to have been "eaten away by disease." In addition, the placement of the house in the centre of town is significant. It implies that everyone who lives here will be at the centre of the events in town. Since both Elizabeth-Jane and Michael are secretly visiting the house, the house already draws the important personages near.

Elizabeth-Jane and Michael continue to act as opposites. By this point, Michael seems to have no affection for Elizabeth-Jane whatsoever, treating her with "absolute indifference." (Yet, as in his relationship with Farfrae, he also seems to regret sending the girl away so quickly.) However, Elizabeth-Jane continues to have a loving spirit. Not only does she promise to return if Michael needs her, she also regards the house as a place where she can find love—she comes there "with a lover's feeling."

Chapter 22: Summary

As Elizabeth-Jane considers going to High-Place Hall to see Lucetta, Michael receives a letter from Lucetta saying that she is staying at High-Place Hall. He has learned that the Hall is being rented by a Miss Templeman, not a Miss Le Sueur (the name by which Michael had known Lucetta in Jersey). Later Lucetta sends him another note: she has taken the name of Templeman from a recently deceased aunt, the woman who left the Hall and her fortune to Lucetta. In this note, Lucetta also explains her choice of companion. When Michael comes to visit his daughter, he can conveniently call upon Lucetta at the same time. Michael is pleased by her inheritance and amused by her tactics to lure him to the hall. He leaves immediately to call on Lucetta, but is told that she is engaged and will see him tomorrow. Annoyed by her "airs," he plans to punish her by staying away from her for a few days.

That evening, Elizabeth-Jane and Lucetta talk. Although she planned to introduce herself as a woman from Bath, she tells Elizabeth-Jane about Jersey, the half-French, half-English region. Elizabeth-Jane is fascinated by the young woman, even if she seems a bit flighty.

The next morning Lucetta eagerly awaits Michael's visit. As she and Elizabeth-Jane watch the town from their window, they watch Michael walking through the market. He accidentally meets Farfrae, but ignores him. Lucetta wonders if the girl is interested in anyone outside.

Two more days pass, and still Michael has not visited. Elizabeth-Jane tells Lucetta that her stepfather will not come because he is angry with her. Lucetta bursts into tears because her scheme is failing. She sends Elizabeth-Jane on several errands, then writes a quick note to Michael, telling him that she will be alone today. When someone finally calls, Lucetta hides behind a curtain. She leaps out, only to discover that the caller is not Michael.

Analysis

The situation that Lucetta suggests acts as a parallel scene to Michael and Susan's plan to fool the residents of Casterbridge. Michael is placed in the position that Susan held. Love does not figure into Michael's plans of marriage either: like Susan, Michael feels that having a wealthy wife can only benefit him "though he was not a fortune-hunter." Lucetta holds the role that Michael had. She suggests that she take the new name and home (as Susan was forced to do). Elizabeth-Jane will again play a part in the courtship: she is again the lure that brings Michael to the house.

Hardy makes Lucetta a stock character as the flighty Frenchwoman, and she serves as a foil to the more upright Elizabeth-Jane. As we saw in Chapter 20, Lucetta is concerned with fashion (while Elizabeth-Jane only flirted with fashion and stuck to her own somber clothing). In this chapter, Lucetta focuses on putting things into pretty French phrases, sitting in pretty poses (as if she were posing for the painter Titian), and manipulating people. How can the somber and shy Elizabeth-Jane ever compare to Lucetta? Although Lucetta manipulates Elizabeth-Jane, she still finds herself telling her new companion her past life. Thus, we see that Lucetta has the capacity for kindness despite all her deception.

Finally, Hardy closes the chapter with a cliffhanger to keep the readers interested in the story. Who is the man? Why has he come? Does he have a connection to Lucetta as well?

Chapter 23: Summary

As it turns out, the visitor is Donald Farfrae, handsome and impeccably dressed. He has come to see Elizabeth-Jane. Lucetta and Farfrae are embarrassed at their surprise encounter, but soon they find that they are becoming attracted to each other. They converse pleasantly, engaging in light, flirtatious comments the whole time.

Underneath the window, a business transaction takes place. A young man must work on a distant farm, leaving his sweetheart behind. Lucetta and Farfrae are both moved by the great emotion shown by the lovers. Farfrae hurries outside to hire the young man, and Lucetta is touched by his kind spirit. Soon after, Farfrae leaves with the promise to visit again, having completely forgotten about Elizabeth-Jane.

Three minutes later, a maid announces that Michael has come to call on Lucetta. Lucetta says she has a headache and will not see him today. Michael leaves. When Elizabeth-Jane returns, Lucetta resolves to keep the girl around as a way to keep Michael from visiting her.

Analysis

Hardy's wry humour shines through in this chapter. Lucetta's invitation to Farfrae to sit is a good example. Farfrae "hesitated, looked at the chair, thought there was no danger in it, and sat down." Such ironic humour is typical of Hardy.

This chapter brings Farfrae back into the story and reminds us of his outlook on things. Farfrae has a cautious manner by nature. He explores the chair and all his options before sitting down. He also has a tender heart, as shown in his desire to keep the young man and his lover together. Finally, he plans to continue all his past obligations with Elizabeth-Jane, showing his honesty and faithfulness.

Lucetta is the opposite in temperament. Instead of being cautious, she openly shows interest in the stranger and begins flirting with him. Although she shows a tender heart in wanting the lovers to stay together, she completely ignores the young man's plan to see Elizabeth-Jane and keeps him for herself. She lies to attract the young man: although she insists that she is not a coquette, her flirtatious manner with Farfrae lies for her. She manipulates people again, keeping Elizabeth-Jane around just to keep Michael away from her. Can Farfrae and Lucetta have a true relationship despite their differences?

Chapter 24: Summary

Elizabeth-Jane is glad to learn that Lucetta will stay. Lucetta's window provides a great view of the marketplace and Farfrae's stall there. Both women secretly steal glances at Farfrae without the other's knowledge.

One Saturday, Lucetta's dresses arrive from London, and Lucetta chooses to wear the new cherry-coloured dress on their trip into town. A new seeding machine called a horse-drill is brought to town, and the women wish to travel into town to see it. As they examine the drill, Michael Henchard speaks to Elizabeth-Jane.

She introduces her stepfather to Lucetta, who is polite. After mocking the horse-drill, Michael leaves, pausing only to murmur "You refused to see me!" to Lucetta. Elizabeth-Jane wonders what the sentence could mean. Suddenly the women hear Farfrae's humming from inside the drill. He reveals that he has purchased this revolutionary machine. As he talks to Lucetta, Elizabeth-Jane notices that the two seem very close. As the women rest at the end of the day, Lucetta comments upon Michael's distance to Elizabeth-Jane.

Curious, Elizabeth-Jane starts to wonder about Lucetta's own past and life, and she decides to keep an eye on her companion. One day she imagines that Lucetta has met Farfrae, and asks a nervous Lucetta about the meeting. Later Lucetta tells the story of her past, making it seem as if it has happened to another woman. Finally, Lucetta asks what the other woman should do now that "she" has grown fond of another man. Elizabeth-Jane cannot give her a definite answer. However, the girl sighs that Lucetta could not tell her the whole truth—for she knows that Lucetta is "she" of the story.

Analysis

The drill serves to remind us of the differences between Farfrae and Michael. Farfrae focuses solely on the business, while Michael has to mix business with personal relationships. Farfrae obviously believes in progress and the use of technology in bringing the drill to town. Michael's stubborn conservative streak causes him to ridicule the machine which is "impossible it should act." There is actually no reason why Michael should be against the machine, except for the "jackanapes" who had it delivered.

The theme of being plagued by a blind fate has already become clear to Susan and Michael. Now the same fate is working against Elizabeth-Jane, in the form of a relationship between Farfrae and Lucetta. It is obvious that Farfrae and Elizabeth-Jane are better suited: Elizabeth-Jane shares his love of change, and they both understand the Scriptures (when Lucetta has a "somewhat limited" knowledge of them). However, she learns of their growing infatuation by means of a scene that parallels the meeting of Farfrae and Elizabeth-Jane. As he did when he met Elizabeth-Jane, he hums a tune that blatantly refers to Lucetta. Despite her disappointment and confusion, Elizabeth-Jane remains stoic and quiet, increasing our respect for her.

Chapter 25: Summary

Farfrae calls upon Lucetta and Elizabeth-Jane frequently. Although Elizabeth-Jane is in the room, Farfrae completely ignores her, choosing to give all his attention to the livelier Lucetta. Soon Elizabeth-Jane realizes that Farfrae is the second man from Lucetta's story—he is blatantly in love with her, with all traces of his past infatuation for Elizabeth-Jane gone.

Michael also calls upon Lucetta. His love for her has increased now that she has proclaimed her love for another man. Lucetta treats him with a cool but cordial air. Michael offers for her hand, and after attempting to change the subject, Lucetta gives an evasive answer. Farfrae rides past as Lucetta and Michael talk, but Michael does not see Lucetta's loving look at Farfrae. Michael leaves, dejected, while Lucetta passionately proclaims that she will forsake the past to love Farfrae. Elizabeth-Jane watches the whole situation and is crushed that the two most important men in her life do not care about her. Farfrae's rejection makes sense because Lucetta is a very desirable woman. However, she cannot understand why her father has become so cold. Nevertheless, she becomes reconciled to being unloved.

Analysis

Hardy brings all the major characters together in the house that sits in the centre of the square. True to his theme, the cruel fate continues to haunt both Michael and Elizabeth-Jane. However, the way each handles the fate speaks volumes about the better person. When Michael is rejected by Lucetta, he implies that he will keep trying to win the woman, even through blackmail: "What is known in your native Jersey may get known here." Elizabeth-Jane, however, takes rejection with a grain of salt. "She... wondered what unwished-for thing Heaven might send her in place of him."

Lucetta reveals her own tragic flaws here. First, like Michael, she is haunted by her past. She is so terrified by her past that she attempts to remake herself: "How you keep on about Jersey! I am English!" Another flaw is her reckless emotion. "I'll love where I choose!" In the following chapters, these flaws will slowly bring her dark fate as well.

Summary and Analysis of Chapters 26-30

Chapter 26: Summary

One morning, Farfrae and Michael pass each other. Farfrae merely nods to his former friend, but Michael stops. He asks the young man if he remembers the story he told about the "second woman," and says that the woman will not have him. Farfrae says that he owes the woman nothing more, and the men part. Farfrae is convinced that the woman of the story is not Lucetta, and Michael is convinced that Farfrae is not the rival for Lucetta's affections. However, soon afterwards, Michael is having tea with Lucetta when Farfrae enters. Lucetta becomes so nervous and fluttery that Michael believes Farfrae is the rival. Elizabeth-Jane, who is watching the scene, is disgusted at everyone's behaviour.

Michael sends for Joshua Jopp, the former applicant for the position of general manager, hoping that Jopp can still serve as a foreman. Jopp, who has been living in the slums of Casterbridge, names a moderate salary. To further persuade Michael, Jopp says that he lived in Jersey when Michael used to work there. Michael eagerly hires him. Jopp's first assignment is to ruin "the Scotsman's" business any way he can. Elizabeth-Jane learns that Michael has hired Jopp, whom she thinks is unfit for the position. When she tries to express her apprehension, Michael merely snaps at her.

The harvest weather always influences the price of grain. This June, the rains foretell a very bad harvest season, sending grain prices up. Michael wants to have proof that the harvest will fail, so he consults a weather diviner, Mr. Fall (who is called Wide-oh behind his back). Mr. Fall predicts that the harvest will be extremely rainy. Spurred by this prediction, Michael buys all the grain he can. However, soon the weather becomes perfect, and Michael loses money selling the corn at lower prices. He loses so much money that he must mortgage much of his property—and running into a sympathetic Farfrae on the way to the bank does not help Michael's mood. Michael fires Jopp for giving him bad advice, but Jopp swears that Michael will be sorry.

Analysis

Elizabeth-Jane is once again the voice of reason when all the other characters are blinded by other passions. Farfrae is blinded by love for Lucetta; Lucetta is blinded by love for Farfrae and fear of Michael; Michael is blinded by a hatred of Farfrae. The reintroduction of Jopp figures heavily in this triangle: he hates Michael and Farfrae, and his connections to Jersey could cause him to have some connection to Lucetta. However, we must remember that Jopp is the villain. He lives in the slums of town, reflecting his true nature. His events and knowledge will inevitably lead to ruin.

The description of the farmer's connection to the weather

is in keeping with the villagers' beliefs earlier in the novel. As stated before, the people derive their strength from the nature and from the pagan beliefs, even as they progress and use the latest technology. The danger is in believing in the old ways too much, as Michael does in his visit to the weather forecaster. Michael believes that this man can accurately predict the weather, which is simply foolish. The man's nickname gives a clue: "Wide-oh" could easily mean "wide off." Farfrae relies on sound business planning and that certain instinct that true people of nature have, and as a result he is a success.

Mr. Fall's name is certainly an allegory. He stands for the season of autumn, or fall—we can tell by his own reliance on "the sun, moon, and stars." His name is also a warning to Michael. Soon Michael will come to a "fall" in status because of his foolishness.

Chapter 27: Summary

Farfrae begins buying grain when the fair harvest weather drives prices down. Just as Michael believes that the diviner could be correct, the weather immediately becomes damp. Farfrae turns a large profit, and Michael knows that the strange fate is again ruining him.

One September evening, Lucetta and Elizabeth-Jane hear a great outcry under the window. The hay wagons of Henchard and Farfrae have crashed, and both wagon drivers are loudly blaming each other. As the men begin a fight, Michael arrives. He blames Farfrae's driver, but Lucetta and Elizabeth-Jane, who saw the whole accident, blame Michael's driver. Michael's driver says that the women are just lying because they love Farfrae. Lucetta hurries into the house before Michael can ask her if it's true. The constable rides up saying that there is only one case to hear in court—the case of a disorderly old woman. Michael agrees to hear the case.

Afterwards, he tries to visit Lucetta, only to learn that she has another "engagement." From his hiding place in the shadows, he watches as Farfrae arrives for Lucetta. Michael follows them to the Market House. Farfrae and Lucetta declare their love for each other, though Lucetta wishes to have her way in some things. Michael leaves, going to Lucetta's home and waiting for her there. When she returns, Michael threatens to reveal their past connections if she does not agree to marry him. With Elizabeth-Jane as a witness, Michael forces Lucetta into accepting him. Elizabeth-Jane wonders why Lucetta is so familiar with her father.

Analysis

Now Michael shows his own gift for clairvoyance in this chapter. He predicts that the conjurer was correct, that Farfrae will be Mayor, and that Lucetta's rival is Farfrae. Hardy adds a sly prediction in his noting that Lucetta had an "engagement" to go out. Of course, Michael's "fetishistic" beliefs, such as clairvoyance and superstition, surface in the face of defeat. In losing his grain and his money, Michael believes that someone is "stirring an unholy brew to confound me!"

Like Michael, Lucetta is haunted by the past—in her case, the past in Jersey. Instead of making it right, however, Lucetta chooses to run away from it, saying, "I don't want to hear it!" Michael behaves as he did in handling the marriage to Susan, in a loveless and bullying manner. His rough manner is made worse by the fact that Farfrae is the chief rival, and he will do anything to ruin Farfrae.

Chapter 28: Summary

As a magistrate, Michael is obliged to preside over the court in the absence of the new Mayor, Dr. Chalkfield. As the constable told him the night before, there is only one case, that of the old woman. Michael looks at the old woman, believing that he knows her, but has no idea why.

Constable Stubberd explains that the old woman was disorderly in a gutter near the church. The old woman says that he is not giving sound testimony, but the magistrates disagree. After stumbling around the curse words that the old woman has said, the constable is stopped by Michael, who wants the woman's testimony. In response, she tells the story of the auction from Weydon-Priors twenty years ago, ending by saying that the man of the story was Michael. Although the magistrates try to stop the woman, Michael admits that the story is true, then steps down from the bench.

Meanwhile, one of Lucetta's servants has heard the story from the old furmity-seller. When Lucetta wonders why so many people are around town today, the servant tells her the whole story. Lucetta has never known why Michael and Susan were separated, so the news comes as a shock to her. She tells Elizabeth-Jane that she must vacation at Port-Bredy for a few days. When Michael calls on Lucetta later that week, Elizabeth-Jane tells him where Lucetta has gone. The next day, Elizabeth-Jane says she has returned, but is walking along the road to Port-Bredy.

Analysis

Coincidence strikes again—what else could explain the furmity-seller's appearance in a town that is some miles away from her home base of Weydon-Priors? It is ironic that she, as a woman of a lower class and one who almost had forgotten the incident when Susan asked, should appear to bring down the gentleman mayor. The scene serves as a parallel scene to Nance Mockridge's accusation against Elizabeth-Jane in Chapter 20.

Hardy's humour shows again in the ineptitude of the court, with the clerk who cannot keep up with the testimony, and the foolish Stubberd who stumbles around curse words. Despite the wry commentary on the court, the magistrates are all convinced the furmity-seller is not to be believed (they have ruled against her two times before her accusation). Michael could have agreed with the magistrates and discounted her claim. However, we must respect him for his display of morality. The confession is also in keeping with his mercurial character as one of his many sudden decisions.

Chapter 29: Summary

Lucetta walks along the road to Port-Bredy, eagerly waiting for Farfrae. Elizabeth-Jane appears to meet Lucetta. Suddenly the women become aware of an old bull that has escaped from his pen. As they run to a nearby barn for protection, the bull begins to chase them. Although the women make it to the barn, the bull enters and is ready to attack the women. Then a hand reaches out to grab the bull by his leading stick. It is Michael, who calmly subdues the bull and rescues the women.

Lucetta cries that she has left her muff in the abandoned barn, and Elizabeth-Jane runs back for it. On her way back to town, she meets Farfrae, who gives her a ride back into town. As they ride, Elizabeth-Jane tells Farfrae about the meeting with the bull and the rescue by Michael. Farfrae is very upset by the news, but does not attempt to find Lucetta for fear of intruding upon her and Michael. He drops Elizabeth-Jane off and goes home to continue packing for his move.

Meanwhile, Michael is helping Lucetta to town. He tells her that he will agree to an "indefinite engagement." Lucetta wants to do something in return for his rescue. Michael begs her to tell the creditor Mr. Grower that they will soon be married, in order to keep Grower from pressing for a payment. Lucetta cannot agree to this, since Grower was a witness to her wedding with Farfrae. After she heard about the auction, she felt unsafe with Michael. She went to Port-Bredy to marry Farfrae. Michael is so enraged that he sends Lucetta away roughly, threatening to reveal their past connection once again.

Analysis

Naturally, the bull is a metaphor for Michael, who like the bull has placed Lucetta and Elizabeth-Jane in danger on several occasions. Like Michael, in Elizabeth-Jane's view the bull does not seem so terrifying, perhaps "having intended a practical joke than a murder." (Look for similar words that Michael uses to describe himself in Chapter 35.)

Irony strikes another blow to Michael in this chapter—the first of many blows that will occur in this section. He has risked himself to save the woman he loves—the woman who is actually his rival's wife. Yet there is an element of suspense present: Michael still has Lucetta's past as a deadly weapon. Despite his anger, he is still honourable enough (or perhaps prideful enough) not to take any of the money that Lucetta offers him for saving her life. This is the first mention of the creditor Mr. Grower in the novel. His name is almost certainly an allegorical one that could represent God, though whether it is the Christian God or a pagan god is unclear. "Grower" hearkens back to the days in village folklore when people believed that certain agricultural gods were responsible for the harvest. Yet Michael and Lucetta seem to speak of him as the judgmental Christian God. Michael says that "it is at [Grower's] hands that I shall suffer if at anybody's," and Lucetta's cry that Grower has witnessed the marriage brings to mind a line from the marriage ceremony: "Those whom God has joined together, let no man put asunder."

Chapter 30: Summary

Donald tells his landlady to move all his belongings to Lucetta's home. The move had been delayed because he had to take care of some business in Port-Bredy. He finally arrives at High-Place Hall to a warm welcome. Together they agree to tell Elizabeth-Jane about their marriage and to ask her to stay at the Hall. Lucetta meets Elizabeth-Jane and hesitantly begins to tell the girl about her past. Elizabeth-Jane wryly notes that she knows who the lady of the story is, and that her father is the first man in the story. She tells Lucetta that she has two "proper" choices: marry Michael, or remain single. When Lucetta flings her hand out, revealing her wedding-ring, Elizabeth-Jane thinks that Lucetta has married Michael. When Lucetta confesses that she has married Farfrae, Elizabeth-Jane is crushed. She quietly moves out of the Hall to an apartment across the street from Michael's rooms. The townspeople, who have been discussing the secret wedding, wonder if Farfrae will live off Lucetta's vast funds.

Analysis

This chapter seems to give illogical behaviours to the characters. Farfrae, strangely enough, seems more concerned with securing his business appointments rather than hurrying home to his new bride. Perhaps Hardy means to hint that Farfrae and Lucetta really are not right for each other.

Elizabeth-Jane also acts strangely in this chapter. We know that Elizabeth-Jane is a stickler for propriety, and would insist that Lucetta marry her father to save face. Yet we cannot explain why Elizabeth-Jane has not heard any of the gossip surrounding the furmity-seller's accusations. Hardy tries to cover up his logical mishap by saying that she is "never knowing what's going on," but even Elizabeth-Jane's too perfect ears would have heard something about her stepfather. Perhaps Hardy is trying to refer back to the quote from that she throws at Lucetta, which translates as, "Though I approve of the better things I see, I follow after the worse." This ironic quote certainly represents Elizabeth-Jane's tendency to support the "worse" characters of Lucetta and Michael.

SUMMARY AND ANALYSIS OF CHAPTERS 31-35

Chapter 31: Summary

Within a day, the furmity-seller's story had become common knowledge in Casterbridge. After such a shocking confession, Henchard's fortunes decrease along with his good name. One of his largest debtors fails, and his employees make bad decisions in purchasing corn. He has lost nearly all his fortune. The creditors take possession of any property Michael has left. During the bankruptcy proceedings, Michael offers everything he has: a gold watch and a money-bag containing spare change. The creditors refuse these items, praising Michael for his honesty. Although he is touched by their compassion, Michael still pawns the watch and uses the money to pay a minor creditor.

Elizabeth-Jane tries to find her father, but writing letters and trying to visit him does no good. She learns that he has moved into Jopp's cottage at Priory Mill, and that he will see no one. As she passes the old business, Abel Whittle tells her that Farfrae owns it now. Farfrae uses the modern equipment, and the men are happy with the working conditions despite the lower salary.

Analysis

The dark fate again haunts Henchard. Despite his noble

act of confession, the townspeople instantly think his act is scandalous—implying the hurtful nature of public opinion once more. Ironically, Michael could have stopped the damage if he had been honest from the beginning. Hardy notes that the damage would not have been as great if the news had been older. Regardless, his debtors fail and all his property is taken. On the other end of the scale, Farfrae has gained the business that Michael has lost due to the same fate.

The punishment that Michael deems fitting for himself is self-destruction. We can see this in his refusal to take the comfort of Elizabeth-Jane and his moving in with his enemy Jopp. Jopp and Michael have a strange, parasitic relationship: Michael stays with Jopp because the man continues to taunt him with his signs of failure. Michael also returns to the depressing and barren side of town, giving Nature a hand in his depression. This chapter also contains a hint of Hardy's intent to connect the series of Wessex novels. One of the men at the bankruptcy proceedings is "a reserved young man named Boldwood." Boldwood appeared in an earlier Wessex novel, Far from the Madding Crowd. This is Hardy's attempt to fashion a reality for his characters and his world.

Chapter 32: Summary

Two bridges on the road leading away from town have long had a reputation for attracting failures and suicides. The poorer people of town visit the near bridge made of brick, while the upper-class people visit the farther one made of stone. Michael frequently visits the stone bridge. One afternoon, Jopp meets him there. He tells Michael that the Farfraes have moved into their new house (Michael's former mansion) and have bought new furniture (Michael's old furniture). Jopp then leaves, satisfied that he has ruined Michael's heart. Michael is bitter at his changed fortune. However, things seem to change when Farfrae comes to visit Michael. He offers Michael a space in his former home, which Michael refuses. Farfrae then offers Michael any furniture that might have sentimental value. Michael begins to think that he may have wronged Farfrae.

Elizabeth-Jane spends most of her days involved in her studies. She does not look out her window at Farfrae and Lucetta, who appear very happy. She hears that Michael has a cold, and leaves to take care of him. At first Michael tries to send her away, but she stays and promises to visit more often. Her visits soon bring him back to health and give him a better outlook on life. He even applies to Farfrae for a job as a hay-trusser. Farfrae employs him, but always sends instructions through a third person.

Michael has now returned to the clothes of a hay-trusser. A ragged blue suit is the last piece of his gentlemanly past. At first he seems very happy with his new life. However, rumors that Farfrae will be elected Mayor are beginning to surface. Upon hearing this and watching the happy Farfraes, Michael slowly grows more angry. When Elizabeth-Jane overhears that Michael is now drinking (after twenty-one years), she hurries to find her father.

Analysis

The bridges of the town are made of brick and stone. They act as metaphors for the differences in lifestyle between the lower classes and the upper classes. The brick bridge symbolizes progress and hope (as brick is the man-made material). The lower classes often come here to think of their misfortunes, but they do not brood on them: "they said they were down on their luck." The misfortunes of the poor are temporary and based upon the whim of fate. The upper classes, however, go to the farther bridge that is made of the more natural stone. The upper classes, like Michael, go there to "muse" on their fate, rather than dismissing it. The stone bridge is farther from town to hide the aristocrats from prying eyes. The stone, the older material, also implies that the aristocrats are rooted in the past.

Farfrae continues his ironic climb to power. He now acquires Michael's house and furniture, making his victory almost complete. Yet he remains kind to Michael, offering him a home and furniture. Elizabeth-Jane also continues to be kind despite all of Michael's rejections, giving him tenderness and someone who cares about him. Michael is in the same situation as he was twenty-one years before. Again he is a hay-trusser who is down on his luck. He has seen another man take his woman away once more. It is natural that such a dire repetition of events should lead Michael to drink once again.

Chapter 33: Summary

Later that Sunday, Michael joins the Casterbridge workers in the weekly discussion and singing that takes place in the Three Mariners. The people welcome him, and offer to sing the Fourth Psalm for him. Michael angrily orders the company to sing the 109th Psalm, a Psalm about a man who has "ill-got riches." As the Farfraes leave church, Michael says that the Psalm is dedicated to Donald, to everyone's shock. Fortunately, Elizabeth-Jane arrives to take her drunken father home. His veiled threats against Farfrae convince her that Farfrae must be warned. Later in the week, Abel Whittle's pitying looks cause Michael to explode. Elizabeth-Jane offers to help, not only to keep Whittle away from her father, but also to see what happens when Michael and Farfrae meet.

Lucetta is never seen out of her husband's company, and she glories in his love. One day, she stumbles into the barn where Michael is working. Michael greets her with a sarcastic servility. The next day Lucetta sends him a note that begs him not to be so bitter the next time they meet. Although Michael realizes this letter could ruin Lucetta, he tosses it into the fire.

Elizabeth-Jane brings Michael tea in an effort to keep him away from stronger drink. One day, she arrives to find her father and Farfrae talking near an open door on the top floor. Michael makes a movement with his arms, as if he plans to push Farfrae out the door and to his death. She is so frightened by this gesture that she resolves to warn Farfrae of the potential danger.

Analysis

Hardy adds the usual smattering of irony to this chapter. The first irony occurs in the Casterbridge custom of meeting for drinks on Sunday. Although the people are gathering in the tavern to discuss the Christian sermon, Hardy likens it to a ritual in "the monolithic circle at Stonehenge." The landlord also has all the tools needed for the ritual in quantities of forty: cups, pipes and chairs. The scene shows the Wessex tendency to combine the Christian with the pagan, and the villagers' tendencies to remain close to the old ways and religions.

Another ironic incident is the dedication of the 109th Psalm to Donald by Michael. Michael intends it to be a prophetic song, but as we can see, the Psalm actually traces Michael's fall. Michael's child is an orphan, and his wife was "a widow plunged in grief." The fruit of all Michael's toil was taken away by "strangers" in the form of creditors. Michael seems to realise how much it impacts his life as he is led away from the tavern.

Michael is obviously more bitter than ever about the quick change in the Farfraes' fortunes. His painfully sarcastic remarks about the feelings of "we of the lower classes" makes that clear. To be fair, the Farfraes are "higher" than the rest of the town: Lucetta's window "aloft" over the marketplace, Farfrae's business taking him to the top of the loft. Michael's threat to push Farfrae from the top of the building symbolizes his desire for Farfrae to "fall from a great height," as Michael did.

Chapter 34: Summary

The next morning, Elizabeth-Jane rises early and goes to meet Farfrae. When she says that Michael may try to injure him, he is incredulous. Farfrae makes light of her fears, but later that day the town clerk says the same. Farfrae came to discuss the terms of a recent agreement. In exchange for the town council's underwriting the costs of a seed shop, Farfrae will pay fifty pounds as down payment. The seed shop was for Michael's "new beginning." At the town clerk's warning, however, Farfrae decides to stop negotiations with the owner of the shop. The disappointed shop owner later tells Michael that the council had wanted to give him a shop, but Farfrae had ruined the plans.

Lucetta greets her husband warmly at the end of the day,

but notices that he is preoccupied. Farfrae confesses that he is confused and hurt by Michael's hatred. Lucetta, afraid that Farfrae will eventually learn of her past indiscretion, suggests that they leave town. Farfrae considers her suggestion until a visitor comes. It is Alderman Vatt, announcing Mayor Chalkfield's death and offering the mayorship to Farfrae. Farfrae accepts, since it is the will of the people and the will of the Powers above.

Soon after, Lucetta accidentally meets Michael in the crowded marketplace. She asks him to return her old letters again, since the death of her aunt prevented her from getting them previously. Michael says he doesn't know where they are, but he will think about finding them. As the town celebrates Farfrae's election, Michael remembers that the letters are right under Lucetta's nose, in the dining-room safe of the old house.

The next day, Farfrae decides to allow Michael into the house to open the safe. Michael finds the letters there. He reminds Farfrae of the story behind the letters, then begins to read them aloud to the bored Farfrae. However, he always stops reading before he reveals the writer.

Analysis

This chapter is filled with irony, all of it caused by the coincidence/ strange fate that has haunted the Henchards. Now it seems that the fate is beginning to turn on Lucetta. Just as she has convinced Farfrae that leaving is the best solution, the city council offers Farfrae the most powerful position in the city government. She wants to keep her past with Michael a secret, yet she continues to meet him in public places. She asks Michael for the letters that are as close as her own living room. Finally, her own words come back to haunt her as Michael reads his love letters to her husband, revealing her tragic flaw as "a creature too unconventionally devoted to you."

The reversal of roles between Farfrae and Michael is complete. Now Farfrae even has Michael's job, and the whole town is pleased. Each level of society, from the upper to the lower classes, is represented in the metaphor of the ringing bells: "brass, wood, catgut, and leather bands." Nevertheless, Farfrae remains cautious: he has premonitions of failure.

Michael has been given several motivations and opportunities for revenge. He believes that Farfrae ruined his chances for getting a shop. Yet he can be seen with Lucetta, and he can reveal who the writer of the letters is...and he doesn't, since the thought "appalled even him. This shows that, despite all his violent thoughts, Michael is still a noble man at heart.

Chapter 35: Summary

Lucetta retired early, but not to sleep. As she amused herself, she heard someone reading something downstairs. Thinking someone was reading about a crime, she tiptoed down the staircase, only to hear her letters in Michael's words. Michael says that he will not destroy the letters, then leaves. As she returns to her room, she fears that Michael has told everything, but Farfrae seems to know nothing of her past. The next morning she writes a note to Michael asking to meet at the Ring that evening. Then she works on making herself appear haggard.

At sunset she meets Michael in the Ring. Seeing the haggard young woman waiting reminds him of his past meeting with Susan, and his heart melts with pity. As she begs for her letters, he thinks that she has placed herself in a very compromising situation. He says that reading the letters was just a practical joke, and he promises to give them back the next morning.

Analysis

Hardy again changes the viewpoint to create sympathy. By seeing the events from Lucetta's viewpoint, we can experience the embarrassment she feels upon hearing her youthful words, her fear that Henchard can ruin her by revealing her past indiscretions to her husband. Although she continues to do foolish things (such as continuing to meet Michael) and manipulative things (such as deliberately planning to look humble to inspire pity) at least we realise why she is doing these things—so that she can be "a faithful and deserving wife." She first believes that the reading of the letters was someone reading about a "crime," an ironic belief since she would regard it as a crime.

Once again, the Ring acts as the Coliseum of Casterbridge, serving as a place for a face-off between the gladiator Michael and the "creature" Lucetta. Lucetta behaves as a wild animal in the encounter, openly scratching at Michael with blatant accusations: "It is all your fault." Michael, ironically, is not affected by her animal tactics, but by her weak, haggard appearance. Michael is also aware of how the scene mirrors his previous meeting in the Ring with Susan. Michael is even motivated by the same feelings that caused his kindness to Susan: not love, but pity.

SUMMARY AND ANALYSIS OF CHAPTERS 36-40

Chapter 36: Summary

When Lucetta returns from the Ring, Jopp is waiting for her. He meekly offers his services to Farfrae as a working partner, and asks Lucetta if she will speak in his favour. Lucetta says she knows nothing about Jopp, but Jopp insists that she knew him from her days in Jersey. Lucetta quickly leaves, fearful that Donald will notice that she is missing.

Jopp returns to his cottage, where Michael is waiting for him. He asks Jopp to take a package (containing Lucetta's letters) to Mrs. Farfrae that night, and Jopp agrees to do so. When Michael retires for the night, Jopp spends some time considering the relationship between Michael and Lucetta from the days in Jersey to the present. Curious and still angry that Lucetta so haughtily rejected him, Jopp opens the package and sees the bundle of letters. However, he seals up the package once again and leaves to deliver it.

On his walk, Jopp meets Mrs. Cuxsom and Nance Mockridge. They invite him to Peter's Finger in Mixen Lane, one of the most morally vile places in Casterbridge. The furmity-seller, who is giving wisdom to the group, asks Jopp what is in the package. Remembering his hatred of Lucetta,

Jopp begins to read the letters aloud. The women are shocked, and murmur that this is a good reason to hold a skimmity ride. Suddenly a stranger enters the pub on his way to Casterbridge. When he asks what a skimmity-ride is, the landlady tells him that it is a funny sight, but expensive. Since the stranger will be in Casterbridge a while, and since he will need to be entertained, he tosses a gold sovereign to the crowd to pay for it. The townspeople eagerly plan the skimmity ride.

The next morning, Jopp delivers the package to the house. Lucetta quickly burns the letters.

Analysis

The pubs of Casterbidge have declined in respectability through the novel just as the patrons of the pubs have declined. Here we have the seedy Peter's Finger inn, situated in the dirtiest and most dangerous side of town. Ironically, the women have the whitest aprons in this dark and dirty section. It is also the home of the once-important "lifeholders," revealing the tendencies of all those in power to make reckless decisions and fall as well. Peter's Finger is an allegorical name. The finger of St. Peter decides which people will reside in heaven or hell. Here the fingers of the townspeople will point towards the sinners they find—Michael and Lucetta.

More elements of suspense are introduced in this chapter. Who is the stranger, and how will he affect the plot, since we know that each character has a significant effect on the story? How will the skimmity ride affect Michael, Lucetta, and Farfrae?

Chapter 37: Summary

Casterbridge learns that a member of the royal family will be passing through town very soon. Farfrae and the council are planning a suitable reception when Michael wanders into the meeting. He wants to join the council in meeting the visitor. At the uneasy glances exchanged by the council members, Farfrae refuses the request. Michael decides that he will meet the visitor anyway.

The royal visitor approaches the crowded and decorated

town. As the visitor's carriage slows, Michael, dressed in shabby clothing, tries to shake the visitor's hand. Farfrae roughly pushes him into the crowd. Elizabeth-Jane, Lucetta, and the spectators are shocked at Michael's behaviour. When someone says that Michael was responsible for Farfrae's rise to power, Lucetta indignantly says that Farfrae won his own success. The royal visitor seems not to have noticed anything. The ceremony is over within moments. The townswomen eagerly plan the skimmity ride, and Jopp announces that it will be held tonight. Coney and Longways, however, decide to write letters telling the Farfraes to stay out of town that night.

Analysis

As usual, Michael refuses to accept his fate. Instead of meeting the visitor as the lower classes will in a large crowd, he must join the council to assert his individuality and his place as a gentleman. His attempt to greet the royal visitor is not really as dangerous or as shocking as the villagers see it: it is merely an attempt to regain some of the dignity that fate has stolen. Of course, Farfrae acts out of a sense of duty and concern for the visitor's safety in pushing Michael back. Yet that has only helped in spurring Michael's anger.

After Farfrae pushes Michael back, Farfrae sees that "his Calpurnia's cheek was pale." Calpurnia was the wife of Julius Caesar. By comparing Lucetta to Calpurnia, Hardy compares Farfrae to Caesar, implying Farfrae's great head for business and government. However, it also implies that Farfrae has a Brutus too, in the form of Michael. Will Michael actually assassinate his leader?

The townswomen seem more excited by the skimmity ride than the townsmen do, and Jopp is the most excited man. This could be a way of implying that Jopp has weaknesses as the women do. The women (as reflected by Nance Mockridge) want the ride to happen because they want to bring shame to the Farfraes and Michael. However, the men have differing ideas, wanting to protect their fellow man Farfrae by warning him in a letter. The women's actions could symbolize the acts of the Fates, the women of Greek mythology who dole out the proper punishments and cut the thread of life.

Chapter 38: Summary

Lucetta rests on her laurels: her hand still feels the shake of the Royal hand, and people are saying that her husband will become a knight. Michael feels the shame and anger of being shoved away by Farfrae. Jopp tells him that he also has been snubbed by Lucetta, but Michael is too busy wallowing in his own misery. Michael plans to challenge Farfrae to a wrestling match, and immediately after dinner he sets out to find Farfrae, telling him to meet him at the granary. As Michael waits, he manages to tie one arm behind his back, since he is stronger than Farfrae.

Soon Farfrae arrives, humming a song that he last hummed at the Three Mariners. The melody moves Michael, who suddenly thinks that he can't fight. Nevertheless, Michael explains why he is attacking Farfrae, and seems determined to fight despite Farfrae's suggestion to cool down. Farfrae narrowly escapes a few blows, but soon Henchard's strength holds Farfrae out the window, three stories up. Again, Michael cannot bring himself to hurt the Scotsman, and Farfrae runs away as Michael lies in the corner. Farfrae tells Whittle that he is now going toward Weatherbury instead of traveling toward Budmouth. Wanting to see his friend but knowing it is too late, Michael goes to the stone bridge. He does not hear the noise coming from the village.

Analysis

The chapter begins with an image of the proud Lucetta, thinking of her victories from the day. A paragraph later, the fallen Michael is angrily brooding about the man that has ruined his life. By setting the former lovers in opposition, Hardy implies that their fates are similar and intertwined. Just as Michael was once of a high status but fell quickly, Hardy implies that Lucetta will fall from her height just as quickly.

The scene that Elizabeth-Jane saw in the same granary in Chapter 33 serves as a parallel scene to the fight here, at first lacking only a female presence. For the second time, Michael has attempted to murder Farfrae, and with very little resistance from Farfrae. Although Michael has the physical strength to kill Farfrae, again he cannot do so because he is honourable at heart, not a murderer. This time, Michael has lowered himself so far that he actually gives up all claims to manhood. He sits in the corner not as a victorious man, but as servile "womanliness." The "unmanning" of Michael is nearly the final blow, ensuring a total defeat in life for him. Donald at first wishes to go to Budmouth, but after he receives the note from the townspeople, he agrees to go to Weatherbury. Not only will his change of plans become important, but also the choice of towns is significant. Budmouth seems to be the place of "mouths," or the place where public opinion can reach him (through the gossip about the skimmity ride). The villagers who care about Farfrae send him to a place that they trust, "Weatherbury." It is fitting that the villagers trust a place that has "weather" in its name, as the connections between the farmer and the weather showed earlier.

Chapter 39: Summary

Farfrae runs downstairs and plans to go to Budmouth as a way to recover from the attack before having to face Lucetta. However, Whittle gives him a note that advises his journey to Weatherbury, and he changes his plans accordingly. The note is from Longways, who is trying to keep the skimmity ride from being a "success." The townspeople do not warn Lucetta, believing that she must bear her scandal.

Lucetta sits in her drawing-room, confident. She overhears some nearby servants wondering which way someone is going. Two stuffed figures, a man and a woman, are riding a donkey. When the description of the woman reaches Lucetta's ears, she leaps to her feet. Elizabeth-Jane immediately enters the room and tries to keep Lucetta away from her window. Lucetta, however, is able to see that the image is of her, and is so shocked that she falls to the floor. Elizabeth-Jane sends for the doctor, who says that Farfrae must be found at Budmouth immediately.

The council members want to arrest the people responsible for the skimmity ride. Mr. Grower leads the council members in searching for the perpetrators. However, Jopp claims to have seen nothing, and at Peter's Finger, the crowd is quiet and orderly.

Analysis

The inept town council tries to find justice once more. Just as their attempts failed in the furmity-seller's trial, so they fail here. The townspeople all show a willingness to lie for each other. Even Grower, perhaps the symbol of a God, cannot fight the fate that Lucetta must experience. The townspeople are destined to make Lucetta see her fate.

What leads to Lucetta's seizure? Hardy attributes it to a fit of epilepsy. Yet epilepsy is usually a lifelong condition, and Lucetta has never had a fit at any other point in the novel. Perhaps Fate has caused her epilepsy, dormant for so long, to return at this point. More likely, the shock of seeing herself in effigy caused her seizure. However, all her flaws led to this point. Her concern for keeping the past hidden and her pride have led to this attack by the townspeople. Her curiosity led her to see the skimmity ride from her window. Her overly passionate nature sends her feelings into a frenzy that may have led to her seizure.

Chapter 40: Summary

Michael has returned towards Casterbridge. He sees the figures on the donkey and knows exactly what is happening, but chooses to go home and sleep. Yet he cannot sleep. In searching for Elizabeth-Jane, he goes to the Farfraes' home. Lucetta's servants tell him everything that has happened, and how someone has been sent to find Donald in Budmouth. Michael knows that Donald is on the way to Weatherbury and Mellstock, and tells everyone, but after his recent unspeakable behaviour, no one believes him. Undaunted, Michael begins running on the road to Mellstock, hoping to catch Farfrae there.

Michael meets Farfrae on the road, telling him that he must come home immediately because his wife is in danger.

Farfrae refuses to believe his attacker—he thinks that Michael is setting up a trap to finish the fight from earlier. Despite Michael's claim that he is true to Farfrae, Farfrae drives toward the next town. Michael returns to town, cursing himself on the way. Jopp meets Michael and says that a "sea-captain" has visited him, though Michael doesn't seem to care.

Later, Farfrae returns home to find that everything is as Henchard has said, and blames himself for not trusting Michael's word. As Farfrae sits by his wife's side, Lucetta tells him about her past with Michael. Michael paces in front of the house all night, making inquiries about the patient. As he paces, he also thinks about Elizabeth-Jane. When a servant finally leaves the house at dawn, she tells Michael that Lucetta has died.

Analysis

In this sad chapter, Lucetta's death parallels the death of Susan before. Lucetta dies from a sudden attack as Susan did. As the dying Susan confessed to her beloved Elizabeth-Jane, Lucetta makes a confession to her beloved Farfrae. The townspeople also disregard any role they had in her death, pretending that the skimmity ride never happened.

More irony adds to the sadness of Lucetta's death. The townspeople saw the skimmity ride as a joke, but it became a deadly trick. Michael, the man who once would have done anything to keep Farfrae and Lucetta apart, is now the only one who can bring Farfrae to Lucetta's side. Farfrae does not believe Michael, because "there might be ironies" in his words of Lucetta's illnesses. Hardy is especially bitter when he points out that the smallest creature in nature is more peaceful that the noblest man: "the sparrows in his way scarcely flying... so little did they believe in human aggression at so early a time."

Finally, the element of suspense introduced is another plan of Fate to take happiness away from Michael. Elizabeth-Jane has been "the pinpoint of light" in the darkness of the skimmity ride and the death. Michael has just realized her worth as the "sea-captain" returns to see Michael. Could it be Newson returning for his daughter?

SUMMARY AND ANALYSIS OF CHAPTERS 41-45

Chapter 41: Summary

Elizabeth-Jane arrives, upset about Lucetta's death. Michael comforts her, tells her to stay with him, and offers to make her some breakfast. As the girl rests, Michael watches her lovingly, convinced he can find happiness with her.

A knock on the door calls Michael away from his thoughts. It is the stranger from Peter's Finger a few weeks ago. He introduces himself as Newson, and Michael becomes very agitated. Newson briefly relates the history of his marriage to Susan and how he came to be "lost at sea." His ship was lost at sea, but he came ashore in Newfoundland. Since Susan was unhappy about their marriage, his "death" was arranged for her benefit. Newson knows that Susan is dead, but he has returned for Elizabeth-Jane. Michael tells him that she died a year ago. Newson shrugs and promises to trouble Michael no longer. Michael is frightened that Newson will learn the truth, so he follows the sailor to ensure that he has safely left town.

When Michael returns home, Elizabeth-Jane has awakened after napping. Michael considers asking her to stay with him, but doesn't, fearing that Newson will return and take her away. They have a lovely breakfast, lingering until it is time for Michael to go to work. Although Elizabeth-Jane promises to return soon, Michael is haunted by the belief that Newson will take her away. He goes to Ten Hatches, the place where the river runs deep, and contemplates his suicide. Suddenly, he sees himself already floating in the water! When he hurries home, Elizabeth-Jane is waiting for him. He takes her to Ten Hatches, where she finds that the image he saw was that of the skimmity ride dummy. She understands what Michael plans to do, so she quickly offers to stay with him and care for him. At this news, Michael changes heart again and becomes a confident new man.

Analysis

Michael and Elizabeth-Jane have completely switched Victorian gender roles, as we can see in this chapter. Michael, once the strong, powerful Mayor, has now fallen to a low that removes all his masculinity. He cares for Elizabeth-Jane as a mother would—cooking for her, keeping the house clean for her, and doing other things "with housewifely care, as if it were an honour to have her in his house." Elizabeth-Jane still remains the tender-hearted and concerned girl. However, her decisions control the now weak-willed and vulnerable Michael. She issues the commands now—"Let us go home"—and is the real provider for her stepfather. "May I live with you, and tend upon you as I used to do?" This marked change in Michael and Elizabeth-Jane's personalities prepares us for the next change in Michael. Once Michael has become more feminine, perhaps he can finally learn to become less bullish and considerate to others. (Of course, that also means that Elizabeth-Jane can become more bullish with her masculinity, as we will see later.)

Irony is used again to create sympathy for Michael. The cruel fate seems to be especially harsh here. Just as Michael has decided that he has "the dream of a future lit by [Elizabeth-Jane's] presence, Newson has arrived to take her away. The skimmity ride effigies that killed Lucetta merely keep Michael alive and die in his place. Although Michael has not completely changed (he still tells a horrible lie just to keep Elizabeth-Jane there), we pity him all the more because he is convinced that he is in "Somebody's hand."

The effigy floating in the water serves as a type of ritual offering, similar to Abraham's sacrifice of the sheep for Issac. Since the townspeople cannot kill Michael, they will sacrifice the effigy by tossing it in the river. At the same time, it serves as a "resurrection" for Michael. When he contemplates suicide, only to see his "dead image" floating in the water, Michael returns to life and becomes fully aware of the consequences of his actions. After this form of resurrection, Michael will go on to save his own world, making him a Christ-like figure.

Chapter 42: Summary

Michael fears that Newson will return for Elizabeth-Jane despite his new attitude. Casterbridge buries Lucetta and quickly forgets her. After a while Farfrae learns of the events that caused her death. At first, he wishes to punish all those responsible. However, soon he realizes that the townspeople did not want their joke to have such a disastrous effect on Lucetta, and he reasons that keeping her history secret will protect all the parties involved. The town council again sets up a seed shop for Michael, allowing him and Elizabeth-Jane to make a respectable living. As Michael continues to worry that Elizabeth-Jane will be taken away, Farfrae decides that his life with Lucetta was doomed to unhappiness from the beginning.

A year passes. Elizabeth-Jane frequently walks on the road to Budmouth twice a week, and she ends up with expensive trinkets, such as muffs and new books, that Michael knows she cannot afford. Upon seeing Farfrae's eyes upon Elizabeth-Jane in the marketplace, however, he begins to suspect that Farfrae is returning to his former love, and he worries that Farfrae will take Elizabeth-Jane away.

Farfrae and Elizabeth-Jane first meet accidentally, but very soon they habitually meet each other as they walk into town. Michael watches from the Ring as Farfrae presents Elizabeth-Jane with a new book everyday. Very soon Farfrae kisses Elizabeth-Jane. Michael, watching the scene, reasons that Farfrae's love will force Elizabeth-Jane to turn against him. He thinks that telling the secret of Elizabeth-Jane's birth to Farfrae will ward the young man off, but cannot bring himself to tell.

Analysis

Even near the end of the book, Hardy introduces some elements of suspense. Will he return, and if he does, what will Elizabeth-Jane do? Will Farfrae and Elizabeth-Jane finally be joined in marriage? Will Michael do anything to halt the wedding or the return of Newson?

Apparently Elizabeth-Jane has finally become learned enough in Latin to be interesting to everyone. As if to reflect her new status, this chapter contains more mythological allusions and Latin phrases to refer to her and those around her. The other young women in the town are compared to the plumes of "Juno's bird" with "Argus eyes." Not only are the townspeople connected to nature (through the comparison to birds), but they are also the gossiping people of before, watching with their own "eyes." Michael has a "solicitus timor" for her love. As usual, however, Elizabeth-Jane does not understand the references—remaining unaware of the eyes upon her and the fear Michael has for her.

Michael is beginning another cycle of success with his seed shop, but we are braced for his downfall. Yet Michael is a changed man this time. He is so weak that he now takes orders from Elizabeth-Jane, "schooling himself to accept her will." He also has more of a regard for his feelings and their effects on others. He is able to consign his emotions on revealing her birth to "the devil," and he feels remorse about his previous actions.

Chapter 43: Summary

The townspeople are shocked that Farfrae is interested in "that bankrupt Henchard's stepdaughter." The young ladies of town indignantly ignore Farfrae. The lower classes, however, are quite pleased with his choice. However, public opinion soon ignores the whole issue entirely, since no one knows what will come of their courtship. Michael worries about his place in Elizabeth-Jane's life. He has now began to watch the daily meetings from an ancient fort called Mai Dun. One day, a stranger walks down the road from Budmouth. Michael realizes that the stranger is Newson, and fears the worst. At home, Elizabeth-Jane shows him a mysterious letter from someone who wants to meet her at Farfrae's this evening. Michael says she may go, and then says he will leave Casterbridge. Despite his stepdaughter's protests, he leaves that evening. Elizabeth-Jane accompanies him to the stone bridge, then watches him walk away. Michael stops for a moment to express his anguish, then continues on his way.

On the walk back to town, Elizabeth-Jane meets Farfrae, who quickly takes her to his house. When she discovers Newson, their reunion is joyful. They eagerly plan the wedding, which will take place with any difficulties now that

Michael is gone. Newson tells the shocked Elizabeth-Jane how Michael kept her away with a lie. Although Newson defends Michael, Elizabeth-Jane is disgusted.

Analysis

Chance and irony strike again. Just as Michael seems to have gained his happiness, Newson has met Farfrae and found that his daughter lives. Although we do not know how Farfrae and Newson met, we can assume that it was merely another chance occurrence, another attempt of Fate to bring down Michael.

Michael describes himself as "Cain... an outcast and a vagabond" in this chapter. His behaviour does parallel that of Cain here. Michael, like Cain, suffered from jealousy of Newson and Farfrae. After killing his daughter in keeping her away from her father, he refuses to be her keeper and leaves her in Casterbridge. However, unlike Cain, Michael feels remorse. While his behaviour was horrible, Hardy has succeeded in making us feel for Michael by describing his viewpoint. We know now that Michael is sorry for his actions and only acts out of love for Elizabeth-Jane.

We hope that there will be a chance for forgiveness. Yet the one person who can forgive Michael, Elizabeth-Jane, refuses to do so. She refuses for the same reasons that other characters refused: she is too deeply rooted in the past. She feels sorry for Michael until her father tells her of the past lie. Although Newson tries to defend Michael's ways, the past lies are so important to her that she refuses to see past them. This will eventually lead her to a smaller downfall—a refusal to see the man who loved her so well.

Chapter 44: Summary

Michael travels for five days. As he travels, he gazes longingly at some of Elizabeth-Jane's things—gloves, handwriting, hair clippings, and the like. He reaches Weydon-Priors, where he reflects on the auction and his failed attempts to fix the wrongs made then. After he has finished there, he leaves for a farm situated on a highway. As he again becomes a hay-trusser, he constantly worries about Elizabeth-Jane's welfare.

One day a passing farmer tells Michael that he has heard of a wedding occurring in Casterbridge on St. Martin's Day. Although he feels his presence in town would not be welcomed, he decides to go there for a chance at forgiveness from Elizabeth-Jane. He stops to buy a wedding gift, a little goldfinch in a cage wrapped in newspaper. Finally he reaches town. Although he regrets his arrival, he nevertheless presents himself as a "humble old friend." He is led into the kitchen, but the housekeeper stops him, asking him to wait until the dance ends. Michael watches the dance, and notices that Elizabeth-Jane is dancing with Newson. When the dance ends, Michael begs for some love from her, but she says she cannot feel love for him. Although he has prepared a list of ways in which he was deceived, Michael merely says that he will not bother them again, and leaves.

Analysis

Michael's travels in this chapter are reflected in the metaphor of the circle: "is wandering... became part of a circle of which Casterbridge formed the centre." Once again, Michael returns to the state that he held in the beginning of the novel. He returns to Weydon-Priors, and again takes the job of hay-trusser. However, as before, he comes to realise the importance of the lost child to his happiness. The metaphor also works to describe the cycle of his rises and falls to power. Frequently, he begins in despair, but slowly works his way to the top of the cycle—reaching a success through his desires. Once he has reached his highest height, fate intervenes to utterly ruin him. There is an implication that the same will occur to Elizabeth-Jane in the way Michael thinks of her day in equal portions: "her sitting down and rising up, her goings and comings."

Yet it is also obvious that this time, Michael's rise to power will be quite different. This is the first time he has truly loved someone enough to constantly think of him. Here Elizabeth-Jane is always on his mind, from his keeping her trinkets to his waiting for any news from Casterbridge. He also has changed in that he feels real remorse for his deed, unlike any of his other decisions within the novel. His love is the one motivation that changes him. Of course, each time he has thought that the person he loved would not forgive him, only to be proven wrong. Ironically, this time he is correct—Elizabeth-Jane, the one person he truly wanted to love, does refuse him. Nevertheless, he still reaches the height of his success. Instead of trying to attach himself to Elizabeth-Jane, he turns and walks away because she wishes it That is the greatest action Michael could do for the angry girl he loves.

The bird serves as a metaphor for Michael himself. The cage represents the self-made prison of his flaws, "plain and small." The bird is a goldfinch, symbolizing the true, golden nature of Michael's character. The newspaper represents the public opinion that covers Michael, just as it covers the bird. What has happened to the bird when Michael leaves the house? We will learn in the next chapter.

Chapter 45: Summary

A month has passed since the wedding. Farfrae hurries home from work everyday, and Elizabeth-Jane is pleased with her new station. Newson stayed in Casterbridge for three days, but his need for the sea is so great that he moves to Budmouth, a place where the sea can be seen.

A week after the wedding, Elizabeth-Jane found a birdcage wrapped in paper with a dead finch inside. Now, a month later, a maid enters the parlor and announces that they understood why it was there. Another maid saw Michael with it as he came to the wedding. Elizabeth-Jane reasons that the bird must have been a wedding gift, and from that moment she feels pity for her stepfather. She asks Farfrae to help her find him.

They finally trace his steps along the road of Weatherbury to Anglebury. Soon the road becomes difficult, and they decide to stop. A man passes them and goes into a nearby cottage. At Elizabeth-Jane's insistence that the man is Abel Whittle, they turn to visit the cottage. Whittle tells them that Michael has died a half-hour before. He gives them a piece of paper that is

Michael's will. The will states that Elizabeth-Jane is not to learn of his death, and that no man is to remember him in any way. Although she weeps that she has just missed her last chance with him, she follows Michael's instructions to the best of her ability. She lives in marriage happily, but also ever sure that she could be pitched into a deep despair at any moment by fate.

Analysis

Hardy delivers the most emotional situations of irony in this final chapter. Just as Elizabeth-Jane has found her father, she again loses him to the sea—and although Newson just lives in Budmouth to see the sea, we know that it is only a matter of time before he leaves again. Michael has been forced to spend the last days of his life with the man whom he considered the lowest of the low. Elizabeth-Jane finally understands the meaning of the present, and goes to find Michael, but arrives too late to extend her love. Even as Elizabeth-Jane lives in a state of contentment, she does not enjoy it for fear that the unkind fate will descend upon her too.

Abel Whittle again takes the role of a Christ figure. Although Michael was a cruel boss to him, he "turns the other cheek" because Michael was kind to his mother years ago. He continues to care for Michael, walking with him despite Michael's order to go back, feeding him and letting him stay in his cottage. Although he is the lowest character in the novel, his kindness makes him the most noble character in the novel.

Michael's connection to Nature is complete as his life ends. His connection to the goldfinch is completed. The goldfish dies of starvation, and Michael will die because he cannot take nourishment. (His starvation is also a metaphor for his life without Elizabeth-Jane: without her love, he is starved for affection.) However, the whole earth seems to become unusually fertile in the wake of Michael's exit. The Farfraes cannot find him because he "had apparently sunk into the earth." Michael's travels have lead him through "Weatherbury," the place that the farmers planned for Farfrae during the skimmity ride. The burial mounds on the road also become fertile places as "the full breasts of Diana Multimammia." The cottage in which Michael spends the last days of his life has Nature entering, with its clay walls, held together by vines of ivy and a floor of leaves. In his loving and forgiving state, Michael and Nature are finally connected. Although fate has dogged him for most of his life, the love for Elizabeth-Jane has brought him to a level of goodness—one that makes him more able to join with Nature.

Chapter 8

Selected Chapters from the Text

Chapter 1

One evening of late summer, before the nineteenth century had reached one-third of its span, a young man and woman, the latter carrying a child, were approaching the large village of Weydon-Priors, in Upper Wessex, on foot. They were plainly but not ill clad, though the thick hoar of dust which had accumulated on their shoes and garments from an obviously long journey lent a disadvantageous shabbiness to their appearance just now.

The man was of fine figure, swarthy, and stern in aspect; and he showed in profile a facial angle so slightly inclined as to be almost perpendicular. He wore a short jacket of brown corduroy, newer than the remainder of his suit, which was a fustian waistcoat with white horn buttons, breeches of the same, tanned leggings, and a straw hat overlaid with black glazed canvas. At his back he carried by a looped strap a rush basket, from which protruded at one end the crutch of a hay-knife, a wimble for hay-bonds being also visible in the aperture. His measured, springless walk was the walk of the skilled countryman as distinct from the desultory shamble of the general labourer; while in the turn and plant of each foot there was, further, a dogged and cynical indifference personal to himself, showing its presence even in the regularly interchanging fustian folds, now in the left leg, now in the right, as he paced along.

What was really peculiar, however, in this couple's progress, and would have attracted the attention of any casual observer otherwise disposed to overlook them, was the perfect silence they preserved. They walked side by side in such a way as to suggest afar off the low, easy, confidential chat of people full of reciprocity; but on closer view it could be discerned that the man was reading, or pretending to read, a ballad sheet which he kept before his eyes with some difficulty by the hand that was passed through the basket strap. Whether this apparent cause were the real cause, or whether it were an assumed one to escape an intercourse that would have been irksome to him, nobody but himself could have said precisely; but his taciturnity was unbroken, and the woman enjoyed no society whatever from his presence. Virtually she walked the highway alone, save for the child she bore. Sometimes the man's bent elbow almost touched her shoulder, for she kept as close to his side as was possible without actual contact, but she seemed to have no idea of taking his arm, nor he of offering it; and far from exhibiting surprise at his ignoring silence she appeared to receive it as a natural thing. If any word at all were uttered by the little group, it was an occasional whisper of the woman to the child—a tiny girl in short clothes and blue boots of knitted yarn—and the murmured babble of the child in reply.

The chief—almost the only—attraction of the young woman's face was its mobility. When she looked down sideways to the girl she became pretty, and even handsome, particularly that in the action her features caught slantwise the rays of the strongly coloured sun, which made transparencies of her eyelids and nostrils and set fire on her lips. When she plodded on in the shade of the hedge, silently thinking, she had the hard, half-apathetic expression of one who deems anything possible at the hands of Time and Chance except, perhaps, fair play. The first phase was the work of Nature, the second probably of civilization.

That the man and woman were husband and wife, and the parents of the girl in arms there could be little doubt. No other than such relationship would have accounted for the atmosphere of stale familiarity which the trio carried along with them like a nimbus as they moved down the road.

The wife mostly kept her eyes fixed ahead, though with little interest—the scene for that matter being one that might have been matched at almost any spot in any county in England at this time of the year; a road neither straight nor crooked, neither level nor hilly, bordered by hedges, trees, and other vegetation, which had entered the blackened-green stage of colour that the doomed leaves pass through on their way to dingy, and yellow, and red. The grassy margin of the bank, and the nearest hedgerow boughs, were powdered by the dust that had been stirred over them by hasty vehicles, the same dust as it lay on the road deadening their footfalls like a carpet; and this, with the aforesaid total absence of conversation, allowed every extraneous sound to be heard.

For a long time there was none, beyond the voice of a weak bird singing a trite old evening song that might doubtless have been heard on the hill at the same hour, and with the self-same trills, quavers, and breves, at any sunset of that season for centuries untold. But as they approached the village sundry distant shouts and rattles reached their ears from some elevated spot in that direction, as yet screened from view by foliage. When the outlying houses of could just be described, the family group was met by a turnip-hoer with his hoe on his shoulder, and his suspended from it. The reader promptly glanced up.

"Any trade doing here?" he asked phlegmatically, designating the village in his van by a wave of the broadsheet. And thinking the labourer did not understand him, he added, "Anything in the hay-trussing line?"

The turnip-hoer had already begun shaking his head. "Why, save the man, what wisdom's in him that 'a should come to Weydon for a job of that sort this time o' year?"

"Then is there any house to let—a little small new cottage just a builded, or such like?" asked the other.

The pessimist still maintained a negative. "Pulling down is more the nater of Weydon. There were five houses cleared away last year, and three this; and the volk nowhere to go—no, not so much as a thatched hurdle; that's the way o' Weydon-Priors."

The hay-trusser, which he obviously was, nodded with some superciliousness. Looking towards the village, he continued, "There is something going on here, however, is there not?" "Ay. 'Tis Fair Day. Though what you hear now is little more than the clatter and scurry of getting away the money o' children and fools, for the real business is done earlier than this. I've been working within sound o't all day, but I didn't go up—not I. 'Twas no business of mine."

The trusser and his family proceeded on their way, and soon entered the Fair-field, which showed standing-places and pens where many hundreds of horses and sheep had been exhibited and sold in the forenoon, but were now in great part taken away. At present, as their informant had observed, but little real business remained on hand, the chief being the sale by auction of a few inferior animals, that could not otherwise be disposed of, and had been absolutely refused by the better class of traders, who came and went early. Yet the crowd was denser now than during the morning hours, the frivolous contingent of visitors, including journeymen out for a holiday, a stray soldier or two come on furlough, village shopkeepers, and the like, having latterly flocked in; persons whose activities found a congenial field among the peep-shows, toy-stands, waxworks, inspired monsters, disinterested medical men who travelled for the public good, thimble-riggers, nick-nack vendors, and readers of Fate.

Neither of our pedestrians had much heart for these things, and they looked around for a refreshment tent among the many which dotted the down. Two, which stood nearest to them in the ochreous haze of expiring sunlight, seemed almost equally inviting. One was formed of new, milk-hued canvas, and bore red flags on its summit; it announced "Good Beer, Ale, and Cyder." The other was less new; a little iron stove-pipe came out of it at the back and in front appeared the placard, "Good Furmity Sold Hear." The man mentally weighed the two inscriptions and inclined to the former tent.

"No—no—the other one," said the woman. "I always like furmity; and so does Elizabeth-Jane; and so will you. It is nourishing after a long hard day."

"I've never tasted it," said the man. However, he gave way to her representations, and they entered the furmity booth forthwith.

A rather numerous company appeared within, seated at the long narrow tables that ran down the tent on each side. At the upper end stood a stove, containing a charcoal fire, over which hung a large three-legged crock, sufficiently polished round the rim to show that it was made of. A haggish creature of about fifty presided, in a white apron, which as it threw an air of respectability over her as far as it extended, was made so wide as to reach nearly round her waist. She slowly stirred the contents of the pot. The dull scrape of her large spoon was audible throughout the tent as she thus kept from burning the mixture of corn in the grain, flour, milk, raisins, currants, and what not, that composed the antiquated slop in which she dealt. Vessels holding the separate ingredients stood on a white-clothed table of boards and trestles close by.

The young man and woman ordered a basin each of the mixture, steaming hot, and sat down to consume it at leisure. This was very well so far, for furmity, as the woman had said, was nourishing, and as proper a food as could be obtained within the four seas; though, to those not accustomed to it, the grains of wheat swollen as large as lemon-pips, which floated on its surface, might have a deterrent effect at first.

But there was more in that tent than met the cursory glance; and the man, with the instinct of a perverse character, scented it quickly. After a mincing attack on his bowl, he watched the hag's proceedings from the corner of his eye, and saw the game she played. He winked to her, and passed up his basin in reply to her nod; when she took a bottle from under the table, slily measured out a quantity of its contents, and tipped the same into the man's furmity. The liquor poured in was rum. The man as slily sent back money in payment.

He found the concoction, thus strongly laced, much more to his satisfaction than it had been in its natural state. His wife had observed the proceeding with much uneasiness; but he persuaded her to have hers laced also, and she agreed to a milder allowance after some misgiving.

The man finished his basin, and called for another, the rum being signalled for in yet stronger proportion. The effect of it was soon apparent in his manner, and his wife but too sadly perceived that in strenuously steering off the rocks of the licensed liquor-tent she had only got into maelstrom depths here amongst the smugglers.

The child began to prattle impatiently, and the wife more than once said to her husband, "Michael, how about our lodging? You know we may have trouble in getting it if we don't go soon."

But he turned a deaf ear to those bird-like chirpings. He talked loud to the company. The child's black eyes, after slow, round, ruminating gazes at the candles when they were lighted, fell together; then they opened, then shut again, and she slept.

At the end of the first basin the man had risen to serenity; at the second he was jovial; at the third, argumentative, at the fourth, the qualities signified by the shape of his face, the occasional clench of his mouth, and the fiery spark of his dark eye, began to tell in his conduct; he was overbearing—even brilliantly quarrelsome.

The conversation took a high turn, as it often does on such occasions. The ruin of good men by bad wives, and, more particularly, the frustration of many a promising youth's high aims and hopes and the extinction of his energies by an early imprudent marriage, was the theme.

"I did for myself that way thoroughly," said the trusser with a contemplative bitterness that was well-night resentful. "I married at eighteen, like the fool that I was; and this is the consequence o't." He pointed at himself and family with a wave of the hand intended to bring out the penuriousness of the exhibition.

The young woman his wife, who seemed accustomed to such remarks, acted as if she did not hear them, and continued her intermittent private words of tender trifles to the sleeping and waking child, who was just big enough to be placed for a moment on the bench beside her when she wished to ease her arms. The man continued—

"I haven't more than fifteen shillings in the world, and yet I am a good experienced hand in my line. I'd challenge England to beat me in the fodder business; and if I were a free man again I'd be worth a thousand pound before I'd done o't. But a fellow never knows these little things till all chance of acting upon 'em is past."

The auctioneer selling the old horses in the field outside could be heard saying, "Now this is the last lot—now who'll take the last lot for a song? Shall I say forty shillings? 'Tis a very promising broodmare, a trifle over five years old, and nothing the matter with the hoss at all, except that she's a little holler in the back and had her left eye knocked out by the kick of another, her own sister, coming along the road."

"For my part I don't see why men who have got wives and don't want 'em, shouldn't get rid of 'em as these gipsy fellows do their old horses," said the man in the tent. "Why shouldn't they put 'em up and sell 'em by auction to men who are in need of such articles? Hey? Why, begad, I'd sell mine this minute if anybody would buy her!" "There's them that would do that," some of the guests replied, looking at the woman, who was by no means ill-favoured.

"True," said a smoking gentleman, whose coat had the fine polish about the collar, elbows, seams, and shoulder-blades that long-continued friction with grimy surfaces will produce, and which is usually more desired on furniture than on clothes. From his appearance he had possibly been in former time groom or coachman to some neighbouring county family. "I've had my breedings in as good circles, I may say, as any man," he added, "and I know true cultivation, or nobody do; and I can declare she's got it—in the bone, mind ye, I say—as much as any female in the fair—though it may want a little bringing out." Then, crossing his legs, he resumed his pipe with a nicely-adjusted gaze at a point in the air.

The fuddled young husband stared for a few seconds at this unexpected praise of his wife, half in doubt of the wisdom of his own attitude towards the possessor of such qualities. But he speedily lapsed into his former conviction, and said harshly—

"Well, then, now is your chance; I am open to an offer for this gem o' creation."

She turned to her husband and murmured, "Michael, you have talked this nonsense in public places before. A joke is a joke, but you may make it once too often, mind!"

"I know I've said it before; I meant it. All I want is a buyer."

At the moment a swallow, one among the last of the season, which had by chance found its way through an opening into the upper part of the tent, flew to and from quick curves above their heads, causing all eyes to follow it absently. In watching the bird till it made its escape the assembled company neglected to respond to the workman's offer, and the subject dropped.

But a quarter of an hour later the man, who had gone on lacing his furmity more and more heavily, though he was either so strong-minded or such an intrepid toper that he still appeared fairly sobre, recurred to the old strain, as in a musical fantasy the instrument fetches up the original theme. "Here—I am waiting to know about this offer of mine. The woman is no good to me. Who'll have her?"

The company had by this time decidedly degenerated, and the renewed inquiry was received with a laugh of appreciation. The woman whispered; she was imploring and anxious: "Come, come, it is getting dark, and this nonsense won't do. If you don't come along, I shall go without you. Come!"

She waited and waited; yet he did not move. In ten minutes the man broke in upon the desultory conversation of the furmity drinkers with. "I asked this question, and nobody answered to 't. Will any Jack Rag or Tom Straw among ye buy my goods?"

The woman's manner changed, and her face assumed the grim shape and colour of which mention has been made.

"Mike, Mike," she said; "this is getting serious. O!—too serious!"

"Will anybody buy her?" said the man.

"I wish somebody would," said she firmly. "Her present

owner is not at all to her liking!" "Nor you to mine," said he. "So we are agreed about that. Gentlemen, you hear? It's an agreement to part. She shall take the girl if she wants to, and go her ways. I'll take my tools, and go my ways. 'Tis simple as Scripture history. Now then, stand up, Susan, and show yourself."

"Don't, my chiel," whispered a buxom staylace dealer in voluminous petticoats, who sat near the woman; "yer good man don't know what he's saying."

The woman, however, did stand up. "Now, who's auctioneer?" cried the hay-trusser.

"I be," promptly answered a short man, with a nose resembling a copper knob, a damp voice, and eyes like button-holes. "Who'll make an offer for this lady?"

The woman looked on the ground, as if she maintained her position by a supreme effort of will.

"Five shillings," said someone, at which there was a laugh.

"No insults," said the husband. "Who'll say a guinea?"

Nobody answered; and the female dealer in staylaces interposed.

"Behave yerself moral, good man, for Heaven's love! Ah, what a cruelty is the poor soul married to! Bed and board is dear at some figures 'pon my 'vation 'tis!"

"Set it higher, auctioneer," said the trusser.

"Two guineas!" said the auctioneer; and no one replied.

"If they don't take her for that, in ten seconds they'll have to give more," said the husband. "Very well. Now auctioneer, add another."

"Three guineas—going for three guineas!" said the rheumy man.

"No bid?" said the husband. "Good Lord, why she's cost me fifty times the money, if a penny. Go on."

"Four guineas!" cried the auctioneer.

"I'll tell ye what—I won't sell her for less than five," said the husband, bringing down his fist so that the basins danced. "I'll sell her for five guineas to any man that will pay me the money, and treat her well; and he shall have her for ever, and never hear aught o' me. But she shan't go for less. Now then—

five guineas—and she's yours. Susan, you agree?" She bowed her head with absolute indifference. "Five guineas," said the auctioneer, "or she'll be withdrawn. Do anybody give it? The last time. Yes or no?"

"Yes," said a loud voice from the doorway.

All eyes were turned. Standing in the triangular opening which formed the door of the tent was a sailor, who, unobserved by the rest, had arrived there within the last two or three minutes. A dead silence followed his affirmation.

"You say you do?" asked the husband, staring at him.

"I say so," replied the sailor.

"Saying is one thing, and paying is another. Where's the money?"

The sailor hesitated a moment, looked anew at the woman, came in, unfolded five crisp pieces of paper, and threw them down upon the tablecloth. They were Bank-of-England notes for five pounds. Upon the face of this he clinked down the shillings severally—one, two, three, four, five.

The sight of real money in full amount, in answer to a challenge for the same till then deemed slightly hypothetical had a great effect upon the spectators. Their eyes became riveted upon the faces of the chief actors, and then upon the notes as they lay, weighted by the shillings, on the table.

Up to this moment it could not positively have been asserted that the man, in spite of his tantalizing declaration, was really in earnest. The spectators had indeed taken the proceedings throughout as a piece of mirthful irony carried to extremes; and had assumed that, being out of work, he was, as a consequence, out of temper with the world, and society, and his nearest kin. But with the demand and response of real cash the jovial frivolity of the scene departed. A lurid colour seemed to fill the tent, and change the aspect of all therein. The mirth-wrinkles left the listeners' faces, and they waited with parting lips.

"Now," said the woman, breaking the silence, so that her low dry voice sounded quite loud, "before you go further, Michael, listen to me. If you touch that money, I and this girl go with the man. Mind, it is a joke no longer."

"A joke? Of course it is not a joke!" shouted her husband, his resentment rising at her suggestion. "I take the money; the sailor takes you. That's plain enough. It has been done elsewhere—and why not here?"

"'Tis quite on the understanding that the young woman is willing," said the sailor blandly. "I wouldn't hurt her feelings for the world."

"Faith, nor I," said her husband. "But she is willing, provided she can have the child. She said so only the other day when I talked o't!"

"That you swear?" said the sailor to her.

"I do," said she, after glancing at her husband's face and seeing no repentance there.

"Very well, she shall have the child, and the bargain's complete," said the trusser. He took the sailor's notes and deliberately folded them, and put them with the shillings in a high remote pocket, with an air of finality.

The sailor looked at the woman and smiled. "Come along!" he said kindly. "The little one too—the more the merrier!" She paused for an instant, with a close glance at him. Then dropping her eyes again, and saying nothing, she took up the child and followed him as he made towards the door. On reaching it, she turned, and pulling off her wedding-ring, flung it across the booth in the hay-trusser's face.

"Mike," she said, "I've lived with thee a couple of years, and had nothing but temper! Now I'm no more to 'ee; I'll try my luck elsewhere. 'Twill be better for me and, both. So good-bye!"

Seizing the sailor's arm with her right hand, and mounting the little girl on her left, she went out of the tent sobbing bitterly.

A stolid look of concern filled the husband's face, as if, after all, he had not quite anticipated this ending; and some of the guests laughed.

"Is she gone?" he said.

"Faith, ay! she's gone clane enough," said some rustics near the door.

He rose and walked to the entrance with the careful tread

of one conscious of his alcoholic load. Some others followed, and they stood looking into the twilight. The difference between the peacefulness of inferior nature and the wilful hostilities of mankind was very apparent at this place. In contrast with the harshness of the act just ended within the tent was the sight of several horses crossing their necks and rubbing each other lovingly as they waited in patience to be harnessed for the homeward journey. Outside the fair, in the valleys and woods, all was quiet. The sun had recently set, and the west heaven was hung with rosy cloud, which seemed permanent, yet slowly changed. To watch it was like looking at some grand feat of stagery from a darkened auditorium. In presence of this scene after the other there was a natural instinct to abjure man as the blot on an otherwise kindly universe; till it was remembered that all terrestrial conditions were intermittent, and that mankind might some night be innocently sleeping when these quiet objects were raging loud.

"Where do the sailor live?" asked a spectator, when they had vainly gazed around.

"God knows that," replied the man who had seen high life. "He's without doubt a stranger here."

"He came in about five minutes ago," said the furmity woman, joining the rest with her hands on her hips. "And then 'a stepped back, and then 'a looked in again. I'm not a penny the better for him."

"Serves the husband well be-right," said the staylace vendor. "A comely respectable body like her—what can a man want more? I glory in the woman's sperrit. I'd ha' done it myself—od send if I wouldn't, if a husband had behaved so to me! I'd go, and 'a might call, and call, till his keacorn was raw; but I'd never come back—no, not till the great trumpet, would I!"

"Well, the woman will be better off," said another of a more deliberative turn. "For seafaring natures be very good shelter for shorn lambs, and the man do seem to have plenty of money, which is what she's not been used to lately, by all showings."

"Mark me—I'll not go after her!" said the trusser,

returning doggedly to his seat. "Let her go! If she's up to such vagaries she must suffer for 'em. She'd no business to take the maid—'tis my maid; and if it were the doing again she shouldn't have her!"

Perhaps from some little sense of having countenanced an indefensible proceeding, perhaps because it was late, the customers thinned away from the tent shortly after this episode. The man stretched his elbows forward on the table leant his face upon his arms, and soon began to snore. The furmity seller decided to close for the night, and after seeing the rum-bottles, milk, corn, raisins, etc., that remained on hand, loaded into the cart, came to where the man reclined. She shook him, but could not wake him. As the tent was not to be struck that night, the fair continuing for two or three days, she decided to let the sleeper, who was obviously no tramp, stay where he was, and his basket with him. Extinguishing the last candle, and lowering the flap of the tent, she left it, and drove away.

Chapter 2

The morning sun was streaming through the crevices of the canvas when the man awoke. A warm glow pervaded the whole atmosphere of the marquee, and a single big blue fly buzzed musically round and round it. Besides the buzz of the fly there was not a sound. He looked about—at the benches—at the table supported by trestles—at his basket of tools—at the stove where the furmity had been boiled—at the empty basins—at some shed grains of wheat—at the corks which dotted the grassy floor. Among the odds and ends he discerned a little shining object, and picked it up. It was his wife's ring.

A confused picture of the events of the previous evening seemed to come back to him, and he thrust his hand into his breast-pocket. A rustling revealed the sailor's bank-notes thrust carelessly in.

This second verification of his dim memories was enough; he knew now they were not dreams. He remained seated, looking on the ground for some time. "I must get out of this as soon as I can," he said deliberately at last, with the air of one who could not catch his thoughts without pronouncing them. "She's gone—to be sure she is—gone with that sailor who bought her, and little Elizabeth-Jane. We walked here, and I had the furmity, and rum in it—and sold her. Yes, that's what's happened and here am I. Now, what am I to do—am I sobre enough to walk, I wonder?" He stood up, found that he was in fairly good condition for progress, unencumbered. Next he shouldered his tool basket, and found he could carry it. Then lifting the tent door he emerged into the open air.

Here the man looked around with gloomy curiosity. The freshness of the September morning inspired and braced him as he stood. He and his family had been weary when they arrived the night before, and they had observed but little of the place; so that he now beheld it as a new thing. It exhibited itself as the top of an open down, bounded on one extreme by a plantation, and approached by a winding road. At the bottom stood the village which lent its name to the upland and the annual fair that was held thereon. The spot stretched downward into valleys, and onward to other uplands, dotted with barrows, and trenched with the remains of prehistoric forts. The whole scene lay under the rays of a newly risen sun, which had not as yet dried a single blade of the heavily dewed grass, whereon the shadows of the yellow and red vans were projected far away, those thrown by the felloe of each wheel being elongated in shape to the orbit of a comet. All the gipsies and showmen who had remained on the ground lay snug within their carts and tents or wrapped in horse-cloths under them, and were silent and still as death, with the exception of an occasional snore that revealed their presence. But the Seven Sleepers had a dog; and dogs of the mysterious breeds that vagrants own, that are as much like cats as dogs and as much like foxes as cats also lay about here. A little one started up under one of the carts, barked as a matter of principle, and quickly lay down again. He was the only positive spectator of the hay-trusser's exit from the Weydon Fair-field.

This seemed to accord with his desire. He went on in silent thought, unheeding the yellowhammers which flitted about the hedges with straws in their bills, the crowns of the mushrooms, and the tinkling of local sheep-bells, whose wearer had had the good fortune not to be included in the fair. When he reached a lane, a good mile from the scene of the previous evening, the man pitched his basket and leant upon a gate. A difficult problem or two occupied his mind.

"Did I tell my name to anybody last night, or didn't I tell my name?" he said to himself; and at last concluded that he did not. His general demeanour was enough to show how he was surprised and nettled that his wife had taken him so literally—as much could be seen in his face, and in the way he nibbled a straw which he pulled from the hedge. He knew that she must have been somewhat excited to do this; moreover, she must have believed that there was some sort of binding force in the transaction. On this latter point he felt almost certain, knowing her freedom from levity of character, and the extreme simplicity of her intellect. There may, too, have been enough recklessness and resentment beneath her ordinary placidity to make her stifle any momentary doubts. On a previous occasion when he had declared during a fuddle that he would dispose of her as he had done, she had replied that she would not hear him say that many times more before it happened, in the resigned tones of a fatalist...."Yet she knows I am not in my senses when I do that!" he exclaimed. "Well, I must walk about till I find her....Seize her, why didn't she know better than bring me into this disgrace!" he roared out. "She wasn't queer if I was. 'Tis like Susan to show such idiotic simplicity. Meek—that meekness has done me more harm than the bitterest temper!"

When he was calmer he turned to his original conviction that he must somehow find her and his little Elizabeth-Jane, and put up with the shame as best he could. It was of his own making, and he ought to bear it. But first he resolved to register an oath, a greater oath than he had ever sworn before: and to do it properly he required a fit place and imagery; for there was something fetichistic in this man's beliefs.

He shouldered his basket and moved on, casting his eyes inquisitively round upon the landscape as he walked, and at the distance of three or four miles perceived the roofs of a village and the tower of a church. He instantly made towards the latter object. The village was quite still, it being that motionless hour of rustic daily life which fills the interval between the departure of the field-labourers to their work, and the rising of their wives and daughters to prepare the breakfast for their return. Hence he reached the church without observation, and the door being only latched he entered. The hay-trusser deposited his basket by the font, went up the nave till he reached the altar-rails, and opening the gate entered the sacrarium, where he seemed to feel a sense of the strangeness for a moment; then he knelt upon the footpace. Dropping his head upon the clamped book which lay on the Communion-table, he said aloud—

"I, Michael Henchard, on this morning of the sixteenth of September, do take an oath before God here in this solemn place that I will avoid all strong liquors for the space of twenty-one years to come, being a year for every year that I have lived. And this I swear upon the book before me; and may I be strook dumb, blind, and helpless, if I break this my oath!"

When he had said it and kissed the big book, the hay-trusser arose, and seemed relieved at having made a start in a new direction. While standing in the porch a moment he saw a thick jet of wood smoke suddenly start up from the red chimney of a cottage near, and knew that the occupant had just lit her fire. He went round to the door, and the housewife agreed to prepare him some breakfast for a trifling payment, which was done. Then he started on the search for his wife and child.

The perplexing nature of the undertaking became apparent soon enough. Though he examined and inquired, and walked hither and thither day after day, no such characters as those he described had anywhere been seen since the evening of the fair. To add to the difficulty he could gain no sound of the sailor's name. As money was short with him he decided, after some hesitation, to spend the sailor's money in the prosecution of this search; but it was equally in vain. The truth was that a certain shyness of revealing his conduct prevented Michael Henchard from following up the investigation with the loud hue-and-cry such a pursuit demanded to render it effectual; and it was probably for this reason that he obtained no clue, though everything was done by him that did not involve an explanation of the circumstances under which he had lost her.

Weeks counted up to months, and still he searched on, maintaining himself by small jobs of work in the intervals. By this time he had arrived at a seaport, and there he derived intelligence that persons answering somewhat to his description had emigrated a little time before. Then he said he would search no longer, and that he would go and settle in the district which he had had for some time in his mind.

Next day he started, journeying south-westward, and did not pause, except for nights' lodgings, till he reached the town of Casterbridge, in a far distant part of Wessex.

Chapter 3

The highroad into the village of Weydon-Priors was again carpeted with dust. The trees had put on as of yore their aspect of dingy green, and where the Henchard family of three had once walked along, two persons not unconnected with the family walked now.

The scene in its broad aspect had so much of its previous character, even to the voices and rattle from the neighbouring village down, that it might for that matter have been the afternoon following the previously recorded episode. Change was only to be observed in details; but here it was obvious that a long procession of years had passed by. One of the two who walked the road was she who had figured as the young wife of Henchard on the previous occasion; now her face had lost much of its rotundity; her skin had undergone a textural change; and though her hair had not lost colour it was considerably thinner than heretofore. She was dressed in the mourning clothes of a widow. Her companion, also in black, appeared as a young woman about eighteen, completely possessed of that ephemeral precious essence youth, which is itself beauty, irrespective of complexion or contour.

A glance was sufficient to inform the eye that this was

Susan Henchard's grown-up daughter. While life's middle summer had set its hardening mark on the mother's face, her former spring-like specialities were transferred so dexterously by Time to the second figure, her child, that the absence of certain facts within her mother's knowledge from the girl's mind would have seemed for the moment, to one reflecting on those facts, to be a curious imperfection in Nature's powers of continuity. They walked with joined hands, and it could be perceived that this was the act of simple affection. The daughter carried in her outer hand a withy basket of old-fashioned make; the mother a blue bundle, which contrasted oddly with her black stuff gown.

Reaching the outskirts of the village they pursued the same track as formerly, and ascended to the fair. Here, too it was evident that the years had told. Certain mechanical improvements might have been noticed in the roundabouts and high-fliers, machines for testing rustic strength and weight, and in the erections devoted to shooting for nuts. But the real business of the fair had considerably dwindled. The new periodical great markets of neighbouring towns were beginning to interfere seriously with the trade carried on here for centuries. The pens for sheep, the tie-ropes for horses, were about half as long as they had been. The stalls of tailors, hosiers, coopers, linen-drapers, and other such trades had almost disappeared, and the vehicles were far less numerous. The mother and daughter threaded the crowd for some little distance, and then stood still.

"Why did we hinder our time by coming in here? I thought you wished to get onward?" said the maiden.

"Yes, my dear Elizabeth-Jane," explained the other. "But I had a fancy for looking up here."

"Why?"

"It was here I first met with Newson—on such a day as this.""First met with father here? Yes, you have told me so before. And now he's drowned and gone from us!" As she spoke the girl drew a card from her pocket and looked at it with a sigh. It was edged with black, and inscribed within a design resembling a mural tablet were the words, "In affectionate memory of Richard Newson, mariner, who was unfortunately lost at sea, in the month of November 184—, aged forty-one years."

"And it was here," continued her mother, with more hesitation, "that I last saw the relation we are going to look for—Mr. Michael Henchard."

"What is his exact kin to us, mother? I have never clearly had it told me."

"He is, or was—for he may be dead—a connection by marriage," said her mother deliberately.

"That's exactly what you have said a score of times before!" replied the young woman, looking about her inattentively. "He's not a near relation, I suppose?"

"Not by any means."

"He was a hay-trusser, wasn't he, when you last heard of him?

"He was."

"I suppose he never knew me?" the girl innocently continued.

Mrs. Henchard paused for a moment, and answered uneasily, "Of course not, Elizabeth-Jane. But come this way." She moved on to another part of the field.

"It is not much use inquiring here for anybody, I should think," the daughter observed, as she gazed round about. "People at fairs change like the leaves of trees; and I daresay you are the only one here to-day who was here all those years ago."

"I am not so sure of that," said Mrs. Newson, as she now called herself, keenly eyeing something under a green bank a little way off. "See there."

The daughter looked in the direction signified. The object pointed out was a tripod of sticks stuck into the earth, from which hung a three-legged crock, kept hot by a smouldering wood fire beneath. Over the pot stooped an old woman haggard, wrinkled, and almost in rags. She stirred the contents of the pot with a large spoon, and occasionally croaked in a broken voice, "Good furmity sold here!"

It was indeed the former mistress of the furmity tent—

once thriving, cleanly, white-aproned, and chinking with money—now tentless, dirty, owning no tables or benches, and having scarce any customers except two small whity-brown boys, who came up and asked for "A ha'p'orth, please—good measure," which she served in a couple of chipped yellow basins of commonest clay.

"She was here at that time," resumed Mrs. Newson, making a step as if to draw nearer.

"Don't speak to her—it isn't respectable!" urged the other.

"I will just say a word—you, Elizabeth-Jane, can stay here." The girl was not loth, and turned to some stalls of coloured prints while her mother went forward. The old woman begged for the latter's custom as soon as she saw her, and responded to Mrs. Henchard-Newson's request for a with more alacrity than she had shown in selling in her younger days. When the soi-disant widow had taken the basin of thin poor slop that stood for the rich concoction of the former time, the hag opened a little basket behind the fire, and looking up slily, whispered, "Just a thought o' rum in it?—smuggled, you know—say two penn'orth—'twill make it slip down like cordial!" Her customer smiled bitterly at this survival of the old trick, and shook her head with a meaning the old woman was far from translating. She pretended to eat a little of the furmity with the leaden spoon offered, and as she did so said blandly to the hag, "You've seen better days?"

"Ah, ma'am—well ye may say it!" responded the old woman, opening the sluices of her heart forthwith. "I've stood in this fair-ground, maid, wife, and widow, these nine-years, and in that time have known what it was to do business with the richest stomachs in the land! Ma'am you'd hardly believe that I was once the owner of a great pavilion-tent that was the attraction of the fair. Nobody could come, nobody could go, without having a dish of Mrs. Goodenough's furmity. I knew the clergy's taste, the dandy gent's taste; I knew the town's taste, the country's taste. I even knowed the taste of the coarse shameless females. But Lord's my life—the world's no memory; straightforward dealings don't bring profit—'tis the sly and the underhand that get on in these times!"

Mrs. Newson glanced round—her daughter was still bending over the distant stalls. "Can you call to mind," she said cautiously to the old woman, "the sale of a wife by her husband in your tent eighteen years ago to-day?"

The hag reflected, and half shook her head. "If it had been a big thing I should have minded it in a moment," she said. "I can mind every serious fight o' married parties, every murder, every manslaughter, even every pocket-picking—leastwise large ones—that 't has been my lot to witness. But a selling? Was it done quiet-like?"

"Well, yes. I think so."

The furmity woman half shook her head again. "And yet," she said, "I do. At any rate, I can mind a man doing something o' the sort—a man in a cord jacket, with a basket of tools; but, Lord bless ye, we don't gi'e it head-room, we don't, such as that. The only reason why I can mind the man is that he came back here to the next year's fair, and told me quite private-like that if a woman ever asked for him I was to say he had gone to—where?—Casterbridge—yes—to Casterbridge, said he. But, Lord's my life, I shouldn't ha' thought of it again!"

Mrs. Newson would have rewarded the old woman as far as her small means afforded had she not discreetly borne in mind that it was by that unscrupulous person's liquor her husband had been degraded. She briefly thanked her informant, and rejoined Elizabeth, who greeted her with, "Mother, do let's get on—it was hardly respectable for you to buy refreshments there. I see none but the lowest do."

"I have learned what I wanted, however," said her mother quietly. "The last time our relative visited this fair he said he was living at Casterbridge. It is a long, long way from here, and it was many years ago that he said it, but there I think we'll go."

With this they descended out of the fair, and went onward to the village, where they obtained a night's lodging.

Chapter 6

Now the group outside the window had within the last few minutes been reinforced by new arrivals, some of them respectable shopkeepers and their assistants, who had come out for a whiff of air after putting up the shutters for the night; some of them of a lower class. Distinct from either there appeared a stranger—a young man of remarkably pleasant aspect—who carried in his hand a carpet-bag of the smart floral pattern prevalent in such articles at that time.

He was ruddy and of a fair countenance, bright-eyed, and slight in build. He might possibly have passed by without stopping at all, or at most for half a minute to glance in at the scene, had not his advent coincided with the discussion on corn and bread, in which event this history had never been enacted. But the subject seemed to arrest him, and he whispered some inquiries of the other bystanders, and remained listening.

When he heard Henchard's closing words, "It can't be done," he smiled impulsively, drew out his pocketbook, and wrote down a few words by the aid of the light in the window. He tore out the leaf, folded and directed it, and seemed about to throw it in through the open sash upon the dining-table; but, on second thoughts, edged himself through the loiterers, till he reached the door of the hotel, where one of the waiters who had been serving inside was now idly leaning against the doorpost.

"Give this to the Mayor at once," he said, handing in his hasty note.

Elizabeth-Jane had seen his movements and heard the words, which attracted her both by their subject and by their accent—a strange one for those parts. It was quaint and northerly.

The waiter took the note, while the young stranger continued—

"And can ye tell me of a respectable hotel that's a little more moderate than this?"

The waiter glanced indifferently up and down the street.

"They say the Three Mariners, just below here, is a very good place," he languidly answered; "but I have never stayed there myself."

The Scotchman, as he seemed to be, thanked him, and strolled on in the direction of the Three Mariners aforesaid, apparently more concerned about the question of an inn than about the fate of his note, now that the momentary impulse of writing it was over. While he was disappearing slowly down the street the waiter left the door, and Elizabeth-Jane saw with some interest the note brought into the dining-room and handed to the Mayor.

Henchard looked at it carelessly, unfolded it with one hand, and glanced it through. Thereupon it was curious to note an unexpected effect. The nettled, clouded aspect which had held possession of his face since the subject of his had been broached, changed itself into one of arrested attention. He read the note slowly, and fell into thought, not moody, but fitfully intense, as that of a man who has been captured by an idea.

By this time toasts and speeches had given place to songs, the wheat subject being quite forgotten. Men were putting their heads together in twos and threes, telling good stories, with pantomimic laughter which reached convulsive grimace. Some were beginning to look as if they did not know how they had come there, what they had come for, or how they were going to get home again; and provisionally sat on with a dazed smile. Square-built men showed a tendency to become hunchbacks; men with a dignified presence lost it in a curious obliquity of figure, in which their features grew disarranged and one-sided, whilst the heads of a few who had dined with extreme thoroughness were somehow sinking into their shoulders, the corners of their mouth and eyes being bent upwards by the subsidence. Only Henchard did not conform to these flexuous changes; he remained stately and vertical, silently thinking.

The clock struck nine. Elizabeth-Jane turned to her companion. "The evening is drawing on, mother," she said. "What do you propose to do?"

She was surprised to find how irresolute her mother had become. "We must get a place to lie down in," she murmured. "I have seen—Mr. Henchard; and that's all I wanted to do."

"That's enough for to-night, at any rate," Elizabeth-Jane replied soothingly. "We can think to-morrow what is best to do about him. The question now is—is it not?—how shall we find a lodging?"

As her mother did not reply Elizabeth-Jane's mind reverted to the words of the waiter, that the Three Mariners was an inn of moderate charges. A recommendation good for one person was probably good for another. "Let's go where the young man has gone to," she said. "He is respectable. What do you say?"

Her mother assented, and down the street they went.

In the meantime the Mayor's thoughtfulness, engendered by the note as stated, continued to hold him in abstraction; till, whispering to his neighbour to take his place, he found opportunity to leave the chair. This was just after the departure of his wife and Elizabeth.

Outside the door of the assembly-room he saw the waiter, and beckoning to him asked who had brought the note which had been handed in a quarter of an hour before.

"A young man, sir—a sort of traveller. He was a Scotchman seemingly."

"Did he say how he had got it?"

"He wrote it himself, sir, as he stood outside the window."

"Oh—wrote it himself....Is the young man in the hotel?"

"No, sir. He went to the Three Mariners, I believe."

The mayor walked up and down the vestibule of the hotel with his hands under his coat tails, as if he were merely seeking a cooler atmosphere than that of the room he had quitted. But there could be no doubt that he was in reality still possessed to the full by the new idea, whatever that might be. At length he went back to the door of the dining-room, paused, and found that the songs, toasts, and conversation were proceeding quite satisfactorily without his presence. The Corporation, private residents, and major and minor tradesmen had, in fact, gone in for comforting beverages to such an extent that they had quite forgotten, not only the Mayor, but all those vast, political, religious, and social differences which they felt necessary to maintain in the daytime, and which separated them like iron grills. Seeing this the Mayor took his hat, and when the waiter had helped him on with a thin holland overcoat, went out and stood under the portico.

Very few persons were now in the street; and his eyes, by

a sort of attraction, turned and dwelt upon a spot about a hundred yards further down. It was the house to which the writer of the note had gone—the Three Mariners—whose two prominent Elizabethan gables, bow-window, and passage-light could be seen from where he stood. Having kept his eyes on it for a while he strolled in that direction.

This ancient house of accommodation for man and beast, now, unfortunately, pulled down, was built of mellow sandstone, with mullioned windows of the same material, markedly out of perpendicular from the settlement of foundations. The bay window projecting into the street, whose interior was so popular among the frequenters of the inn, was closed with shutters, in each of which appeared a heart-shaped aperture, somewhat more attenuated in the right and left ventricles than is seen in Nature.

Inside these illuminated holes, at a distance of about three inches, were ranged at this hour, as every passer knew, the ruddy polls of Billy Wills the glazier, Smart the shoemaker, Buzzford the general dealer, and others of a secondary set of worthies, of a grade somewhat below that of the diners at the King's Arms, each with his yard of clay.

A four-centred Tudor arch was over the entrance, and over the arch the signboard, now visible in the rays of an opposite lamp. Hereon the Mariners, who had been represented by the artist as persons of two dimensions only—in other words, flat as a shadow—were standing in a row in paralyzed attitudes. Being on the sunny side of the street the three comrades had suffered largely from warping, splitting, fading, and shrinkage, so that they were but a half-invisible film upon the reality of the grain, and knots, and nails, which composed the signboard. As a matter of fact, this state of things was not so much owing to Stannidge the landlord's neglect, as from the lack of a painter in Casterbridge who would undertake to reproduce the features of men so traditional.

A long, narrow, dimly-lit passage gave access to the inn, within which passage the horses going to their stalls at the back, and the coming and departing human guests, rubbed shoulders indiscriminately, the latter running no slight risk of having their toes trodden upon by the animals. The good stabling and the good ale of the Mariners, though somewhat difficult to reach on account of there being but this narrow way to both, were nevertheless perseveringly sought out by the sagacious old heads who knew what was what in Casterbridge.

Henchard stood without the inn for a few instants; then lowering the dignity of his presence as much as possible by buttoning the brown holland coat over his shirt-front, and in other ways toning himself down to his ordinary everyday appearance, he entered the inn door.

Chapter 8

Thus they parted; and Elizabeth-Jane and her mother remained each in her thoughts over their meal, the mother's face being strangely bright since Henchard's avowal of shame for a past action. The quivering of the partition to its core presented denoted that Donald Farfrae had again rung his bell, no doubt to have his supper removed; for humming a tune, and walking up and down, he seemed to be attracted by the lively bursts of conversation and melody from the general company below. He sauntered out upon the landing, and descended the staircase.

When Elizabeth-Jane had carried down his supper tray, and also that used by her mother and herself, she found the bustle of serving to be at its height below, as it always was at this hour. The young woman shrank from having anything to do with the ground-floor serving, and crept silently about observing the scene—so new to her, fresh from the seclusion of a seaside cottage. In the general sitting-room, which was large, she remarked the two or three dozen strong-backed chairs that stood round against the wall, each fitted with its genial occupant; the sanded floor; the black settle which, projecting endwise from the wall within the door, permitted Elizabeth to be a spectator of all that went on without herself being particularly seen.

The young Scotchman had just joined the guests. These, in addition to the respectable master-tradesmen occupying the seats of privileges in the bow-window and its neighbourhood, included an inferior set at the unlighted end, whose seats were mere benches against the wall, and who drank from cups instead of from glasses. Among the latter she noticed some of those personages who had stood outside the windows of the King's Arms.

Behind their backs was a small window, with a wheel ventilator in one of the panes, which would suddenly start off spinning with a jingling sound, as suddenly stop, and as suddenly start again.

While thus furtively making her survey the opening words of a song greeted her ears from the front of the settle, in a melody and accent of peculiar charm. There had been some singing before she came down; and now the Scotchman had made himself so soon at home that, at the request of some of the master-tradesmen, he, too, was favouring the room with a ditty. Elizabeth-Jane was fond of music; she could not help pausing to listen; and the longer she listened the more she was enraptured. She had never heard any singing like this and it was evident that the majority of the audience had not heard such frequently, for they were attentive to a much greater degree than usual. They neither whispered, nor drank, nor dipped their pipe-stems in their ale to moisten them, nor pushed the mug to their neighbours. The singer himself grew emotional, till she could imagine a tear in his eye as the words went on:—

"It's hame, and it's hame, hame fain would I be,
O hame, hame, hame to my ain countree!
There's an eye that ever weeps, and a fair face will be fain,
As I pass through Annan Water with my bonnie bands again;
When the flower is in the bud, and the leaf upon the tree,
The lark shall sing me hame to my ain countree!"

There was a burst of applause, and a deep silence which was even more eloquent than the applause. It was of such a kind that the snapping of a pipe-stem too long for him by old Solomon Longways, who was one of those gathered at the shady end of the room, seemed a harsh and irreverent act. Then the ventilator in the window-pane spasmodically started off for a new spin, and the pathos of Donald's song was temporarily effaced.

"'Twas not amiss—not at all amiss!" muttered Christopher Coney, who was also present. And removing his pipe a finger's breadth from his lips, he said aloud, "Draw on with the next verse, young gentleman, please."

"Yes. Let's have it again, stranger," said the glazier, a stout, bucket-headed man, with a white apron rolled up round his waist. "Folks don't lift up their hearts like that in this part of the world." And turning aside, he said in undertones, "Who is the young man?—Scotch, d'ye say?"

"Yes, straight from the mountains of Scotland, I believe," replied Coney.

Young Farfrae repeated the last verse. It was plain that nothing so pathetic had been heard at the Three Mariners for a considerable time. The difference of accent, the excitability of the singer, the intense local feeling, and the seriousness with which he worked himself up to a climax, surprised this set of worthies, who were only too prone to shut up their emotions with caustic words.

"Danged if our country down here is worth singing about like that!" continued the glazier, as the Scotchman again melodized with a dying fall, "My ain countree!" "When you take away from among us the fools and the rogues, and the lammigers, and the wanton hussies, and the slatterns, and such like, there's cust few left to ornament a song with in Casterbridge, or the country round."

"True," said Buzzford, the dealer, looking at the grain of the table. "Casterbridge is a old, hoary place o' wickedness, by all account. 'Tis recorded in history that we rebelled against the King one or two hundred years ago, in the time of the Romans, and that lots of us was hanged on Gallows Hill, and quartered, and our different jints sent about the country like butcher's meat; and for my part I can well believe it."

"What did ye come away from yer own country for, young maister, if ye be so wownded about it?" inquired Christopher Coney, from the background, with the tone of a man who preferred the original subject. "Faith, it wasn't worth your while on our account, for as Maister Billy Wills says, we be bruckle folk here—the best o' us hardly honest sometimes, what with hard winters, and so many mouths to fill, and Goda'mighty sending his little taties so terrible small to fill 'em with. We don't think about flowers and fair faces, not we—except in the shape o' cauliflowers and pigs' chaps."

"But, no!" said Donald Farfrae, gazing round into their faces with earnest concern; "the best of ye hardly honest—not that surely? None of ye has been stealing what didn't belong to him?"

"Lord! no, no!" said Solomon Longways, smiling grimly. "That's only his random way o' speaking. 'A was always such a man of underthoughts." (And reprovingly towards Christopher): "Don't ye be so over-familiar with a gentleman that ye know nothing of—and that's travelled a'most from the North Pole."

Christopher Coney was silenced, and as he could get no public sympathy, he mumbled his feelings to himself: "Be dazed, if I loved my country half as well as the young feller do, I'd live by claning my neighbour's pigsties afore I'd go away! For my part I've no more love for my country than I have for Botany Bay!"

"Come," said Longways; "let the young man draw onward with his ballet, or we shall be here all night."

"That's all of it," said the singer apologetically.

"Soul of my body, then we'll have another!" said the general dealer.

"Can you turn a strain to the ladies, sir?" inquired a fat woman with a figured purple apron, the waiststring of which was overhung so far by her sides as to be invisible.

"Let him breathe-let him breathe, Mother Cuxsom. He hain't got his second wind yet," said the master glazier.

"Oh yes, but I have!" exclaimed the young man; and he at once rendered "O Nannie" with faultless modulations, and another or two of the like sentiment, winding up at their earnest request with "Auld Lang Syne."

By this time he had completely taken possession of the

hearts of the Three Mariners' inmates, including even old Coney. Notwithstanding an occasional odd gravity which awoke their sense of the ludicrous for the moment, they began to view him through a golden haze which the tone of his mind seemed to raise around him. Casterbridge had sentiment-Casterbridge had romance; but this stranger's sentiment was of differing quality. Or rather, perhaps, the difference was mainly superficial; he was to them like the poet of a new school who takes his contemporaries by storm; who is not really new, but is the first to articulate what all his listeners have felt, though but dumbly till then.

The silent landlord came and leant over the settle while the young man sang; and even Mrs. Stannidge managed to unstick herself from the framework of her chair in the bar and get as far as the door-post, which movement she accomplished by rolling herself round, as a cask is trundled on the chine by a drayman without losing much of its perpendicular.

"And are you going to bide in Casterbridge, sir?" she asked.

"Ah-no!" said the Scotchman, with melancholy fatality in his voice, "I'm only passing thirrough! I am on my way to Bristol, and on frae there to foreign parts."

"We be truly sorry to hear it," said Solomon Longways. "We can ill afford to lose tuneful wynd-pipes like yours when they fall among us. And verily, to mak' acquaintance with a man a-come from so far, from the land o' perpetual snow, as we may say, where wolves and wild boars and other dangerous animalcules be as common as blackbirds here-about-why, 'tis a thing we can't do every day; and there's good sound information for bide-at-homes like we when such a man opens his mouth."

"Nay, but ye mistake my country," said the young man, looking round upon them with tragic fixity, till his eye lighted up and his cheek kindled with a sudden enthusiasm to right their errors. "There are not perpetual snow and wolves at all in it!-except snow in winter, and-well-a little in summer just sometimes, and a 'gaberlunzie' or two stalking about here and there, if ye may call them dangerous. Eh, but you should take a summer jarreny to Edinboro', and Arthur's Seat, and all round there, and then go on to the lochs, and all the Highland scenery-in May and June-and you would never say 'tis the land of wolves and perpetual snow!"

"Of course not-it stands to reason," said Buzzford. "'Tis barren ignorance that leads to such words. He's a simple home-spun man, that never was fit for good company-think nothing of him, sir." "And do ye carry your flock bed, and your quilt, and your crock, and your bit of chiney? or do ye go in bare bones, as I may say?" inquired Christopher Coney.

"I've sent on my luggage-though it isn't much; for the voyage is long." Donald's eyes dropped into a remote gaze as he added: "But I said to myself, 'Never a one of the prizes of life will I come by unless I undertake it!' and I decided to go."

A general sense of regret, in which Elizabeth-Jane shared not least, made itself apparent in the company. As she looked at Farfrae from the back of the settle she decided that his statements showed him to be no less thoughtful than his fascinating melodies revealed him to be cordial and impassioned. She admired the serious light in which he looked at serious things. He had seen no jest in ambiguities and roguery, as the Casterbridge toss-pots had done; and rightly not-there was none. She disliked those wretched humours of Christopher Coney and his tribe; and he did not appreciate them. He seemed to feel exactly as she felt about life and its surroundings-that they were a tragical rather than a comical thing; that though one could be gay on occasion, moments of gaiety were interludes, and no part of the actual drama. It was extraordinary how similar their views were.

Though it was still early the young Scotchman expressed his wish to retire, whereupon the landlady whispered to Elizabeth to run upstairs and turn down his bed. She took a candlestick and proceeded on her mission, which was the act of a few moments only. When, candle in hand, she reached the top of the stairs on her way down again, Mr. Farfrae was at the foot coming up. She could not very well retreat; they met and passed in the turn of the staircase.

She must have appeared interesting in some way-her plain

dress-or rather, possibly, in consequence of it, for she was a girl characterized by earnestness and soberness of mien, with which simple drapery accorded well. Her face flushed, too, at the slight awkwardness of the meeting, and she passed him with her eyes bent on the candle-flame that she carried just below her nose. Thus it happened that when confronting her he smiled; and then, with the manner of a temporarily light-hearted man, who has started himself on a flight of song whose momentum he cannot readily check, he softly tuned an old ditty that she seemed to suggest-

"As I came in by my bower door,
As day was waxin' wearie,
Oh wha came tripping down the stair
But bonnie Peg my dearie."

Elizabeth-Jane, rather disconcerted, hastened on; and the Scotchman's voice died away, humming more of the same within the closed door of his room.

Here the scene and sentiment ended for the present. When soon after, the girl rejoined her mother, the latter was still in thought-on quite another matter than a young man's song.

"We've made a mistake," she whispered (that the Scotchman might not overhear). "On no account ought ye to have helped serve here to-night. Not because of ourselves, but for the sake of him. If he should befriend us, and take us up, and then find out what you did when staying here, 'twould grieve and wound his natural pride as Mayor of the town."

Elizabeth, who would perhaps have been more alarmed at this than her mother had she known the real relationship, was not much disturbed about it as things stood. Her "he" was another man than her poor mother's. "For myself," she said, "I didn't at all mind waiting a little upon him. He's so respectable, and educated-far above the rest of 'em in the inn. They thought him very simple not to know their grim broad way of talking about themselves here. But of course he didn't know-he was too refined in his mind to know such things!" Thus she earnestly pleaded.

Meanwhile, the "he" of her mother was not so far away as even they thought. After leaving the Three Mariners he had sauntered up and down the empty High Street, passing and repassing the inn in his promenade. When the Scotchman sang his voice had reached Henchard's ears through the holes in the window-shutters, and had led him to pause outside them a long while.

"To be sure, to be sure, how that fellow does draw me!" he had said to himself. "I suppose 'tis because I'm so lonely. I'd have given him a third share in the business to have stayed!"

Chapter 10

While she still sat under the Scotchman's eyes a man came up to the door, reaching it as Henchard opened the door of the inner office to admit Elizabeth. The newcomer stepped forward like the quicker cripple at Bethesda, and entered in her stead. She could hear his words to Henchard: "Joshua Jopp, sir-by appointment-the new manager."

"The new manager!-he's in his office," said Henchard bluntly.

"In his office!" said the man, with a stultified air.

"I mentioned Thursday," said Henchard; "and as you did not keep your appointment, I have engaged another manager. At first I thought he must be you. Do you think I can wait when business is in question?"

"You said Thursday or Saturday, sir," said the newcomer, pulling out a letter.

"Well, you are too late," said the corn-factor. "I can say no more."

"You as good as engaged me," murmured the man.

"Subject to an interview," said Henchard. "I am sorry for you-very sorry indeed. But it can't be helped."

There was no more to be said, and the man came out, encountering Elizabeth-Jane in his passage. She could see that his mouth twitched with anger, and that bitter disappointment was written in his face everywhere.

Elizabeth-Jane now entered, and stood before the master of the premises. His dark pupils-which always seemed to have a red spark of light in them, though this could hardly be a physical fact-turned indifferently round under his dark brows until they rested on her figure. "Now then, what is it, my young woman?" he said blandly.

"Can I speak to you-not on business, sir?" said she.

"Yes-I suppose." He looked at her more thoughtfully.

"I am sent to tell you, sir," she innocently went on, "that a distant relative of yours by marriage, Susan Newson, a sailor's widow, is in the town, and to ask whether you would wish to see her."

The rich rouge-et-noir of his countenance underwent a slight change. "Oh-Susan is-still alive?" he asked with difficulty.

"Yes, sir."

"Are you her daughter?"

"Yes, sir-her only daughter."

"What-do you call yourself-your Christian name?"

"Elizabeth-Jane, sir."

"Newson?"

"Elizabeth-Jane Newson."

This at once suggested to Henchard that the transaction of his early married life at Weydon Fair was unrecorded in the family history. It was more than he could have expected. His wife had behaved kindly to him in return for his unkindness, and had never proclaimed her wrong to her child or to the world.

"I am-a good deal interested in your news," he said. "And as this is not a matter of business, but pleasure, suppose we go indoors."

It was with a gentle delicacy of manner, surprising to Elizabeth, that he showed her out of the office and through the outer room, where Donald Farfrae was overhauling bins and samples with the inquiring inspection of a beginner in charge. Henchard preceded her through the door in the wall to the suddenly changed scene of the garden and flowers, and onward into the house. The dining-room to which he introduced her still exhibited the remnants of the lavish breakfast laid for Farfrae. It was furnished to profusion with heavy mahogany furniture of the deepest red-Spanish hues. Pembroke tables, with leaves hanging so low that they well-nigh touched the floor, stood against the walls on legs and feet shaped like those of an elephant, and on one lay three huge folio volumes-a Family Bible, a "Josephus," and a "Whole Duty of Man." In the chimney comer was a fire-grate with a fluted semicircular back, having urns and festoons cast in relief thereon, and the chairs were of the kind which, since that day, has cast lustre upon the names of Chippendale and Sheraton, though, in point of fact, their patterns may have been such as those illustrious carpenters never saw or heard of.

"Sit down-Elizabeth-Jane-sit down," he said, with a shake in his voice as he uttered her name, and sitting down himself he allowed his hands to hang between his knees while he looked upon the carpet. "Your mother, then, is quite well?"

"She is rather worn out, sir, with travelling."

"A sailor's widow-when did he die?"

"Father was lost last spring."

Henchard winced at the word "father," thus applied. "Do you and she come from abroad-America or Australia?" he asked.

"No. We have been in England some years. I was twelve when we came here from Canada."

"Ah; exactly." By such conversation he discovered the circumstances which had enveloped his wife and her child in such total obscurity that he had long ago believed them to be in their graves. These things being clear, he returned to the present. "And where is your mother staying?"

"At the Three Mariners."

"And you are her daughter Elizabeth-Jane?" repeated Henchard. He arose, came close to her, and glanced in her face. "I think," he said, suddenly turning away with a wet eye, "you shall take a note from me to your mother. I should like to see her....She is not left very well off by her late husband?" His eye fell on Elizabeth's clothes, which, though a respectable suit of black, and her very best, were decidedly old-fashioned even to Casterbridge eyes.

"Not very well," she said, glad that he had divined this without her being obliged to express it.

He sat down at the table and wrote a few lines, next taking

from his pocket-book a five-pound note, which he put in the envelope with the letter, adding to it, as by an afterthought, five shillings. Sealing the whole up carefully, he directed it to "Mrs. Newson, Three Mariners Inn," and handed the packet to Elizabeth.

"Deliver it to her personally, please," said Henchard. "Well, I am glad to see you here, Elizabeth-Jane-very glad. We must have a long talk together-but not just now."

He took her hand at parting, and held it so warmly that she, who had known so little friendship, was much affected, and tears rose to her aerial-grey eyes. The instant that she was gone Henchard's state showed itself more distinctly; having shut the door he sat in his dining-room stiffly erect, gazing at the opposite wall as if he read his history there.

"Begad!" he suddenly exclaimed, jumping up. "I didn't think of that. Perhaps these are impostors-and Susan and the child dead after all!"

However, a something in Elizabeth-Jane soon assured him that, as regarded her, at least, there could be little doubt. And a few hours would settle the question of her mother's identity; for he had arranged in his note to see her that evening.

"It never rains but it pours!" said Henchard. His keenly excited interest in his new friend the Scotchman was now eclipsed by this event, and Donald Farfrae saw so little of him during the rest of the day that he wondered at the suddenness of his employer's moods.

In the meantime Elizabeth had reached the inn. Her mother, instead of taking the note with the curiosity of a poor woman expecting assistance, was much moved at sight of it. She did not read it at once, asking Elizabeth to describe her reception, and the very words Mr. Henchard used. Elizabeth's back was turned when her mother opened the letter. It ran thus:-

"Meet me at eight o'clock this evening, if you can, at the Ring on the Budmouth road. The place is easy to find. I can say no more now. The news upsets me almost. The girl seems to be in ignorance. Keep her so till I have seen you. M. H."

He said nothing about the enclosure of five guineas. The

amount was significant; it may tacitly have said to her that he bought her back again. She waited restlessly for the close of the day, telling Elizabeth-Jane that she was invited to see Mr. Henchard; that she would go alone. But she said nothing to show that the place of meeting was not at his house, nor did she hand the note to Elizabeth.

Chapter 12

On entering his own door after watching his wife out of sight, the Mayor walked on through the tunnel-shaped passage into the garden, and thence by the back door towards the stores and granaries. A light shone from the office-window, and there being no blind to screen the interior Henchard could see Donald Farfrae still seated where he had left him, initiating himself into the managerial work of the house by overhauling the books. Henchard entered, merely observing, "Don't let me interrupt you, if ye will stay so late."

He stood behind Farfrae's chair, watching his dexterity in clearing up the numerical fogs which had been allowed to grow so thick in Henchard's books as almost to baffle even the Scotchman's perspicacity. The corn-factor's mien was half admiring, and yet it was not without a dash of pity for the tastes of any one who could care to give his mind to such finnikin details. Henchard himself was mentally and physically unfit for grubbing subtleties from soiled paper; he had in a modern sense received the education of Achilles, and found penmanship a tantalizing art.

"You shall do no more to-night," he said at length, spreading his great hand over the paper. "There's time enough to-morrow. Come indoors with me and have some supper. Now you shall! I am determined on't." He shut the account-books with friendly force.

Donald had wished to get to his lodgings; but he already saw that his friend and employer was a man who knew no moderation in his requests and impulses, and he yielded gracefully. He liked Henchard's warmth, even if it inconvenienced him; the great difference in their characters adding to the liking. They locked up the office, and the young man followed his companion through the private little door which, admitting directly into Henchard's garden, permitted a passage from the utilitarian to the beautiful at one step. The garden was silent, dewy, and full of perfume. It extended a long way back from the house, first as lawn and flower-beds, then as fruit-garden, where the long-tied espaliers, as old as the old house itself, had grown so stout, and cramped, and gnarled that they had pulled their stakes out of the ground and stood distorted and writhing in vegetable agony, like leafy Laocoons. The flowers which smelt so sweetly were not discernible; and they passed through them into the house.

The hospitalities of the morning were repeated, and when they were over Henchard said, "Pull your chair round to the fireplace, my dear fellow, and let's make a blaze-there's nothing I hate like a black grate, even in September." He applied a light to the laid-in fuel, and a cheerful radiance spread around.

"It is odd," said Henchard, "that two men should meet as we have done on a purely business ground, and that at the end of the first day I should wish to speak to 'ee on a family matter. But, damn it all, I am a lonely man, Farfrae: I have nobody else to speak to; and why shouldn't I tell it to 'ee?"

"I'll be glad to hear it, if I can be of any service," said Donald, allowing his eyes to travel over the intricate of the chimney-piece, representing garlanded lyres, shields, and quivers, on either side of a draped ox-skull, and flanked by heads of Apollo and Diana in low relief.

"I've not been always what I am now," continued Henchard, his firm deep voice being ever so little shaken. He was plainly under that strange influence which sometimes prompts men to confide to the new-found friend what they will not tell to the old. "I began life as a working hay-trusser, and when I was eighteen I married on the strength o' my calling. Would you think me a married man?"

"I heard in the town that you were a widower."

"Ah, yes-you would naturally have heard that. Well, I lost my wife nineteen years ago or so-by my own fault....This is how it came about. One summer evening I was travelling for employment, and she was walking at my side, carying the baby, our only child. We came to a booth in a country fair. I was a drinking man at that time." Henchard paused a moment, threw himself back so that his elbow rested on the table, his forehead being shaded by his hand, which, however, did not hide the marks of introspective inflexibility on his features as he narrated in fullest detail the incidents of the transaction with the sailor. The tinge of indifference which had at first been visible in the Scotchman now disappeared.

Henchard went on to describe his attempts to find his wife; the oath he swore; the solitary life he led during the years which followed. "I have kept my oath for nineteen years," he went on; "I have risen to what you see me now."

"Ay!"

"Well-no wife could I hear of in all that time; and being by nature something of a woman-hater, I have found it no hardship to keep mostly at a distance from the sex. No wife could I hear of, I say, till this very day. And now-she has come back."

"Come back, has she!"

"This morning-this very morning. And what's to be done?"

"Can ye no' take her and live with her, and make some amends?"

"That's what I've planned and proposed. But, Farfrae," said Henchard gloomily, "by doing right with Susan I wrong another innocent woman."

"Ye don't say that?"

"In the nature of things, Farfrae, it is almost impossible that a man of my sort should have the good fortune to tide through twenty years o' life without making more blunders than one. It has been my custom for many years to run across to Jersey in the the way of business, particularly in the potato and root season. I do a large trade wi' them in that line. Well, one autumn when stopping there I fell quite ill, and in my illness I sank into one of those gloomy fits I sometimes suffer from, on account o' the loneliness of my domestic life, when the world seems to have the blackness of hell, and, like Job, I could curse the day that gave me birth."

"Ah, now, I never feel like it," said Farfrae.

"Then pray to God that you never may, young man. While in this state I was taken pity on by a woman-a young lady I should call her, for she was of good family, well bred, and well educated-the daughter of some harum-scarum military officer who had got into difficulties, and had his pay sequestrated. He was dead now, and her mother too, and she was as lonely as I. This young creature was staying at the boarding-house where I happened to have my lodging; and when I was pulled down she took upon herself to nurse me. From that she got to have a foolish liking for me. Heaven knows why, for I wasn't worth it. But being together in the same house, and her feeling warm, we got naturally intimate. I won't go into particulars of what our relations were. It is enough to say that we honestly meant to marry.

There arose a scandal, which did me no harm, but was of course ruin to her. Though, Farfrae, between you and me, as man and man, I solemnly declare that philandering with womankind has neither been my vice nor my virtue. She was terribly careless of appearances, and I was perhaps more, because o' my dreary state; and it was through this that the scandal arose.

At last I was well, and came away. When I was gone she suffered much on my account, and didn't forget to tell me so in letters one after another; till latterly, I felt I owed her something, and thought that, as I had not heard of Susan for so long, I would make this other one the only return I could make, and ask her if she would run the risk of Susan being alive (very slight as I believed) and marry me, such as I was. She jumped for joy, and we should no doubt soon have been married-but, behold, Susan appears!"

Donald showed his deep concern at a complication so far beyond the degree of his simple experiences.

"Now see what injury a man may cause around him! Even after that wrong-doing at the fair when I was young, if I had never been so selfish as to let this giddy girl devote herself to me over at Jersey, to the injury of her name, all might now be well. Yet, as it stands, I must bitterly disappoint one of these women; and it is the second. My first duty is to Susan-there's no doubt about that." "They are both in a very melancholy position, and that's true!" murmured Donald. "They are! For myself I don't care-'twill all end one way. But these two." Henchard paused in reverie. "I feel I should like to treat the second, no less than the first, as kindly as a man can in such a case."

"Ah, well, it cannet be helped!" said the other, with philosophic woefulness. "You mun write to the young lady, and in your letter you must put it plain and honest that it turns out she cannet be your wife, the first having come back; that ye cannet see her more; and that-ye wish her weel."

"That won't do. 'Od seize it, I must do a little more than that! I must-though she did always brag about her rich uncle or rich aunt, and her expectations from 'em-I must send a useful sum of money to her, I suppose-just as a little recompense, poor girl....Now, will you help me in this, and draw up an explanation to her of all I've told ye, breaking it as gently as you can? I'm so bad at letters."

"And I will."

"Now, I haven't told you quite all yet. My wife Susan has my daughter with her-the baby that was in her arms at the fair; and this girl knows nothing of me beyond that I am some sort of relation by marriage. She has grown up in the belief that the sailor to whom I made over her mother, and who is now dead, was her father, and her mother's husband.

What her mother has always felt, she and I together feel now-that we can't proclaim our disgrace to the girl by letting her know the truth. Now what would you do?-I want your advice."

"I think I'd run the risk, and tell her the truth. She'll forgive ye both."

"Never!" said Henchard. "I am not going to let her know the truth. Her mother and I be going to marry again; and it will not only help us to keep our child's respect, but it will be more proper. Susan looks upon herself as the sailor's widow, and won't think o' living with me as formerly without another religious ceremony-and she's right."

Farfrae thereupon said no more. The letter to the young

Jersey woman was carefully framed by him, and the interview ended, Henchard saying, as the Scotchman left, "I feel it a great relief, Farfrae, to tell some friend o' this! You see now that the Mayor of Casterbridge is not so thriving in his mind as it seems he might be from the state of his pocket."

"I do. And I'm sorry for ye!" said Farfrae.

When he was gone Henchard copied the letter, and, enclosing a cheque, took it to the post-office, from which he walked back thoughtfully. "Can it be that it will go off so easily!" he said. "Poor thing-God knows! Now then, to make amends to Susan!"

Chapter 14

A Martinmas summer of Mrs. Henchard's life set in with her entry into her husband's large house and respectable social orbit; and it was as bright as such summers well can be. Lest she should pine for deeper affection than he could give he made a point of showing some semblance of it in external action. Among other things he had the iron railings, that had smiled sadly in dull rust for the last eighty years, painted a bright green, and the heavy-barred, small-paned Georgian sash windows enlivened with three coats of white. He was as kind to her as a man, mayor, and churchwarden could possibly be. The house was large, the rooms lofty, and the landings wide; and the two unassuming women scarcely made a perceptible addition to its contents.

To Elizabeth-Jane the time was a most triumphant one. The freedom she experienced, the indulgence with which she was treated, went beyond her expectations. The reposeful, easy, affluent life to which her mother's marriage had introduced her was, in truth, the beginning of a great change in Elizabeth. She found she could have nice personal possessions and ornaments for the asking, and, as the mediaeval saying puts it, "Take, have, and keep, are pleasant words." With peace of mind came development, and with development beauty. Knowledge-the result of great natural insight-she did not lack; learning, accomplishment-those, alas, she had not; but as the winter and spring passed by her thin face and figure filled out in rounder and softer curves; the lines and contractions upon her young brow went away; the muddiness of skin which she had looked upon as her lot by nature departed with a change to abundance of good things, and a bloom came upon her cheek. Perhaps, too, her grey, thoughtful eyes revealed an arch gaiety sometimes; but this was infrequent; the sort of wisdom which looked from their pupils did not readily keep company with these lighter moods. Like all people who have known rough times, light-heartedness seemed to her too irrational and inconsequent to be indulged in except as a reckless dram now and then; for she had been too early habituated to anxious reasoning to drop the habit suddenly. She felt none of those ups and downs of spirit which beset so many people without cause; never-to paraphrase a recent poet-never a gloom in Elizabeth-Jane's soul but she well knew how it came there; and her present cheerfulness was fairly proportionate to her solid guarantees for the same.

It might have been supposed that, given a girl rapidly becoming good-looking, comfortably circumstanced, and for the first time in her life commanding ready money, she would go and make a fool of herself by dress. But no. The reasonableness of almost everything that Elizabeth did was nowhere more conspicuous than in this question of clothes. To keep in the rear of opportunity in matters of indulgence is as valuable a habit as to keep abreast of opportunity in matters of enterprise. This unsophisticated girl did it by an innate perceptiveness that was almost genius. Thus she refrained from bursting out like a water-flower that spring, and clothing herself in puffings and knick-knacks, as most of the Casterbridge girls would have done in her circumstances. Her triumph was tempered by circumspection, she had still that field-mouse fear of the coulter of destiny despite fair promise, which is common among the thoughtful who have suffered early from poverty and oppression.

"I won't be too gay on any account," she would say to herself. "It would be tempting Providence to hurl mother and me down, and afflict us again as He used to do."

We now see her in a black silk bonnet, velvet mantle or silk spencer, dark dress, and carrying a sunshade. In this latter article she drew the line at fringe, and had it plain edged, with a little ivory ring for keeping it closed. It was odd about the necessity for that sunshade. She discovered that with the clarification of her complexion and the birth of pink cheeks her skin had grown more sensitive to the sun's rays. She protected those cheeks forthwith, deeming spotlessness part of womanliness.

Henchard had become very fond of her, and she went out with him more frequently than with her mother now. Her appearance one day was so attractive that he looked at her critically.

"I happened to have the ribbon by me, so I made it up," she faltered, thinking him perhaps dissatisfied with some rather bright trimming she had donned for the first time.

"Ay-of course-to be sure," he replied in his leonine way. "Do as you like-or rather as your mother advises ye. 'Od send-I've nothing to say to't!"

Indoors she appeared with her hair divided by a parting that arched like a white rainbow from ear to ear. All in front of this line was covered with a thick encampment of curls; all behind was dressed smoothly, and drawn to a knob.

The three members of the family were sitting at breakfast one day, and Henchard was looking silently, as he often did, at this head of hair, which in colour was brown-rather light than dark. "I thought Elizabeth-Jane's hair-didn't you tell me that Elizabeth-Jane's hair promised to be black when she was a baby?" he said to his wife.

She looked startled, jerked his foot warningly, and murmured, "Did I?"

As soon as Elizabeth was gone to her own room Henchard resumed. "Begad, I nearly forgot myself just now! What I meant was that the girl's hair certainly looked as if it would be darker, when she was a baby."

"It did; but they alter so," replied Susan.

"Their hair gets darker, I know-but I wasn't aware it lightened ever?"

"O yes." And the same uneasy expression came out on her face, to which the future held the key. It passed as Henchard went on:

"Well, so much the better. Now Susan, I want to have her called Miss Henchard-not Miss Newson. Lots o' people do it already in carelessness-it is her legal name-so it may as well be made her usual name-I don't like t'other name at all for my own flesh and blood. I'll advertise it in the Casterbridge paper-that's the way they do it. She won't object."

"No. O no. But-"

"Well, then, I shall do it," he said, peremptorily. "Surely, if she's willing, you must wish it as much as I?"

"O yes-if she agrees let us do it by all means," she replied.

Then Mrs. Henchard acted somewhat inconsistently; it might have been called falsely, but that her manner was emotional and full of the earnestness of one who wishes to do right at great hazard. She went to Elizabeth-Jane, whom she found sewing in her own sitting-room upstairs, and told her what had been proposed about her surname. "Can you agree-is it not a slight upon Newson-now he's dead and gone?" Elizabeth reflected. "I'll think of it, mother," she answered.

When, later in the day, she saw Henchard, she adverted to the matter at once, in a way which showed that the line of feeling started by her mother had been persevered in. "Do you wish this change so very much, sir?" she asked.

"Wish it? Why, my blessed fathers, what an ado you women make about a trifle! I proposed it-that's all. Now, 'Lizabeth-Jane, just please yourself. Curse me if I care what you do. Now, you understand, don't 'ee go agreeing to it to please me."

Here the subject dropped, and nothing more was said, and nothing was done, and Elizabeth still passed as Miss Newson, and not by her legal name.

Meanwhile the great corn and hay traffic conducted by Henchard throve under the management of Donald Farfrae as it had never thriven before. It had formerly moved in jolts; now it went on oiled casters. The old crude viva voce system of Henchard, in which everything depended upon his memory, and bargains were made by the tongue alone, was swept away. Letters and ledgers took the place of "I'll do't," and "you shall hae't"; and, as in all such cases of advance, the rugged picturesqueness of the old method disappeared with its inconveniences.

The position of Elizabeth-Jane's room-rather high in the house, so that it commanded a view of the hay-stores and granaries across the garden-afforded her opportunity for accurate observation of what went on there. She saw that Donald and Mr. Henchard were inseparables. When walking together Henchard would lay his arm familiarly on his manager's shoulder, as if Farfrae were a younger brother, bearing so heavily that his slight frame bent under the weight. Occasionally she would hear a perfect cannonade of laughter from Henchard, arising from something Donald had said, the latter looking quite innocent and not laughing at all. In Henchard's somewhat lonely life he evidently found the young man as desirable for comradeship as he was useful for consultations. Donald's brightness of intellect maintained in the corn-factor the admiration it had won at the first hour of their meeting. The poor opinion, and but ill-concealed, that he entertained of the slim Farfrae's physical girth, strength, and dash was more than counterbalanced by the immense respect he had for his brains.

Her quiet eye discerned that Henchard's tigerish affection for the younger man, his constant liking to have Farfrae near him, now and then resulted in a tendency to domineer, which, however, was checked in a moment when Donald exhibited marks of real offence. One day, looking down on their figures from on high, she heard the latter remark, as they stood in the doorway between the garden and yard, that their habit of walking and driving about together rather neutralized Farfrae's value as a second pair of eyes, which should be used in places where the principal was not. "'Od damn it," cried Henchard, "what's all the world! I like a fellow to talk to. Now come along and hae some supper, and don't take too much thought about things, or ye'll drive me crazy."

When she walked with her mother, on the other hand, she

often beheld the Scotchman looking at them with a curious interest. The fact that he had met her at the Three Mariners was insufficient to account for it, since on the occasions on which she had entered his room he had never raised his eyes. Besides, it was at her mother more particularly than at herself that he looked, to 's half-conscious, simple-minded, perhaps pardonable, disappointment. Thus she could not account for this interest by her own attractiveness, and she decided that it might be apparent only-a way of turning his eyes that Mr. Farfrae had.

She did not divine the ample explanation of his manner, without personal vanity, that was afforded by the fact of Donald being the depositary of Henchard's confidence in respect of his past treatment of the pale, chastened mother who walked by her side. Her conjectures on that past never went further than faint ones based on things casually heard and seen-mere guesses that Henchard and her mother might have been lovers in their younger days, who had quarrelled and parted.

Casterbridge, as has been hinted, was a place deposited in the block upon a corn-field. There was no suburb in the modern sense, or transitional intermixture of town and down. It stood, with regard to the wide fertile land adjoining, clean-cut and distinct, like a chess-board on a green tablecloth. The farmer's boy could sit under his barley-mow and pitch a stone into the office-window of the town-clerk; reapers at work among the sheaves nodded to acquaintances standing on the pavement-corner; the red-robed judge, when he condemned a sheep-stealer, pronounced sentence to the tune of Baa, that floated in at the window from the remainder of the flock browsing hard by; and at executions the waiting crowd stood in a meadow immediately before the drop, out of which the cows had been temporarily driven to give the spectators room.

The corn grown on the upland side of the borough was garnered by farmers who lived in an eastern purlieu called Durnover. Here wheat-ricks overhung the old Roman street, and thrust their eaves against the church tower; barns, with doorways as high as the gates of Solomon's temple, opened directly upon the main thoroughfare. Barns indeed were so numerous as to alternate with every half-dozen houses along the way. Here lived burgesses who daily walked the fallow; shepherds in an intra-mural squeeze. A street of farmers' homesteads-a street ruled by a mayor and corporation, yet echoing with the thump of the flail, the flutter of the winnowing-fan, and the purr of the milk into the pails-a street which had nothing urban in it whatever-this was the Durnover end of Casterbridge.

Henchard, as was natural, dealt largely with this nursery or bed of small farmers close at hand-and his waggons were often down that way. One day, when arrangements were in progress for getting home corn from one of the aforesaid farms, Elizabeth-Jane received a note by hand, asking her to oblige the writer by coming at once to a granary on Durnover Hill. As this was the granary whose contents Henchard was removing, she thought the request had something to do with his business, and proceeded thither as soon as she had put on her bonnet. The granary was just within the farm-yard, and stood on stone staddles, high enough for persons to walk under. The gates were open, but nobody was within. However, she entered and waited. Presently she saw a figure approaching the gate-that of Donald Farfrae. He looked up at the church clock, and came in. By some unaccountable shyness, some wish not to meet him there alone, she quickly ascended the step-ladder leading to the granary door, and entered it before he had seen her. Farfrae advanced, imagining himself in solitude, and a few drops of rain beginning to fall he moved and stood under the shelter where she had just been standing. Here he leant against one of the staddles, and gave himself up to patience. He, too, was plainly expecting some one; could it be herself? If so, why? In a few minutes he looked at his watch, and then pulled out a note, a duplicate of the one she had herself received.

This situation began to be very awkward, and the longer she waited the more awkward it became. To emerge from a door just above his head and descend the ladder, and show she had been in hiding there, would look so very foolish that she still waited on. A winnowing machine stood close beside her, and to relieve her suspense she gently moved the handle; whereupon a cloud of wheat husks flew out into her face, and covered her clothes and bonnet, and stuck into the fur of her victorine. He must have heard the slight movement for he looked up, and then ascended the steps.

"Ah-it's Miss Newson," he said as soon as he could see into the granary. "I didn't know you were there. I have kept the appointment, and am at your service."

"O Mr. Farfrae," she faltered, "so have I. But I didn't know it was you who wished to see me, otherwise I-"

"I wished to see you? O no-at least, that is, I am afraid there may be a mistake."

"Didn't you ask me to come here? Didn't you write this?" Elizabeth held out her note.

"No. Indeed, at no hand would I have thought of it! And for you-didn't you ask me? This is not your writing?" And he held up his.

"By no means."

"And is that really so! Then it's somebody wanting to see us both. Perhaps we would do well to wait a little longer."

Acting on this consideration they lingered, Elizabeth-Jane's face being arranged to an expression of preternatural composure, and the young Scot, at every footstep in the street without, looking from under the granary to see if the passer were about to enter and declare himself their summoner. They watched individual drops of rain creeping down the thatch of the opposite rick-straw after straw-till they reached the bottom; but nobody came, and the granary roof began to drip.

"The person is not likely to be coming," said Farfrae. "It's a trick perhaps, and if so, it's a great pity to waste our time like this, and so much to be done."

"'Tis a great liberty," said Elizabeth.

"It's true, Miss Newson. We'll hear news of this some day depend on't, and who it was that did it. I wouldn't stand for it hindering myself; but you, Miss Newson--"

"I don't mind-much,' she replied.

"Neither do I."

They lapsed again into silence. "You are anxious to get back to Scotland, I suppose, Mr. Farfrae?" she inquired.

"O no, Miss Newson. Why would I be?"

"I only supposed you might be from the song you sang at the Three Mariners-about Scotland and home, I mean-which you seemed to feel so deep down in your heart; so that we all felt for you."

"Ay-and I did sing there-I did--But, Miss Newson"-and Donald's voice musically undulated between two semi-tones as it always did when he became earnest-"it's well you feel a song for a few minutes, and your eyes they get quite tearful; but you finish it, and for all you felt you don't mind it or think of it again for a long while. O no, I don't want to go back! Yet I'll sing the song to you wi' pleasure whenever you like. I could sing it now, and not mind at all?"

"Thank you, indeed. But I fear I must go-rain or no."

"Ay! Then, Miss Newson, ye had better say nothing about this hoax, and take no heed of it. And if the person should say anything to you, be civil to him or her, as if you did not mind it-so you'll take the clever person's laugh away." In speaking his eyes became fixed upon her dress, still sown with wheat husks. "There's husks and dust on you. Perhaps you don't know it?" he said, in tones of extreme delicacy. "And it's very bad to let rain come upon clothes when there's chaff on them. It washes in and spoils them. Let me help you-blowing is the best."

As Elizabeth neither assented nor dissented Donald Farfrae began blowing her back hair, and her side hair, and her neck, and the crown of her bonnet, and the fur of her victorine, Elizabeth saying, "O, thank you," at every puff. At last she was fairly clean, though Farfrae, having got over his first concern at the situation, seemed in no manner of hurry to be gone.

"Ah-now I'll go and get ye an umbrella," he said.

She declined the offer, stepped out and was gone. Farfrae walked slowly after, looking thoughtfully at her diminishing figure, and whistling in undertones, "As I came down through Cannobie."

Chapter 15

At first Miss Newson's budding beauty was not regarded with much interest by anybody in Casterbridge. Donald Farfrae's gaze, it is true, was now attracted by the Mayor's so-called step-daughter, but he was only one. The truth is that she was but a poor illustrative instance of the prophet Baruch's sly definition: "The virgin that loveth to go gay."

When she walked abroad she seemed to be occupied with an inner chamber of ideas, and to have slight need for visible objects. She formed curious resolves on checking gay fancies in the matter of clothes, because it was inconsistent with her past life to blossom gaudily the moment she had become possessed of money. But nothing is more insidious than the evolution of wishes from mere fancies, and of wants from mere wishes. Henchard gave Elizabeth-Jane a box of delicately-tinted gloves one spring day. She wanted to wear them to show her appreciation of his kindness, but she had no bonnet that would harmonize. As an artistic indulgence she thought she would have such a bonnet. When she had a bonnet that would go with the gloves she had no dress that would go with the bonnet. It was now absolutely necessary to finish; she ordered the requisite article, and found that she had no sunshade to go with the dress. In for a penny in for a pound; she bought the sunshade, and the whole structure was at last complete.

Everybody was attracted, and some said that her bygone simplicity was the art that conceals art, the "delicate imposition" of Rochefoucauld; she had produced an effect, a contrast, and it had been done on purpose. As a matter of fact this was not true, but it had its result; for as soon as Casterbridge thought her artful it thought her worth notice. "It is the first time in my life that I have been so much admired," she said to herself; "though perhaps it is by those whose admiration is not worth having."

But Donald Farfrae admired her, too; and altogether the time was an exciting one; sex had never before asserted itself in her so strongly, for in former days she had perhaps been too impersonally human to be distinctively feminine. After an unprecedented success one day she came indoors, went upstairs, and leant upon her bed face downwards quite forgetting the possible creasing and damage. "Good Heaven," she whispered, "can it be? Here am I setting up as the town beauty!"

When she had thought it over, her usual fear of exaggerating appearances engendered a deep sadness. "There is something wrong in all this," she mused. "If they only knew what an unfinished girl I am-that I can't talk Italian, or use globes, or show any of the accomplishments they learn at boarding schools, how they would despise me! Better sell all this finery and buy myself grammar-books and dictionaries and a history of all the philosophies!"

She looked from the window and saw Henchard and Farfrae in the hay-yard talking, with that impetuous cordiality on the Mayor's part, and genial modesty on the younger man's, that was now so generally observable in their intercourse. Friendship between man and man; what a rugged strength there was in it, as evinced by these two. And yet the seed that was to lift the foundation of this friendship was at that moment taking root in a chink of its structure.

It was about six o'clock; the men were dropping off homeward one by one. The last to leave was a round-shouldered, blinking young man of nineteen or twenty, whose mouth fell ajar on the slightest provocation, seemingly because there was no chin to support it. Henchard called aloud to him as he went out of the gate, "Here-Abel Whittle!"

Whittle turned, and ran back a few steps. "Yes, sir," he said, in breathless deprecation, as if he knew what was coming next.

"Once more-be in time to-morrow morning. You see what's to be done, and you hear what I say, and you know I'm not going to be trifled with any longer."

"Yes, sir." Then Abel Whittle left, and Henchard and Farfrae; and Elizabeth saw no more of them.

Now there was good reason for this command on Henchard's part. Poor Abel, as he was called, had an inveterate habit of over-sleeping himself and coming late to his work. His anxious will was to be among the earliest; but if his comrades omitted to pull the string that he always tied round his great toe and left hanging out the window for that purpose, his will was as wind. He did not arrive in time.

As he was often second hand at the hay-weighing, or at the crane which lifted the sacks, or was one of those who had to accompany the waggons into the country to fetch away stacks that had been purchased, this affliction of Abel's was productive of much inconvenience. For two mornings in the present week he had kept the others waiting nearly an hour; hence Henchard's threat. It now remained to be seen what would happen to-morrow.

Six o'clock struck, and there was no Whittle. At half-past six Henchard entered the yard; the waggon was horsed that Abel was to accompany; and the other man had been waiting twenty minutes. Then Henchard swore, and Whittle coming up breathless at that instant, the corn-factor turned on him, and declared with an oath that this was the last time; that if he were behind once more, by God, he would come and drag him out o' bed.

"There is sommit wrong in my make, your worshipful!" said Abel, "especially in the inside, whereas my poor dumb brain gets as dead as a clot afore I've said my few scrags of prayers. Yes-it came on as a stripling, just afore I'd got man's wages, whereas I never enjoy my bed at all, for no sooner do I lie down than I be asleep, and afore I be awake I be up. I've fretted my gizzard green about it, maister, but what can I do? Now last night, afore I went to bed, I only had a scantling o' cheese and-"

"I don't want to hear it!" roared Henchard. "To-morrow the waggons must start at four, and if you're not here, stand clear. I'll mortify thy flesh for thee!"

"But let me clear up my points, your worshipful--"

Henchard turned away.

"He asked me and he questioned me, and then 'a wouldn't hear my points!" said Abel, to the yard in general. "Now, I shall twitch like a moment-hand all night to-night for fear o' him!"

The journey to be taken by the waggons next day was a long one into Blackmoor Vale, and at four o'clock lanterns were moving about the yard. But Abel was missing. Before either of the other men could run to Abel's and warn him Henchard appeared in the garden doorway. "Where's Abel Whittle? Not come after all I've said? Now I'll carry out my word, by my blessed fathers-nothing else will do him any good! I'm going up that way."

Henchard went off, entered Abel's house, a little cottage in Back Street, the door of which was never locked because the inmates had nothing to lose. Reaching Whittle's bedside the corn-factor shouted a bass note so vigorously that Abel started up instantly, and beholding Henchard standing over him, was galvanized into spasmodic movements which had not much relation to getting on his clothes.

"Out of bed, sir, and off to the granary, or you leave my employ to-day! 'Tis to teach ye a lesson. March on; never mind your breeches!"

The unhappy Whittle threw on his sleeve waistcoat, and managed to get into his boots at the bottom of the stairs, while Henchard thrust his hat over his head. Whittle then trotted on down Back Street, Henchard walking sternly behind.

Just at this time Farfrae, who had been to Henchard's house to look for him, came out of the back gate, and saw something white fluttering in the morning gloom, which he soon perceived to be part of Abel's shirt that showed below his waistcoat.

"For maircy's sake, what object's this?" said Farfrae, following Abel into the yard, Henchard being some way in the rear by this time.

"Ye see, Mr. Farfrae," gibbered Abel with a resigned smile of terror, "he said he'd mortify my flesh if so be I didn't get up sooner, and now he's a-doing on't! Ye see it can't be helped, Mr. Farfrae; things do happen queer sometimes! Yes-I'll go to Blackmoor Vale half naked as I be, since he do command; but I shall kill myself afterwards; I can't outlive the disgrace, for the women-folk will be looking out of their winders at my mortification all the way along, and laughing me to scorn as a man 'ithout breeches! You know how I feel such things, Maister Farfrae, and how forlorn thoughts get hold upon me. Yes-I shall do myself harm-I feel it coming on!" "Get back home, and slip on your breeches, and come to wark like a man! If ye go not, you'll ha'e your death standing there!"

"I'm afeard I mustn't! Mr. Henchard said--"

"I don't care what Mr. Henchard said, nor anybody else! 'Tis simple foolishness to do this. Go and dress yourself instantly Whittle."

"Hullo, hullo!" said Henchard, coming up behind. "Who's sending him back?"

All the men looked towards Farfrae.

"I am," said Donald. "I say this joke has been carried far enough."

"And I say it hasn't! Get up in the waggon, Whittle."

"Not if I am manager," said Farfrae. "He either goes home, or I march out of this yard for good."

Henchard looked at him with a face stern and red. But he paused for a moment, and their eyes met. Donald went up to him, for he saw in Henchard's look that he began to regret this.

"Come," said Donald quietly, "a man o' your position should ken better, sir! It is tyrannical and no worthy of you."

"'Tis not tyrannical!" murmured Henchard, like a sullen boy. "It is to make him remember!" He presently added, in a tone of one bitterly hurt: "Why did you speak to me before them like that, Farfrae? You might have stopped till we were alone. Ah-I know why! I've told ye the secret o' my life-fool that I was to do't-and you take advantage of me!"

"I had forgot it," said Farfrae simply.

Henchard looked on the ground, said nothing more, and turned away. During the day Farfrae learnt from the men that Henchard had kept Abel's old mother in coals and snuff all the previous winter, which made him less antagonistic to the corn-factor. But Henchard continued moody and silent, and when one of the men inquired of him if some oats should be hoisted to an upper floor or not, he said shortly, "Ask Mr. Farfrae. He's master here!"

Morally he was; there could be no doubt of it. Henchard, who had hitherto been the most admired man in his circle, was the most admired no longer. One day the daughters of a deceased farmer in Durnover wanted an opinion of the value of their haystack, and sent a messenger to ask Mr. Farfrae to oblige them with one. The messenger, who was a child, met in the yard not Farfrae, but Henchard.

"Very well," he said. "I'll come."

"But please will Mr. Farfrae come?" said the child.

"I am going that way....Why Mr. Farfrae?" said Henchard, with the fixed look of thought. "Why do people always want Mr. Farfrae?"

"I suppose because they like him so-that's what they say."

"Oh-I see-that's what they say-hey? They like him because he's cleverer than Mr. Henchard, and because he knows more; and, in short, Mr. Henchard can't hold a candle to him-hey?"

"Yes-that's just it, sir-some of it."

"Oh, there's more? Of course there's more! What besides? Come, here's a sixpence for a fairing."

"'And he's better tempered, and Henchard's a fool to him,' they say. And when some of the women were a-walking home they said, 'He's a diment-he's a chap o' wax-he's the best-he's the horse for my money,' says they. And they said, 'He's the most understanding man o' them two by long chalks. I wish he was the master instead of Henchard,' they said."

"They'll talk any nonsense," Henchard replied with covered gloom. "Well, you can go now. And I am coming to value the hay, d'ye hear?-I." The boy departed, and Henchard murmured, "Wish he were master here, do they?"

He went towards Durnover. On his way he overtook Farfrae. They walked on together, Henchard looking mostly on the ground.

"You're no yoursel' the day?" Donald inquired.

"Yes, I am very well," said Henchard.

"But ye are a bit down-surely ye are down? Why, there's nothing to be angry about! 'Tis splendid stuff that we've got from Blackmoor Vale. By the by, the people in Durnover want their hay valued."

"Yes. I am going there."

"I'll go with ye."

As Henchard did not reply Donald practised a piece of music sotto voce, till, getting near the bereaved people's door, he stopped himself with-

"Ah, as their father is dead I won't go on with such as that. How could I forget?"

"Do you care so very much about hurting folks' feelings?" observed Henchard with a half sneer. "You do, I know-especially mine!"

"I am sorry if I have hurt yours, sir," replied Donald, standing still, with a second expression of the same sentiment in the regretfulness of his face. "Why should you say it-think it?" The cloud lifted from Henchard's brow, and as Donald finished the corn-merchant turned to him, regarding his breast rather than his face.

"I have been hearing things that vexed me," he said. "'Twas that made me short in my manner-made me overlook what you really are. Now, I don't want to go in here about this hay-Farfrae, you can do it better than I. They sent for 'ee, too. I have to attend a meeting of the Town Council at eleven, and 'tis drawing on for't."

They parted thus in renewed friendship, Donald forbearing to ask Henchard for meanings that were not very plain to him. On Henchard's part there was now again repose; and yet, whenever he thought of Farfrae, it was with a dim dread; and he often regretted that he had told the young man his whole heart, and confided to him the secrets of his life.

Chapter 18

There came a shock which had been foreseen for some time by Elizabeth, as the box passenger foresees the approaching jerk from some channel across the highway.

Her mother was ill-too unwell to leave her room. Henchard, who treated her kindly, except in moments of irritation, sent at once for the richest, busiest doctor, whom he supposed to be the best. Bedtime came, and they burnt a light all night. In a day or two she rallied.

Elizabeth, who had been staying up, did not appear at breakfast on the second morning, and Henchard sat down alone. He was startled to see a letter for him from Jersey in a writing he knew too well, and had expected least to behold again. He took it up in his hands and looked at it as at a picture, a vision, a vista of past enactments; and then he read it as an unimportant finale to conjecture.

The writer said that she at length perceived how impossible it would be for any further communications to proceed between them now that his re-marriage had taken place. That such reunion had been the only straightforward course open to him she was bound to admit.

"On calm reflection, therefore," she went on, "I quite forgive you for landing me in such a dilemma, remembering that you concealed nothing before our ill-advised acquaintance; and that you really did set before me in your grim way the fact of there being a certain risk in intimacy with you, slight as it seemed to be after fifteen or sixteen years of silence on your wife's part. I thus look upon the whole as a misfortune of mine, and not a fault of yours.

"So that, Michael, I must ask you to overlook those letters with which I pestered you day after day in the heat of my feelings. They were written whilst I thought your conduct to me cruel; but now I know more particulars of the position you were in I see how inconsiderate my reproaches were.

"Now you will, I am sure, perceive that the one condition which will make any future happiness possible for me is that the past connection between our lives be kept secret outside this isle. Speak of it I know you will not; and I can trust you not to write of it. One safe-guard more remains to be mentioned-that no writings of mine, or trifling articles belonging to me, should be left in your possession through neglect or forgetfulness. To this end may I request you to return to me any such you may have, particularly the letters written in the first abandonment of feeling.

"For the handsome sum you forwarded to me as a plaster to the wound I heartily thank you.

"I am now on my way to Bristol, to see my only relative. She is rich, and I hope will do something for me. I shall return through Casterbridge and Budmouth, where I shall take the packet-boat. Can you meet me with the letters and other trifles? I shall be in the coach which changes horses at the Antelope Hotel at half-past five Wednesday evening; I shall be wearing a Paisley shawl with a red centre, and thus may easily be found. I should prefer this plan of receiving them to having them sent.-I remain still, yours; ever,

LUCETTA: Henchard breathed heavily. "Poor thing-better you had not known me! Upon my heart and soul, if ever I should be left in a position to carry out that marriage with thee, I OUGHT to do it-I ought to do it, indeed!"

The contingency that he had in his mind was, of course, the death of Mrs. Henchard.

As requested, he sealed up Lucetta's letters, and put the parcel aside till the day she had appointed; this plan of returning them by hand being apparently a little ruse of the young lady for exchanging a word or two with him on past times. He would have preferred not to see her; but deeming that there could be no great harm in acquiescing thus far, he went at dusk and stood opposite the coach-office.

The evening was chilly, and the coach was late. Henchard crossed over to it while the horses were being changed; but there was no Lucetta inside or out. Concluding that something had happened to modify her arrangements he gave the matter up and went home, not without a sense of relief. Meanwhile Mrs. Henchard was weakening visibly. She could not go out of doors any more.

One day, after much thinking which seemed to distress her, she said she wanted to write something. A desk was put upon her bed with pen and paper, and at her request she was left alone. She remained writing for a short time, folded her paper carefully, called Elizabeth-Jane to bring a taper and wax, and then, still refusing assistance, sealed up the sheet, directed it, and locked it in her desk. She had directed it in these words:-

"MR. MICHAEL HENCHARD. NOT TO BE OPENED TILL 'S WEDDING-DAY."

The latter sat up with her mother to the utmost of her strength night after night. To learn to take the universe seriously there is no quicker way than to watch-to be a "waker," as the country-people call it. Between the hours at which the last toss-pot went by and the first sparrow shook himself, the silence in Casterbridge-barring the rare sound of the watchman-was broken in Elizabeth's ear only by the time-piece in the bedroom ticking frantically against the clock on the stairs; ticking harder and harder till it seemed to clang like a gong; and all this while the girl asking herself why she was born, why sitting in a room, and blinking at the candle; why things around her had taken the shape they wore in preference to every other possible shape.

Why they stared at her so helplessly, as if waiting for the touch of some wand that should release them from terrestrial constraint; what that chaos called consciousness, which spun in her at this moment like a top, tended to, and began in. Her eyes fell together; she was awake, yet she was asleep.

A word from her mother roused her. Without preface, and as the continuation of a scene already progressing in her mind, Mrs. Henchard said: "You remember the note sent to you and Mr. Farfrae-asking you to meet some one in Durnover Barton-and that you thought it was a trick to make fools of you?"

"Yes."

"It was not to make fools of you-it was done to bring you together. 'Twas I did it."

"Why?" said Elizabeth, with a start.

"I-wanted you to marry Mr. Farfrae."

"O mother!" Elizabeth-Jane bent down her head so much that she looked quite into her own lap. But as her mother did not go on, she said, "What reason?"

"Well, I had a reason. 'Twill out one day. I wish it could have been in my time! But there-nothing is as you wish it! Henchard hates him."

"Perhaps they'll be friends again," murmured the girl.

"I don't know-I don't know." After this her mother was silent, and dozed; and she spoke on the subject no more.

Some little time later on Farfrae was passing Henchard's house on a Sunday morning, when he observed that the blinds were all down. He rang the bell so softly that it only sounded a single full note and a small one; and then he was informed that Mrs. Henchard was dead-just dead-that very hour. At the town-pump there were gathered when he passed a few old inhabitants, who came there for water whenever they had, as at present, spare time to fetch it, because it was purer from that original fount than from their own wells. Mrs. Cuxsom, who had been standing there for an indefinite time with her pitcher, was describing the incidents of Mrs. Henchard's death, as she had learnt them from the nurse.

"And she was white as marble-stone," said Mrs. Cuxsom. "And likewise such a thoughtful woman, too-ah, poor soul-that a' minded every little thing that wanted tending. 'Yes,' says she, 'when I'm gone, and my last breath's blowed, look in the top drawer o' the chest in the back room by the window, and you'll find all my coffin clothes, a piece of flannel-that's to put under me, and the little piece is to put under my head; and my new stockings for my feet-they are folded alongside, and all my other things.

And there's four ounce pennies, the heaviest I could find, a-tied up in bits of linen, for weights-two for my right eye and two for my left,' she said. 'And when you've used 'em, and my eyes don't open no more, bury the pennies, good souls and don't ye go spending 'em, for I shouldn't like it. And open the windows as soon as I am carried out, and make it as cheerful as you can for Elizabeth-Jane.'"

"Ah, poor heart!"

"Well, and Martha did it, and buried the ounce pennies in the garden. But if ye'll believe words, that man, Christopher Coney, went and dug 'em up, and spent 'em at the Three Mariners. 'Faith,' he said, 'why should death rob life o' fourpence? Death's not of such good report that we should respect 'en to that extent,' says he."

"'Twas a cannibal deed!" deprecated her listeners.

"Gad, then I won't quite ha'e it," said Solomon Longways. "I say it to-day, and 'tis a Sunday morning, and I wouldn't speak wrongfully for a zilver zixpence at such a time. I don't see noo harm in it. To respect the dead is sound doxology; and I wouldn't sell skellintons-leastwise respectable skellintons-to be varnished for 'natomies, except I were out o' work. But money is scarce, and throats get dry. Why SHOULD death rob life o' fourpence? I say there was no treason in it."

"Well, poor soul; she's helpless to hinder that or anything now," answered Mother Cuxsom. "And all her shining keys will be took from her, and her cupboards opened; and little things a' didn't wish seen, anybody will see; and her wishes and ways will all be as nothing!"

Chapter 20

Of all the enigmas which ever confronted a girl there can have been seldom one like that which followed Henchard's announcement of himself to Elizabeth as her father. He had done it in an ardour and an agitation which had half carried the point of affection with her; yet, behold, from the next morning onwards his manner was constrained as she had never seen it before.

The coldness soon broke out into open chiding. One grievous failing of Elizabeth's was her occasional pretty and picturesque use of dialect words-those terrible marks of the beast to the truly genteel.

It was dinner-time-they never met except at meals-and she happened to say when he was rising from table, wishing to show him something, "If you'll bide where you be a minute, father, I'll get it."

"'Bide where you be,'" he echoed sharply, "Good God, are you only fit to carry wash to a pig-trough, that ye use such words as those?"

She reddened with shame and sadness.

"I meant 'Stay where you are,' father," she said, in a low, humble voice. "I ought to have been more careful."

He made no reply, and went out of the room.

The sharp reprimand was not lost upon her, and in time it came to pass that for "fay" she said "succeed"; that she no longer spoke of "dumbledores" but of "humble bees"; no longer said of young men and women that they "walked together," but that they were "engaged"; that she grew to talk of "greggles" as "wild hyacinths"; that when she had not slept she did not quaintly tell the servants next morning that she had been "hag-rid," but that she had "suffered from indigestion." These improvements, however, are somewhat in advance of the story. Henchard, being uncultivated himself, was the bitterest critic the fair girl could possibly have had of her own lapses-really slight now, for she read omnivorously. A gratuitous ordeal was in store for her in the matter of her handwriting. She was passing the door one evening, and had occasion to go in for something. It was not till she had opened the door that she knew the Mayor was there in the company of a man with whom he transacted business.

"Here, Elizabeth-Jane," he said, looking round at her, "just write down what I tell you-a few words of an agreement for me and this gentleman to sign. I am a poor tool with a pen."

"Be jowned, and so be I," said the gentleman.

She brought forward blotting-book, paper, and ink, and sat down.

"Now then-'An agreement entered into this sixteenth day of October'-write that first."

She started the pen in an elephantine march across the sheet. It was a splendid round, bold hand of her own conception, a style that would have stamped a woman as Minerva's own in more recent days. But other ideas reigned then: Henchard's creed was that proper young girls wrote ladies'-hand-nay, he believed that bristling characters were as innate and inseparable a part of refined womanhood as sex itself. Hence when, instead of scribbling, like the Princess Ida,-

"In such a hand as when a field of corn

Bows all its ears before the roaring East,"

Elizabeth-Jane produced a line of chain-shot and sand-bags, he reddened in angry shame for her, and, peremptorily saying, "Never mind-I'll finish it," dismissed her there and then.

Her considerate disposition became a pitfall to her now. She was, it must be admitted, sometimes provokingly and unnecessarily willing to saddle herself with manual labours. She would go to the kitchen instead of ringing, "Not to make Phoebe come up twice." She went down on her knees, shovel in hand, when the cat overturned the coal-scuttle; moreover, she would persistently thank the parlour-maid for everything, till one day, as soon as the girl was gone from the room, Henchard broke out with, "Good God, why dostn't leave off thanking that girl as if she were a goddess-born! Don't I pay her a dozen pound a year to do things for 'ee?" Elizabeth shrank so visibly at the exclamation that he became sorry a few minutes after, and said that he did not mean to be rough.

These domestic exhibitions were the small protruding needlerocks which suggested rather than revealed what was underneath. But his passion had less terror for her than his coldness. The increasing frequency of the latter mood told her the sad news that he disliked her with a growing dislike. The more interesting that her appearance and manners became under the softening influences which she could now command, and in her wisdom did command, the more she seemed to estrange him. Sometimes she caught him looking at her with a louring invidiousness that she could hardly bear. Not knowing his secret it was cruel mockery that she should for the first time excite his animosity when she had taken his surname.

But the most terrible ordeal was to come. Elizabeth had latterly been accustomed of an afternoon to present a cup of cider or ale and bread-and-cheese to Nance Mockridge, who worked in the yard wimbling hay-bonds. Nance accepted this offering thankfully at first; afterwards as a matter of course. On a day when Henchard was on the premises he saw his step-daughter enter the hay-barn on this errand; and, as there was no clear spot on which to deposit the provisions, she at once set to work arranging two trusses of hay as a table, Mockridge meanwhile standing with her hands on her hips, easefully looking at the preparations on her behalf.

"Elizabeth, come here!" said Henchard; and she obeyed.

"Why do you lower yourself so confoundedly?" he said with suppressed passion. "Haven't I told you o't fifty times? Hey? Making yourself a drudge for a common workwoman of such a character as hers! Why, ye'll disgrace me to the dust!"

Now these words were uttered loud enough to reach Nance inside the barn door, who fired up immediately at the slur upon her personal character. Coming to the door she cried regardless of consequences, "Come to that, Mr. Henchard, I can let 'ee know she've waited on worse!"

"Then she must have had more charity than sense," said Henchard.

"O no, she hadn't. 'Twere not for charity but for hire; and at a public-house in this town!"

"It is not true!" cried Henchard indignantly.

"Just ask her," said Nance, folding her naked arms in such a manner that she could comfortably scratch her elbows.

Henchard glanced at Elizabeth-Jane, whose complexion, now pink and white from confinement, lost nearly all of the former colour. "What does this mean?" he said to her. "Anything or nothing?"

"It is true," said Elizabeth-Jane. "But it was only-"

"Did you do it, or didn't you? Where was it?"

"At the Three Mariners; one evening for a little while, when we were staying there."

Nance glanced triumphantly at Henchard, and sailed into the barn; for assuming that she was to be discharged on the instant she had resolved to make the most of her victory. Henchard, however, said nothing about discharging her. Unduly sensitive on such points by reason of his own past, he had the look of one completely ground down to the last indignity. Elizabeth followed him to the house like a culprit; but when she got inside she could not see him. Nor did she see him again that day.

Convinced of the scathing damage to his local repute and position that must have been caused by such a fact, though it had never before reached his own ears, Henchard showed a positive distaste for the presence of this girl not his own, whenever he encountered her. He mostly dined with the farmers at the market-room of one of the two chief hotels, leaving her in utter solitude. Could he have seen how she made use of those silent hours he might have found reason to reserve his judgment on her quality. She read and took notes incessantly, mastering facts with painful laboriousness, but never flinching from her self-imposed task. She began the study of Latin, incited by the Roman characteristics of the town she lived in. "If I am not well-informed it shall be by no fault of my own," she would say to herself through the tears that would occasionally glide down her peachy cheeks when she was fairly baffled by the portentous obscurity of many of these educational works.

Thus she lived on, a dumb, deep-feeling, great-eyed creature, construed by not a single contiguous being; quenching with patient fortitude her incipient interest in Farfrae, because it seemed to be one-sided, unmaidenly, and unwise. True, that for reasons best known to herself, she had, since Farfrae's dismissal, shifted her quarters from the back room affording a view of the yard (which she had occupied with such zest) to a front chamber overlooking the street; but as for the young man, whenever he passed the house he seldom or never turned his head.

Winter had almost come, and unsettled weather made her still more dependent upon indoor resources. But there were certain early winter days in Casterbridge-days of firmamental exhaustion which followed angry south-westerly tempests-when, if the sun shone, the air was like velvet. She seized on these days for her periodical visits to the spot where her mother lay buried-the still-used of the old Roman-British city, whose curious feature was this, its continuity as a place of sepulture. Mrs. Henchard's dust mingled with the dust of women who lay ornamented with glass hair-pins and amber necklaces, and men who held in their mouths coins of Hadrian, Posthumus, and the Constantines.

Half-past ten in the morning was about her hour for seeking this spot-a time when the town avenues were deserted as the avenues of Karnac. Business had long since passed down them into its daily cells, and Leisure had not arrived there. So Elizabeth-Jane walked and read, or looked over the edge of the book to think, and thus reached the churchyard.

There, approaching her mother's grave she saw a solitary dark figure in the middle of the gravel-walk. This figure, too, was reading; but not from a book: the words which engrossed it being the inscription on Mrs. Henchard's tombstone. The personage was in mourning like herself, was about her age and size, and might have been her wraith or double, but for the fact that it was a lady much more beautifully dressed than she. Indeed, comparatively indifferent as Elizabeth-Jane was to dress, unless for some temporary whim or purpose, her eyes were arrested by the artistic perfection of the lady's appearance. Her gait, too, had a flexuousness about it, which seemed to avoid angularity. It was a revelation to Elizabeth that human beings could reach this stage of external development-she had never suspected it. She felt all the freshness and grace to be stolen from herself on the instant by the neighbourhood of such a stranger. And this was in face of the fact that Elizabeth could now have been writ handsome, while the young lady was simply pretty.

Had she been envious she might have hated the woman; but she did not do that-she allowed herself the pleasure of feeling fascinated. She wondered where the lady had come from. The stumpy and practical walk of honest homeliness which mostly prevailed there, the two styles of dress thereabout, the simple and the mistaken, equally avouched that this figure was no Casterbridge woman's, even if a book in her hand resembling a guide-book had not also suggested it. The stranger presently moved from the tombstone of Mrs. Henchard, and vanished behind the corner of the wall. Elizabeth went to the tomb herself; beside it were two distinct in the soil, signifying that the lady had stood there a long time. She returned homeward, musing on what she had seen, as she might have mused on a rainbow or the Northern Lights, a rare butterfly or a cameo.

Interesting as things had been out of doors, at home it turned out to be one of her bad days. Henchard, whose two years' mayoralty was ending, had been made aware that he was not to be chosen to fill a vacancy in the list of aldermen; and that Farfrae was likely to become one of the Council. This caused the unfortunate discovery that she had played the waiting-maid in the town of which he was Mayor to rankle in his mind yet more poisonously. He had learnt by personal inquiry at the time that it was to Donald Farfrae-that treacherous upstart-that she had thus humiliated herself. And though Mrs. Stannidge seemed to attach no great importance to the incident-the cheerful souls at the Three Mariners having exhausted its aspects long ago-such was Henchard's haughty spirit that the simple thrifty deed was regarded as little less than a social catastrophe by him.

Ever since the evening of his wife's arrival with her daughter there had been something in the air which had changed his luck. That dinner at the King's Arms with his friends had been Henchard's Austerlitz: he had had his successes since, but his course had not been upward. He was not to be numbered among the aldermen-that Peerage of burghers-as he had expected to be, and the consciousness of this soured him to-day.

"Well, where have you been?" he said to her with offhand laconism.

"I've been strolling in the Walks and churchyard, father, till I feel quite leery." She clapped her hand to her mouth, but too late.

This was just enough to incense Henchard after the other crosses of the day. "I WON'T have you talk like that!" he thundered. "'Leery,' indeed. One would think you worked upon a farm! One day I learn that you lend a hand in. Then I hear you talk like a clodhopper. I'm burned, if it goes on, this house can't hold us two."

The only way of getting a single pleasant thought to go to sleep upon after this was by recalling the lady she had seen that day, and hoping she might see her again.

Meanwhile Henchard was sitting up, thinking over his jealous folly in forbidding Farfrae to pay his addresses to this girl who did not belong to him, when if he had allowed them to go on he might not have been encumbered with her. At last he said to himself with satisfaction as he jumped up and went to the writing-table: "Ah! he'll think it means peace, and a marriage portion-not that I don't want my house to be troubled with her, and no portion at all!" He wrote as follows:-

Sir,-On consideration, I don't wish to interfere with your courtship of Elizabeth-Jane, if you care for her. I therefore withdraw my objection; excepting in this-that the business be not carried on in my house.-

Yours,

M. HENCHARD

Mr. Farfrae.

The morrow, being fairly fine, found Elizabeth-Jane again in the churchyard, but while looking for the lady she was startled by the apparition of Farfrae, who passed outside the gate. He glanced up for a moment from a pocket-book in which he appeared to be making figures as he went; whether or not he saw her he took no notice, and disappeared.

Unduly depressed by a sense of her own superfluity she thought he probably scorned her; and quite broken in spirit sat down on a bench. She fell into painful thought on her position, which ended with her saying quite loud, "O, I wish I was dead with dear mother!"

Behind the bench was a little promenade under the wall where people sometimes walked instead of on the gravel. The bench seemed to be touched by something, she looked round, and a face was bending over her, veiled, but still distinct, the face of the young woman she had seen yesterday.

Elizabeth-Jane looked confounded for a moment, knowing she had been overheard, though there was pleasure in her confusion. "Yes, I heard you," said the lady, in a vivacious voice, answering her look. "What can have happened?"

"I don't-I can't tell you," said Elizabeth, putting her hand to her face to hide a quick flush that had come.

There was no movement or word for a few seconds; then the girl felt that the young lady was sitting down beside her.

"I guess how it is with you," said the latter. "That was your mother." She waved her hand towards the tombstone. Elizabeth looked up at her as if inquiring of herself whether there should be confidence. The lady's manner was so desirous, so anxious, that the girl decided there should be confidence. "It was my mother," she said, "my only friend."

"But your father, Mr. Henchard. He is living?"

"Yes, he is living," said Elizabeth-Jane.

"Is he not kind to you?"

"I've no wish to complain of him."

"There has been a disagreement?"

"A little."

"Perhaps you were to blame," suggested the stranger.

"I was-in many ways," sighed the meek Elizabeth. "I swept up the coals when the servants ought to have done it; and I said I was leery;-and he was angry with me."

The lady seemed to warm towards her for that reply. "Do you know the impression your words give me?" she said ingenuously. "That he is a hot-tempered man-a little proud-perhaps ambitious; but not a bad man." Her anxiety not to condemn Henchard while siding with Elizabeth was curious.

"O no; certainly not BAD," agreed the honest girl. "And he has not even been unkind to me till lately-since mother died. But it has been very much to bear while it has lasted. All is owing to my defects, I daresay; and my defects are owing to my history."

"What is your history?"

Elizabeth-Jane looked wistfully at her questioner. She found that her questioner was looking at her, turned her eyes down; and then seemed compelled to look back again. "My history is not gay or attractive," she said. "And yet I can tell it, if you really want to know."

The lady assured her that she did want to know; whereupon Elizabeth-Jane told the tale of her life as she understood it, which was in general the true one, except that the sale at the fair had no part therein.

Contrary to the girl's expectation her new friend was not shocked. This cheered her; and it was not till she thought of returning to that home in which she had been treated so roughly of late that her spirits fell.

"I don't know how to return," she murmured. "I think of going away. But what can I do? Where can I go?"

"Perhaps it will be better soon," said her friend gently. "So I would not go far. Now what do you think of this: I shall soon want somebody to live in my house, partly as housekeeper, partly as companion; would you mind coming to me? But perhaps-"

"O yes," cried Elizabeth, with tears in her eyes. "I would, indeed-I would do anything to be independent; for then perhaps my father might get to love me. But, ah!"

"What?"

"I am no accomplished person. And a companion to you must be that."

"O, not necessarily."

"Not? But I can't help using rural words sometimes, when I don't mean to."

"Never mind, I shall like to know them."

"And-O, I know I shan't do!"-she cried with a distressful laugh. "I accidentally learned to write round hand instead of ladies'-hand. And, of course, you want some one who can write that?"

"Well, no."

"What, not necessary to write ladies'-hand?" cried the joyous Elizabeth.

"Not at all."

"But where do you live?"

"In Casterbridge, or rather I shall be living here after twelve o'clock to-day."

Elizabeth expressed her astonishment.

"I have been staying at Budmouth for a few days while my house was getting ready. The house I am going into is that one they call High-Place Hall-the old stone one looking down the lane to the market. Two or three rooms are fit for occupation, though not all: I sleep there to-night for the first time. Now will you think over my proposal, and meet me here the first fine day next week, and say if you are still in the same mind?"

Elizabeth, her eyes shining at this prospect of a change from an unbearable position, joyfully assented; and the two parted at the gate of the churchyard.

Chapter 22

We go back for a moment to the preceding night, to account for Henchard's attitude.

At the hour when Elizabeth-Jane was contemplating her

stealthy reconnoitring excursion to the abode of the lady of her fancy, he had been not a little amazed at receiving a letter by hand in Lucetta's well-known characters. The self-repression, the resignation of her previous communication had vanished from her mood; she wrote with some of the natural lightness which had marked her in their early acquaintance.

HIGH-PLACE HALL MY DEAR MR. HENCHARD: Don't be surprised. It is for your good and mine, as I hope, that I have come to live at Casterbridge-for how long I cannot tell. That depends upon another; and he is a man, and a merchant, and a Mayor, and one who has the first right to my affections.

Seriously, mon ami, I am not so light-hearted as I may seem to be from this. I have come here in consequence of hearing of the death of your wife-whom you used to think of as dead so many years before! Poor woman, she seems to have been a sufferer, though uncomplaining, and though weak in intellect not an imbecile.

I am glad you acted fairly by her. As soon as I knew she was no more, it was brought home to me very forcibly by my conscience that I ought to endeavour to disperse the shade which my etourderie flung over my name, by asking you to carry out your promise to me. I hope you are of the same mind, and that you will take steps to this end. As, however, I did not know how you were situated, or what had happened since our separation, I decided to come and establish myself here before communicating with you.

You probably feel as I do about this. I shall be able to see you in a day or two. Till then, farewell.-Yours,

LUCETTA: P.S.-I was unable to keep my appointment to meet you for a moment or two in passing through Casterbridge the other day. My plans were altered by a family event, which it will surprise you to hear of.

Henchard had already heard that High-Place Hall was being prepared for a tenant. He said with a puzzled air to the first person he encountered, "Who is coming to live at the Hall?" "A lady of the name of Templeman, I believe, sir," said his informant.

Henchard thought it over. "Lucetta is related to her, I

suppose," he said to himself. "Yes, I must put her in her proper position, undoubtedly." It was by no means with the oppression that would once have accompanied the thought that he regarded the moral necessity now; it was, indeed, with interest, if not warmth.

His bitter disappointment at finding Elizabeth-Jane to be none of his, and himself a childless man, had left an emotional void in Henchard that he unconsciously craved to fill. In this frame of mind, though without strong feeling, he had strolled up the alley and into High-Place Hall by the postern at which Elizabeth had so nearly encountered him. He had gone on thence into the court, and inquired of a man whom he saw unpacking china from a crate if Miss Le Sueur was living there. Miss Le Sueur had been the name under which he had known Lucetta-or "Lucette," as she had called herself at that time.

The man replied in the negative; that Miss Templeman only had come. Henchard went away, concluding that Lucetta had not as yet settled in.

He was in this interested stage of the inquiry when he witnessed Elizabeth-Jane's departure the next day. On hearing her announce the address there suddenly took possession of him the strange thought that Lucetta and Miss Templeman were one and the same person, for he could recall that in her season of intimacy with him the name of the rich relative whom he had deemed somewhat a mythical personage had been given as Templeman.

Though he was not a, the possibility that Lucetta had been sublimed into a lady of means by some munificent testament on the part of this relative lent a charm to her image which it might not otherwise have acquired. He was getting on towards the dead level of middle age, when material things increasingly possess the mind.

But Henchard was not left long in suspense. Lucetta was rather addicted to scribbling, as had been shown by the torrent of letters after the fiasco in their marriage arrangements, and hardly had Elizabeth gone away when another note came to the Mayor's house from High-Place Hall.

"I am in residence," she said, "and comfortable, though

getting here has been a wearisome undertaking. You probably know what I am going to tell you, or do you not? My good Aunt Templeman, the banker's widow, whose very existence you used to doubt, much more her affluence, has lately died, and bequeathed some of her property to me. I will not enter into details except to say that I have taken her name-as a means of escape from mine, and its wrongs.

"I am now my own mistress, and have chosen to reside in Casterbridge-to be tenant of High-Place Hall, that at least you may be put to no trouble if you wish to see me. My first intention was to keep you in ignorance of the changes in my life till you should meet me in the street; but I have thought better of this.

"You probably are aware of my arrangement with your daughter, and have doubtless laughed at the-what shall I call it?-practical joke of my getting her to live with me. But my first meeting with her was purely an accident. Do you see, Michael, partly why I have done it?-why, to give you an excuse for coming here as if to visit HER, and thus to form my acquaintance naturally. She is a dear, good girl, and she thinks you have treated her with undue severity. You may have done so in your haste, but not deliberately, I am sure. As the result has been to bring her to me I am not disposed to upbraid you.-In haste, yours always,

LUCETTA.

The excitement which these announcements produced in Henchard's gloomy soul was to him most pleasurable. He sat over his dining-table long and dreamily, and by an almost mechanical transfer the sentiments which had run to waste since his estrangement from Elizabeth-Jane and Donald Farfrae gathered around Lucetta before they had grown dry. She was plainly in a very coming-on disposition for marriage. But what else could a poor woman be who had given her time and her heart to him so thoughtlessly, at that former time, as to lose her credit by it? Probably conscience no less than affection had brought her here. On the whole he did not blame her.

"The artful little woman!" he said, smiling (with reference to Lucetta's adroit and pleasant manoeuvre with).

To feel that he would like to see Lucetta was with Henchard to start for her house. He put on his hat and went. It was between eight and nine o'clock when he reached her door. The answer brought him was that Miss Templeman was engaged for that evening; but that she would be happy to see him the next day.

"That's rather like giving herself airs!" he thought. "And considering what we-" But after all, she plainly had not expected him, and he took the refusal quietly. Nevertheless he resolved not to go next day. "These cursed women-there's not an inch of straight grain in 'em!" he said.

Let us follow the train of Mr. Henchard's thought as if it were a clue line, and view the interior of High-Place Hall on this particular evening.

On Elizabeth-Jane's arrival she had been phlegmatically asked by an elderly woman to go upstairs and take off her things. She replied with great earnestness that she would not think of giving that trouble, and on the instant divested herself of her bonnet and cloak in the passage. She was then conducted to the first floor on the landing, and left to find her way further alone.

The room disclosed was prettily furnished as a boudoir or small drawing-room, and on a sofa with two cylindrical pillows reclined a dark-haired, large-eyed, pretty woman, of unmistakably French extraction on one side or the other. She was probably some years older than Elizabeth, and had a sparkling light in her eye. In front of the sofa was a small table, with a pack of cards scattered upon it faces upward.

The attitude had been so full of abandonment that she bounded up like a spring on hearing the door open.

Perceiving that it was Elizabeth she lapsed into ease, and came across to her with a reckless skip that innate grace only prevented from being boisterous.

"Why, you are late," she said, taking hold of 's hands.

"There were so many little things to put up."

"And you seem dead-alive and tired. Let me try to enliven you by some wonderful tricks I have learnt, to kill time. Sit there and don't move." She gathered up the pack of cards, pulled the table in front of her, and began to deal them rapidly, telling Elizabeth to choose some.

"Well, have you chosen?" she asked flinging down the last card.

"No," stammered Elizabeth, arousing herself from a reverie. "I forgot, I was thinking of-you, and me-and how strange it is that I am here."

Miss Templeman looked at Elizabeth-Jane with interest, and laid down the çards. "Ah! never mind," she said. "I'll lie here while you sit by me; and we'll talk."

Elizabeth drew up silently to the head of the sofa, but with obvious pleasure. It could be seen that though in years she was younger than her entertainer in manner and general vision she seemed more of the sage. Miss Templeman deposited herself on the sofa in her former flexuous position, and throwing her arm above her brow-somewhat in the pose of a well-known conception of Titian's-talked up at Elizabeth-Jane invertedly across her forehead and arm.

"I must tell you something," she said. "I wonder if you have suspected it. I have only been mistress of a large house and fortune a little while."

"Oh-only a little while?" murmured Elizabeth-Jane, her countenance slightly falling.

"As a girl I lived about in garrison towns and elsewhere with my father, till I was quite flighty and unsettled. He was an officer in the army. I should not have mentioned this had I not thought it best you should know the truth."

"Yes, yes." She looked thoughtfully round the room-at the little square piano with brass inlayings, at the, at the lamp, at the fair and dark kings and queens on the card-table, and finally at the inverted face of Lucetta Templeman, whose large lustrous eyes had such an odd effect upside down.

Elizabeth's mind ran on acquirements to an almost morbid degree. "You speak French and Italian fluently, no doubt," she said. "I have not been able to get beyond a wretched bit of Latin yet."

"Well, for that matter, in my native isle speaking French does not go for much. It is rather the other way."

"Where is your native isle?"

It was with rather more reluctance that Miss Templeman said, "Jersey. There they speak French on one side of the street and English on the other, and a mixed tongue in the middle of the road. But it is a long time since I was there. Bath is where my people really belong to, though my ancestors in Jersey were as good as anybody in England. They were the Le Sueurs, an old family who have done great things in their time. I went back and lived there after my father's death. But I don't value such past matters, and am quite an English person in my feelings and tastes."

Lucetta's tongue had for a moment outrun her discretion. She had arrived at Casterbridge as a Bath lady, and there were obvious reasons why Jersey should drop out of her life. But Elizabeth had tempted her to make free, and a deliberately formed resolve had been broken.

It could not, however, have been broken in safer company. Lucetta's words went no further, and after this day she was so much upon her guard that there appeared no chance of her identification with the young Jersey woman who had been Henchard's dear comrade at a critical time. Not the least amusing of her safeguards was her resolute avoidance of a French word if one by accident came to her tongue more readily than its English equivalent. She shirked it with the suddenness of the weak Apostle at the accusation, "Thy speech bewrayeth thee!" Expectancy sat visibly upon Lucetta the next morning. She dressed herself for Mr. Henchard, and restlessly awaited his call before mid-day; as he did not come she waited on through the afternoon. But she did not tell Elizabeth that the person expected was the girl's stepfather.

They sat in adjoining windows of the same room in Lucetta's great stone mansion, netting, and looking out upon the market, which formed an animated scene. Elizabeth could see the crown of her stepfather's hat among the rest beneath, and was not aware that Lucetta watched the same object with yet intenser interest. He moved about amid the throng, at this point lively as an ant-hill; elsewhere more reposeful, and broken up by stalls of fruit and vegetables.

The farmers as a rule preferred the open carrefour for their transactions, despite its inconvenient jostlings and the danger from crossing vehicles, to the gloomy sheltered market-room provided for them. Here they surged on this one day of the week, forming a little world of leggings, switches, and sample-bags; men of extensive stomachs, sloping like mountain sides; men whose heads in walking swayed as the trees in November gales; who in conversing varied their attitudes much, lowering themselves by spreading their knees, and thrusting their hands into the pockets of remote inner jackets. Their faces radiated tropical warmth; for though when at home their countenances varied with the seasons, their market-faces all the year round were glowing little fires.

All over-clothes here were worn as if they were an inconvenience, a hampering necessity. Some men were well dressed; but the majority were careless in that respect, appearing in suits which were historical records of their wearer's deeds, sun-scorchings, and daily struggles for many years past. Yet many carried ruffled cheque-books in their pockets which regulated at the bank hard by a balance of never less than four figures. In fact, what these gibbous human shapes specially represented was ready money-money insistently ready-not ready next year like a nobleman's-often not merely ready at the bank like a professional man's, but ready in their large plump hands.

It happened that to-day there rose in the midst of them all two or three tall apple-trees standing as if they grew on the spot; till it was perceived that they were held by men from the cider-districts who came here to sell them, bringing the clay of their county on their boots. Elizabeth-Jane, who had often observed them, said, "I wonder if the same trees come every week?"

"What trees?" said Lucetta, absorbed in watching for Henchard. Elizabeth replied vaguely, for an incident checked her. Behind one of the trees stood Farfrae, briskly discussing a sample-bag with a farmer. Henchard had come up, accidentally encountering the young man, whose face seemed to inquire, "Do we speak to each other?"

She saw her stepfather throw a shine into his eye which answered "No!" Elizabeth-Jane sighed.

"Are you particularly interested in anybody out there?" said Lucetta.

"O, no," said her companion, a quick red shooting over her face.

Luckily Farfrae's figure was immediately covered by the apple-tree.

Lucetta looked hard at her. "Quite sure?" she said.

"O yes," said Elizabeth-Jane.

Again Lucetta looked out. "They are all farmers, I suppose?" she said.

"No. There's Mr. Bulge-he's a wine merchant; there's Benjamin Brownlet-a horse dealer; and Kitson, the pig breeder; and Yopper, the auctioneer; besides maltsters, and millers-and so on." Farfrae stood out quite distinctly now; but she did not mention him.

The Saturday afternoon slipped on thus desultorily. The market changed from the sample-showing hour to the idle hour before starting homewards, when tales were told. Henchard had not called on Lucetta though he had stood so near. He must have been too busy, she thought. He would come on Sunday or Monday.

The days came but not the visitor, though Lucetta repeated her dressing with scrupulous care. She got disheartened. It may at once be declared that Lucetta no longer bore towards Henchard all that warm allegiance which had characterized her in their first acquaintance, the then unfortunate issue of things had chilled pure love considerably. But there remained a conscientious wish to bring about her union with him, now that there was nothing to hinder it-to right her position-which in itself was a happiness to sigh for. With strong social reasons on her side why their marriage should take place there had ceased to be any worldly reason on his why it should be postponed, since she had succeeded to fortune.

Tuesday was the great Candlemas fair. At breakfast she said to Elizabeth-Jane quite coolly: "I imagine your father may call to see you to-day. I suppose he stands close by in the market-place with the rest of the corn-dealers?"

She shook her head. "He won't come."

"Why?"

"He has taken against me," she said in a husky voice.

"You have quarreled more deeply than I know of."

Elizabeth, wishing to shield the man she believed to be her father from any charge of unnatural dislike, said "Yes."

"Then where you are is, of all places, the one he will avoid?"

Elizabeth nodded sadly.

Lucetta looked blank, twitched up her lovely eyebrows and lip, and burst into hysterical sobs. Here was a disaster-her ingenious scheme completely stultified.

"O, my dear Miss Templeman-what's the matter?" cried her companion.

"I like your company much!" said Lucetta, as soon as she could speak.

"Yes, yes-and so do I yours!" Elizabeth chimed in soothingly.

"But-but-" She could not finish the sentence, which was, naturally, that if Henchard had such a rooted dislike for the girl as now seemed to be the case, Elizabeth-Jane would have to be got rid of-a disagreeable necessity.

A provisional resource suggested itself. "Miss Henchard-will you go on an errand for me as soon as breakfast is over?-Ah, that's very good of you. Will you go and order-" Here she enumerated several commissions at sundry shops, which would occupy Elizabeth's time for the next hour or two, at least. "And have you ever seen the Museum?" Elizabeth-Jane had not.

"Then you should do so at once. You can finish the morning by going there. It is an old house in a back street-I forget where-but you'll find out-and there are crowds of interesting things-skeletons, teeth, old pots and pans, ancient boots and shoes, birds' eggs-all charmingly instructive. You'll be sure to stay till you get quite hungry."

Elizabeth hastily put on her things and departed. "I

wonder why she wants to get rid of me to-day!" she said sorrowfully as she went. That her absence, rather than her services or instruction, was in request, had been readily apparent to Elizabeth-Jane, simple as she seemed, and difficult as it was to attribute a motive for the desire.

She had not been gone ten minutes when one of Lucetta's servants was sent to Henchard's with a note. The contents were briefly:-

DEAR MICHAEL: You will be standing in view of my house for two or three hours in the course of your business, so do please call and see me. I am sadly disappointed that you have not come before, for can I help anxiety about my own equivocal relation to you?-especially now my aunt's fortune has brought me more prominently before society? Your daughter's presence here may be the cause of your neglect; and I have therefore sent her away for the morning. Say you come on business-I shall be quite alone.

LUCETTA: When the messenger returned her mistress gave directions that if a gentleman called he was to be admitted at once, and sat down to await results.

Sentimentally she did not much care to see him-his delays had wearied her, but it was necessary; and with a sigh she arranged herself picturesquely in the chair; first this way, then that; next so that the light fell over her head. Next she flung herself on the couch in the cyma-recta curve which so became her, and with her arm over her brow looked towards the door. This, she decided, was the best position after all, and thus she remained till a man's step was heard on the stairs.

Whereupon Lucetta, forgetting her curve (for Nature was too strong for Art as yet), jumped up and ran and hid herself behind one of the window-curtains in a freak of timidity. In spite of the waning of passion the situation was an agitating one-she had not seen Henchard since his temporary parting from her in Jersey. She could hear the servant showing the visitor into the room, shutting the door upon him, and leaving as if to go and look for her mistress. Lucetta flung back the curtain with a nervous greeting. The man before her was not Henchard.

Chapter 25

The next phase of the supersession of Henchard in Lucetta's heart was an experiment in calling on her performed by Farfrae with some apparent trepidation. Conventionally speaking he conversed with both Miss Templeman and her companion; but in fact it was rather that Elizabeth sat invisible in the room. Donald appeared not to see her at all, and answered her wise little remarks with curtly indifferent monosyllables, his looks and faculties hanging on the woman who could boast of a more Protean variety in her phases, moods, opinions, and also principles, than could Elizabeth. Lucetta had persisted in dragging her into the circle; but she had remained like an awkward third point which that circle would not touch.

Susan Henchard's daughter bore up against the frosty ache of the treatment, as she had borne up under worse things, and contrived as soon as possible to get out of the inharmonious room without being missed. The Scotchman seemed hardly the same Farfrae who had danced with her and walked with her in a delicate poise between love and friendship-that period in the history of a love when alone it can be said to be unalloyed with pain.

She stoically looked from her bedroom window, and contemplated her fate as if it were written on the top of the church-tower hard by. "Yes," she said at last, bringing down her palm upon the sill with a pat: "HE is the second man of that story she told me!"

All this time Henchard's smouldering sentiments towards Lucetta had been fanned into higher and higher inflammation by the circumstances of the case. He was discovering that the young woman for whom he once felt a pitying warmth which had been almost chilled out of him by reflection, was, when now qualified with a slight inaccessibility and a more matured beauty, the very being to make him satisfied with life. Day after day proved to him, by her silence, that it was no use to think of bringing her round by holding aloof; so he gave in, and called upon her again, Elizabeth-Jane being absent.

He crossed the room to her with a heavy tread of some

awkwardness, his strong, warm gaze upon her-like the sun beside the moon in comparison with Farfrae's modest look-and with something of a hail-fellow bearing, as, indeed, was not unnatural. But she seemed so transubstantiated by her change of position, and held out her hand to him in such cool friendship, that he became deferential, and sat down with a perceptible loss of power. He understood but little of fashion in dress, yet enough to feel himself inadequate in appearance beside her whom he had hitherto been dreaming of as almost his property. She said something very polite about his being good enough to call. This caused him to recover balance. He looked her oddly in the face, losing his awe.

"Why, of course I have called, Lucetta," he said. "What does that nonsense mean? You know I couldn't have helped myself if I had wished-that is, if I had any kindness at all. I've called to say that I am ready, as soon as custom will permit, to give you my name in return for your devotion and what you lost by it in thinking too little of yourself and too much of me; to say that you can fix the day or month, with my full consent, whenever in your opinion it would be seemly: you know more of these things than I."

"It is full early yet," she said evasively.

"Yes, yes; I suppose it is. But you know, Lucetta, I felt directly my poor ill-used Susan died, and when I could not bear the idea of marrying again, that after what had happened between us it was my duty not to let any unnecessary delay occur before putting things to rights. Still, I wouldn't call in a hurry, because-well, you can guess how this money you've come into made me feel." His voice slowly fell; he was conscious that in this room his accents and manner wore a roughness not observable in the street. He looked about the room at the novel hangings and ingenious furniture with which she had surrounded herself.

"Upon my life I didn't know such furniture as this could be bought in Casterbridge," he said.

"Nor can it be " said she. "Nor will it till fifty years more of civilization have passed over the town. It took a waggon and four horses to get it here."

"H'm. It looks as if you were living on capital."

"O no, I am not."

"So much the better. But the fact is, your setting up like this makes my beaming towards you rather awkward."

"Why?"

An answer was not really needed, and he did not furnish one. "Well," he went on, "there's nobody in the world I would have wished to see enter into this wealth before you, Lucetta, and nobody, I am sure, who will become it more." He turned to her with congratulatory admiration so fervid that she shrank somewhat, notwithstanding that she knew him so well.

"I am greatly obliged to you for all that," said she, rather with an air of speaking ritual. The stint of reciprocal feeling was perceived, and Henchard showed chagrin at once-nobody was more quick to show that than he.

"You may be obliged or not for't. Though the things I say may not have the polish of what you've lately learnt to expect for the first time in your life, they are real, my lady Lucetta."

"That's rather a rude way of speaking to me," pouted Lucetta, with stormy eyes.

"Not at all!" replied Henchard hotly. "But there, there, I don't wish to quarrel with 'ee. I come with an honest proposal for silencing your Jersey enemies, and you ought to be thankful."

"How can you speak so!" she answered, firing quickly. "Knowing that my only crime was the indulging in a foolish girl's passion for you with too little regard for correctness, and that I was what I call innocent all the time they called me guilty, you ought not to be so cutting! I suffered enough at that worrying time, when you wrote to tell me of your wife's return and my consequent dismissal, and if I am a little independent now, surely the privilege is due to me!"

"Yes, it is," he said. "But it is not by what is, in this life, but by what appears, that you are judged; and I therefore think you ought to accept me-for your own good name's sake. What is known in your native Jersey may get known here."

"How you keep on about Jersey! I am English!"

"Yes, yes. Well, what do you say to my proposal?"

For the first time in their acquaintance Lucetta had the move; and yet she was backward. "For the present let things be," she said with some embarrassment. "Treat me as an acquaintance, and I'll treat you as one. Time will-" She stopped; and he said nothing to fill the gap for awhile, there being no pressure of half acquaintance to drive them into speech if they were not minded for it.

"That's the way the wind blows, is it?" he said at last grimly, nodding an affirmative to his own thoughts.

A yellow flood of reflected sunlight filled the room for a few instants. It was produced by the passing of a load of newly trussed hay from the country, in a waggon marked with Farfrae's name. Beside it rode Farfrae himself on. Lucetta's face became-as a woman's face becomes when the man she loves rises upon her gaze like an apparition.

A turn of the eye by Henchard, a glance from the window, and the secret of her inaccessibility would have been revealed. But Henchard in estimating her tone was looking down so plumb-straight that he did not note the warm consciousness upon Lucetta's face.

"I shouldn't have thought it-I shouldn't have thought it of women!" he said emphatically by-and-by, rising and shaking himself into activity; while Lucetta was so anxious to divert him from any suspicion of the truth that she asked him to be in no hurry. Bringing him some apples she insisted upon paring one for him.

He would not take it. "No, no; such is not for me," he said drily, and moved to the door. At going out he turned his eye upon her.

"You came to live in Casterbridge entirely on my account," he said. "Yet now you are here you won't have anything to say to my offer!"

He had hardly gone down the staircase when she dropped upon the sofa and jumped up again in a fit of desperation. "I WILL love him!" she cried passionately; "as for HIM-he's hot-tempered and stern, and it would be madness to bind myself to him knowing that. I won't be a slave to the past-I'll love where I choose!"

Yet having decided to break away from Henchard one might have supposed her capable of aiming higher than Farfrae. But Lucetta reasoned nothing: she feared hard words from the people with whom she had been earlier associated; she had no relatives left; and with native lightness of heart took kindly to what fate offered. Elizabeth-Jane, surveying the position of Lucetta between her two lovers from the crystalline sphere of a straightforward mind, did not fail to perceive that her father, as she called him, and Donald Farfrae became more desperately enamoured of her friend every day. On Farfrae's side it was the unforced passion of youth. On Henchard's the artificially stimulated coveting of maturer age.

The pain she experienced from the almost absolute obliviousness to her existence that was shown by the pair of them became at times half dissipated by her sense of its humourousness. When Lucetta had pricked her finger they were as deeply concerned as if she were dying; when she herself had been seriously sick or in danger they uttered a conventional word of sympathy at the news, and forgot all about it immediately. But, as regarded Henchard, this perception of hers also caused her some filial grief; she could not help asking what she had done to be neglected so, after the professions of solicitude he had made. As regarded Farfrae, she thought, after honest reflection, that it was quite natural. What was she beside Lucetta?-as one of the "meaner beauties of the night," when the moon had risen in the skies.

She had learnt the lesson of renunciation, and was as familiar with the wreck of each day's wishes as with the diurnal setting of the sun. If her earthly career had taught her few book philosophies it had at least well practised her in this. Yet her experience had consisted less in a series of pure disappointments than in a series of substitutions. Continually it had happened that what she had desired had not been granted her, and that what had been granted her she had not desired. So she viewed with an approach to equanimity the new cancelled days when Donald had been her undeclared lover, and wondered what thing Heaven might send her in place of him.

Chapter 28

The next morning Henchard went to the Town Hall below Lucetta's house, to attend Petty Sessions, being still a magistrate for the year by virtue of his late position as Mayor. In passing he looked up at her windows, but nothing of her was to be seen.

Henchard as a Justice of the Peace may at first seem to be an even greater incongruity than Shallow and Silence themselves. But his rough and ready perceptions, his sledge-hammer directness, had often served him better than nice legal knowledge in despatching such simple business as fell to his hands in this Court. To-day Dr. Chalkfield, the Mayor for the year, being absent, the corn-merchant took the big chair, his eyes still abstractedly stretching out of the window to the ashlar front of High-Place Hall.

There was one case only, and the offender stood before him. She was an old woman of mottled countenance, attired in a shawl of that nameless tertiary hue which comes, but cannot be made-a hue neither tawny, russet, hazel, nor ash; a sticky black bonnet that seemed to have been worn in the country of the Psalmist where the clouds drop fatness; and an apron that had been white in time so comparatively recent as still to contrast visibly with the rest of her clothes. The steeped aspect of the woman as a whole showed her to be no native of the country-side or even of a country-town.

She looked cursorily at Henchard and the second magistrate, and Henchard looked at her, with a momentary pause, as if she had reminded him indistinctly of somebody or something which passed from his mind as quickly as it had come. "Well, and what has she been doing?" he said, looking down at the charge sheet.

"She is charged, sir, with the offence of disorderly female and nuisance," whispered Stubberd.

"Where did she do that?" said the other magistrate.

"By the church, sir, of all the horrible places in the world!- I caught her in the act, your worship."

"Stand back then," said Henchard, "and let's hear what you've got to say."

Stubberd was sworn in, the magistrate's clerk dipped his pen, Henchard being no note-taker himself, and the constable began-

"Hearing a' illegal noise I went down the street at minutes past eleven P.M. on the night of the fifth instinct, Hannah Dominy. When I had-

"Don't go so fast, Stubberd," said the clerk.

The constable waited, with his eyes on the clerk's pen, till the latter stopped scratching and said, "yes." Stubberd continued: "When I had proceeded to the spot I saw defendant at another spot, namely, the gutter." He paused, watching the point of the clerk's pen again.

"Gutter, yes, Stubberd."

"Spot measuring twelve feet nine inches or thereabouts from where I-" Still careful not to outrun the clerk's penmanship Stubberd pulled up again; for having got his evidence by heart it was immaterial to him whereabouts he broke off.

"I object to that," spoke up the old woman, "'spot measuring twelve feet nine or thereabouts from where I,' is not sound testimony!"

The magistrates consulted, and the second one said that the bench was of opinion that twelve feet nine inches from a man on his oath was admissible.

Stubberd, with a suppressed gaze of victorious rectitude at the old woman, continued: "Was standing myself. She was wambling about quite dangerous to the thoroughfare and when I approached to draw near she committed the nuisance, and insulted me."

"'Insulted me.'...Yes, what did she say?"

"She said, 'Put away that dee lantern,' she says."

"Yes."

"Says she, 'Dost hear, old turmit-head? Put away that dee lantern. I have floored fellows a dee sight finer-looking than a dee fool like thee, you son of a bee, dee me if I haint,' she says.

"I object to that conversation!" interposed the old woman. "I was not capable enough to hear what I said, and what is said out of my hearing is not evidence."

There was another stoppage for consultation, a book was referred to, and finally Stubberd was allowed to go on again. The truth was that the old woman had appeared in court so many more times than the magistrates themselves, that they were obliged to keep a sharp look-out upon their procedure. However, when Stubberd had rambled on a little further Henchard broke out impatiently, "Come-we don't want to hear any more of them cust dees and bees! Say the words out like a man, and don't be so modest, Stubberd; or else leave it alone!" Turning to the woman, "Now then, have you any questions to ask him, or anything to say?"

"Yes," she replied with a twinkle in her eye; and the clerk dipped his pen.

"Twenty years ago or thereabout I was selling of furmity in a tent at Weydon Fair--"

"'Twenty years ago'-well, that's beginning at the beginning; suppose you go back to the Creation!" said the clerk, not without satire.

But Henchard stared, and quite forgot what was evidence and what was not.

"A man and a woman with a little child came into my tent," the woman continued. "They sat down and had a basin apiece. Ah, Lord's my life! I was of a more respectable station in the world then than I am now, being a land smuggler in a large way of business; and I used to season my furmity with rum for them who asked for't. I did it for the man; and then he had more and more; till at last he quarrelled with his wife, and offered to sell her to the highest bidder. A sailor came in and bid five guineas, and paid the money, and led her away. And the man who sold his wife in that fashion is the man sitting there in the great big chair." The speaker concluded by nodding her head at Henchard and folding her arms.

Everybody looked at Henchard. His face seemed strange, and in tint as if it had been powdered over with ashes. "We don't want to hear your life and adventures," said the second magistrate sharply, filling the pause which followed. "You've been asked if you've anything to say bearing on the case."

"That bears on the case. It proves that he's no better than

I, and has no right to sit there in judgment upon me." "'Tis a concocted story," said the clerk. "So hold your tongue!"

"No-'tis true." The words came from Henchard. "'Tis as true as the light," he said slowly. "And upon my soul it does prove that I'm no better than she! And to keep out of any temptation to treat her hard for her revenge, I'll leave her to you."

The sensation in the court was indescribably great. Henchard left the chair, and came out, passing through a group of people on the steps and outside that was much larger than usual; for it seemed that the old furmity dealer had mysteriously hinted to the denizens of the lane in which she had been lodging since her arrival, that she knew a queer thing or two about their great local man Mr. Henchard, if she chose to tell it. This had brought them hither.

"Why are there so many idlers round the Town Hall today?" said Lucetta to her servant when the case was over. She had risen late, and had just looked out of the window.

"Oh, please, ma'am, 'tis this larry about Mr. Henchard. A woman has proved that before he became a gentleman he sold his wife for five guineas in a booth at a fair."

In all the accounts which Henchard had given her of the separation from his wife Susan for so many years, of his belief in her death, and so on, he had never clearly explained the actual and immediate cause of that separation. The story she now heard for the first time.

A gradual misery overspread Lucetta's face as she dwelt upon the promise wrung from her the night before. At bottom, then, Henchard was this. How terrible a contingency for a woman who should commit herself to his care.

During the day she went out to the Ring and to other places, not coming in till nearly dusk. As soon as she saw Elizabeth-Jane after her return indoors she told her that she had resolved to go away from home to the seaside for a few days-to Port-Bredy; Casterbridge was so gloomy.

Elizabeth, seeing that she looked wan and disturbed, encouraged her in the idea, thinking a change would afford her relief. She could not help suspecting that the gloom which seemed to have come over Casterbridge in Lucetta's eyes might be partially owing to the fact that Farfrae was away from home.

Elizabeth saw her friend depart for Port-Bredy, and took charge of High-Place Hall till her return. After two or three days of solitude and incessant rain Henchard called at the house. He seemed disappointed to hear of Lucetta's absence and though he nodded with outward indifference he went away handling his beard with a nettled mien.

The next day he called again. "Is she come now?" he asked.

"Yes. She returned this morning," replied his. "But she is not indoors. She has gone for a walk along the turnpike-road to Port-Bredy. She will be home by dusk."

After a few words, which only served to reveal his restless impatience, he left the house again.

Chapter 30

Farfrae's words to his landlady had referred to the removal of his boxes and other effects from his late lodgings to Lucetta's house. The work was not heavy, but it had been much hindered on account of the frequent pauses necessitated by exclamations of surprise at the event, of which the good woman had been briefly informed by letter a few hours earlier.

At the last moment of leaving Port-Bredy, Farfrae, like John Gilpin, had been detained by important customers, whom, even in the exceptional circumstances, he was not the man to neglect. Moreover, there was a convenience in Lucetta arriving first at her house. Nobody there as yet knew what had happened; and she was best in a position to break the news to the inmates, and give directions for her husband's accommodation. He had, therefore, sent on his two-days' bride in a hired brougham, whilst he went across the country to a certain group of wheat and barley ricks a few miles off, telling her the hour at which he might be expected the same evening. This accounted for her trotting out to meet him after their separation of four hours.

By a strenuous effort, after leaving Henchard she calmed herself in readiness to receive Donald at High-Place Hall when he came on from his lodgings. One supreme fact empowered her to this, the sense that, come what would, she had secured him. Half-an-hour after her arrival he walked in, and she met him with a relieved gladness, which a month's perilous absence could not have intensified.

"There is one thing I have not done; and yet it is important," she said earnestly, when she had finished talking about the adventure with the bull. "That is, broken the news of our marriage to my dear Elizabeth-Jane."

"Ah, and you have not?" he said thoughtfully. "I gave her a lift from the barn homewards; but I did not tell her either; for I thought she might have heard of it in the town, and was keeping back her congratulations from shyness, and all that."

"She can hardly have heard of it. But I'll find out; I'll go to her now. And, Donald, you don't mind her living on with me just the same as before? She is so quiet and unassuming."

"O no, indeed I don't," Farfrae answered with, perhaps, a faint awkwardness. "But I wonder if she would care to?"

"O yes!" said Lucetta eagerly. "I am sure she would like to. Besides, poor thing, she has no other home."

Farfrae looked at her and saw that she did not suspect the secret of her more reserved friend. He liked her all the better for the blindness. "Arrange as you like with her by all means," he said. "It is I who have come to your house, not you to mine."

"I'll run and speak to her," said Lucetta.

When she got upstairs to Elizabeth-Jane's room the latter had taken off her out-door things, and was resting over a book. Lucetta found in a moment that she had not yet learnt the news.

"I did not come down to you, Miss Templeman," she said simply. "I was coming to ask if you had quite recovered from your fright, but I found you had a visitor. What are the bells ringing for, I wonder? And the band, too, is playing. Somebody must be married; or else they are practising for Christmas."

Lucetta uttered a vague "Yes," and seating herself by the other young woman looked musingly at her. "What a lonely creature you are," she presently said; "never knowing what's going on, or what people are talking about everywhere with keen interest. You should get out, and gossip about as other women do, and then you wouldn't be obliged to ask me a question of that kind. Well, now, I have something to tell you.

Elizabeth-Jane said she was so glad, and made herself receptive.

"I must go rather a long way back," said Lucetta, the difficulty of explaining herself satisfactorily to the pondering one beside her growing more apparent at each syllable. "You remember that trying case of conscience I told you of some time ago-about the first lover and the second lover?" She let out in jerky phrases a leading word or two of the story she had told.

"O yes-I remember the story of YOUR FRIEND," said Elizabeth drily, regarding the irises of Lucetta's eyes as though to catch their exact shade. "The two lovers-the old one and the new: how she wanted to marry the second, but felt she ought to marry the first; so that she neglected the better course to follow the evil, like the poet Ovid I've just been construing: 'Video meliora proboque, deteriora sequor.'"

"O no; she didn't follow evil exactly!" said Lucetta hastily.

"But you said that she-or as I may say you"-answered Elizabeth, dropping the mask, "were in honour and conscience bound to marry the first?"

Lucetta's blush at being seen through came and went again before she replied anxiously, "You will never breathe this, will you, Elizabeth-Jane?"

"Certainly not, if you say not.

"Then I will tell you that the case is more complicated-worse, in fact-than it seemed in my story. I and the first man were thrown together in a strange way, and felt that we ought to be united, as the world had talked of us. He was a widower, as he supposed. He had not heard of his first wife for many years. But the wife returned, and we parted. She is now dead, and the husband comes paying me addresses again, saying, 'Now we'll complete our purposes.' But, Elizabeth-Jane, all this amounts to a new courtship of me by him; I was absolved from all vows by the return of the other woman."

"Have you not lately renewed your promise?" said the

younger with quiet surmise. She had divined Man Number One.

"That was wrung from me by a threat."

"Yes, it was. But I think when any one gets coupled up with a man in the past so unfortunately as you have done she ought to become his wife if she can, even if she were not the sinning party."

Lucetta's countenance lost its sparkle. "He turned out to be a man I should be afraid to marry," she pleaded. "Really afraid! And it was not till after my renewed promise that I knew it."

"Then there is only one course left to honesty. You must remain a single woman."

"But think again! Do consider--"

"I am certain," interrupted her companion hardily. "I have guessed very well who the man is. My father; and I say it is him or nobody for you."

Any suspicion of impropriety was to Elizabeth-Jane like a red rag to a bull. Her craving for correctness of procedure was, indeed, almost vicious. Owing to her early troubles with regard to her mother a semblance of irregularity had terrors for her which those whose names are safeguarded from suspicion know nothing of. "You ought to marry Mr. Henchard or nobody-certainly not another man!" she went on with a quivering lip in whose movement two passions shared.

"I don't admit that!" said Lucetta passionately.

"Admit it or not, it is true!"

Lucetta covered her eyes with her right hand, as if she could plead no more, holding out her left to Elizabeth-Jane.

"Why, you HAVE married him!" cried the latter, jumping up with pleasure after a glance at Lucetta's fingers. "When did you do it? Why did you not tell me, instead of teasing me like this? How very honourable of you! He did treat my mother badly once, it seems, in a moment of intoxication. And it is true that he is stern sometimes. But you will rule him entirely, I am sure, with your beauty and wealth and accomplishments. You are the woman he will adore, and we shall all three be happy together now!"

"O, my Elizabeth-Jane!" cried Lucetta distressfully. "'Tis somebody else that I have married! I was so desperate-so afraid of being forced to anything else-so afraid of revelations that would quench his love for me, that I resolved to do it offhand, come what might, and purchase a week of happiness at any cost!"

"You-have-married Mr. Farfrae!" cried Elizabeth-Jane, in Nathan tones

Lucetta bowed. She had recovered herself.

"The bells are ringing on that account," she said. "My husband is downstairs. He will live here till a more suitable house is ready for us; and I have told him that I want you to stay with me just as before."

"Let me think of it alone," the girl quickly replied, corking up the turmoil of her feeling with grand control.

"You shall. I am sure we shall be happy together."

Lucetta departed to join Donald below, a vague uneasiness floating over her joy at seeing him quite at home there. Not on account of her friend Elizabeth did she feel it: for of the bearings of Elizabeth-Jane's emotions she had not the least suspicion; but on Henchard's alone.

Now the instant decision of Susan Henchard's daughter was to dwell in that house no more. Apart from her estimate of the propriety of Lucetta's conduct, Farfrae had been so nearly her avowed lover that she felt she could not abide there.

It was still early in the evening when she hastily put on her things and went out. In a few minutes, knowing the ground, she had found a suitable lodging, and arranged to enter it that night. Returning and entering noiselessly she took off her pretty dress and arrayed herself in a plain one, packing up the other to keep as her best; for she would have to be very economical now. She wrote a note to leave for Lucetta, who was closely shut up in the drawing-room with Farfrae; and then Elizabeth-Jane called a man with a wheel-barrow; and seeing her boxes put into it she trotted off down the street to her rooms. They were in the street in which Henchard lived, and almost opposite his door.

Here she sat down and considered the means of

subsistence. The little annual sum settled on her by her stepfather would keep body and soul together. A wonderful skill in netting of all sorts-acquired in childhood by making seines in Newson's home-might serve her in good stead; and her studies, which were pursued unremittingly, might serve her in still better.

By this time the marriage that had taken place was known throughout Casterbridge; had been discussed noisily on kerbstones, confidentially behind counters, and jovially at the Three Mariners. Whether Farfrae would sell his business and set up for a gentleman on his wife's money, or whether he would show independence enough to stick to his trade in spite of his brilliant alliance, was a great point of interest.

Chapter 32

Two bridges stood near the lower part of Casterbridge town. The first, of weather-stained brick, was immediately at the end of High Street, where a diverging branch from that thoroughfare ran round to the low-lying Durnover lanes; so that the precincts of the bridge formed the merging point of respectability and indigence. The second bridge, of stone, was further out on the highway-in fact, fairly in the meadows, though still within the town boundary.

These bridges had speaking countenances. Every projection in each was worn down to obtuseness, partly by weather, more by friction from generations of loungers, whose toes and heels had from year to year made restless movements against these parapets, as they had stood there meditating on the aspect of affairs. In the case of the more friable bricks and stones even the flat faces were worn into hollows by the same mixed mechanism. The masonry of the top was clamped with iron at each joint; since it had been no uncommon thing for desperate men to wrench the coping off and throw it down the river, in reckless defiance of the magistrates.

For to this pair of bridges gravitated all the failures of the town; those who had failed in business, in love, in sobriety, in crime. Why the unhappy hereabout usually chose the bridges for their meditations in preference to a railing, a gate, or a stile, was not so clear. There was a marked difference of quality between the personages who haunted the near bridge of brick and the personages who haunted the far one of stone. Those of lowest character preferred the former, adjoining the town; they did not mind the glare of the public eye. They had been of comparatively no account during their successes; and though they might feel dispirited, they had no particular sense of shame in their ruin. Their hands were mostly kept in their pockets; they wore a leather strap round their hips or knees, and boots that required a great deal of lacing, but seemed never to get any. Instead of sighing at their adversities they spat, and instead of saying the iron had entered into their souls they said they were down on their luck. Jopp in his time of distress had often stood here; so had Mother Cuxsom, Christopher Coney, and poor Abel Whittle.

The miserables who would pause on the remoter bridge were of a politer stamp. They included bankrupts, hypochondriacs, persons who were what is called "out of a situation" from fault or lucklessness, the inefficient of the professional class-shabby-genteel men, who did not know how to get rid of the weary time between breakfast and dinner, and the yet more weary time between dinner and dark. The eye of this species were mostly directed over the parapet upon the running water below. A man seen there looking thus fixedly into the river was pretty sure to be one whom the world did not treat kindly for some reason or other. While one in straits on the townward bridge did not mind who saw him so, and kept his back to the parapet to survey the passers-by, one in straits on this never faced the road, never turned his head at coming footsteps, but, sensitive to his own condition, watched the current whenever a stranger approached, as if some strange fish interested him, though every finned thing had been poached out of the river years before.

There and thus they would muse; if their grief were the grief of oppression they would wish themselves kings; if their grief were poverty, wish themselves millionaires; if sin, they would wish they were saints or angels; if despised love, that they were some much-courted Adonis of county fame. Some had been known to stand and think so long with this fixed gaze downward that eventually they had allowed their poor carcases to follow that gaze; and they were discovered the next morning out of reach of their troubles, either here or in the deep pool called Blackwater, a little higher up the river.

To this bridge came Henchard, as other unfortunates had come before him, his way thither being by the riverside path on the chilly edge of the town. Here he was standing one windy afternoon when Durnover church clock struck five. While the gusts were bringing the notes to his ears across the damp intervening flat a man passed behind him and greeted Henchard by name. Henchard turned slightly and saw that the corner was Jopp, his old foreman, now employed elsewhere, to whom, though he hated him, he had gone for lodgings because Jopp was the one man in Casterbridge whose observation and opinion the fallen corn-merchant despised to the point of indifference.

Henchard returned him a scarcely perceptible nod, and Jopp stopped.

"He and she are gone into their new house to-day," said Jopp.

"Oh," said Henchard absently. "Which house is that?"

"Your old one."

"Gone into my house?" And starting up Henchard added, " MY house of all others in the town!"

"Well, as somebody was sure to live there, and you couldn't, it can do 'ee no harm that he's the man."

It was quite true: he felt that it was doing him no harm. Farfrae, who had already taken the yards and stores, had acquired possession of the house for the obvious convenience of its contiguity. And yet this act of his taking up residence within those roomy chambers while he, their former tenant, lived in a cottage, galled Henchard indescribably.

Jopp continued: "And you heard of that fellow who bought all the best furniture at your sale? He was bidding for no other than Farfrae all the while! It has never been moved out of the house, as he'd already got the lease."

"My furniture too! Surely he'll buy my body and soul

likewise!" "There's no saying he won't, if you be willing to sell." And having planted these wounds in the heart of his once imperious master Jopp went on his way; while Henchard stared and stared into the racing river till the bridge seemed moving backward with him.

The low land grew blacker, and the sky a deeper grey, When the landscape looked like a picture blotted in with ink, another traveller approached the great stone bridge. He was driving a gig, his direction being also townwards. On the round of the middle of the arch the gig stopped. "Mr Henchard?" came from it in the voice of Farfrae. Henchard turned his face.

Finding that he had guessed rightly Farfrae told the man who accompanied him to drive home; while he alighted and went up to his former friend.

"I have heard that you think of emigrating, Mr. Henchard?" he said. "Is it true? I have a real reason for asking."

Henchard withheld his answer for several instants, and then said, "Yes; it is true. I am going where you were going to a few years ago, when I prevented you and got you to bide here. 'Tis turn and turn about, isn't it! Do ye mind how we stood like this in the Chalk Walk when I persuaded 'ee to stay? You then stood without a chattel to your name, and I was the master of the house in corn Street. But now I stand without a stick or a rag, and the master of that house is you."

"Yes, yes; that's so! It's the way o' the warrld," said Farfrae.

"Ha, ha, true!" cried Henchard, throwing himself into a mood of jocularity. "Up and down! I'm used to it. What's the odds after all!"

"Now listen to me, if it's no taking up your time," said Farfrae, "just as I listened to you. Don't go. Stay at home."

"But I can do nothing else, man!" said Henchard scornfully. "The little money I have will just keep body and soul together for a few weeks, and no more. I have not felt inclined to go back to journey-work yet; but I can't stay doing nothing, and my best chance is elsewhere."

"No; but what I propose is this-if ye will listen. Come and live in your old house. We can spare some rooms very well-I am sure my wife would not mind it at all-until there's an opening for ye."

Henchard started. Probably the picture drawn by the unsuspecting Donald of himself under the same roof with Lucetta was too striking to be received with equanimity. "No, no," he said gruffly; "we should quarrel."

"You should hae a part to yourself," said Farfrae; "and nobody to interfere wi' you. It will be a deal healthier than down there by the river where you live now."

Still Henchard refused. "You don't know what you ask," he said. "However, I can do no less than thank 'ee."

They walked into the town together side by side, as they had done when Henchard persuaded the young Scotchman to remain. "Will you come in and have some supper?" said Farfrae when they reached the middle of the town, where their paths diverged right and left.

"No, no."

"By-the-bye, I had nearly forgot. I bought a good deal of your furniture.

"So I have heard."

"Well, it was no that I wanted it so very much for myself; but I wish ye to pick out all that you care to have-such things as may be endeared to ye by associations, or particularly suited to your use. And take them to your own house-it will not be depriving me, we can do with less very well, and I will have plenty of opportunities of getting more."

"What-give it to me for nothing?" said Henchard. "But you paid the creditors for it!"

"Ah, yes; but maybe it's worth more to you than it is to me."

Henchard was a little moved. "I-sometimes think I've wronged 'ee!" he said, in tones which showed the disquietude that the night shades hid in his face. He shook Farfrae abruptly by the hand, and hastened away as if unwilling to betray himself further. Farfrae saw him turn through the thoroughfare into Bull Stake and vanish down towards the Priory Mill.

Meanwhile Elizabeth-Jane, in an upper room no larger than the Prophet's chamber, and with the silk attire of her palmy days packed away in a box, was netting with great industry between the hours which she devoted to studying such books as she could get hold of.

Her lodgings being nearly opposite her stepfather's former residence, now Farfrae's, she could see Donald and Lucetta speeding in and out of their door with all the bounding enthusiasm of their situation. She avoided looking that way as much as possible, but it was hardly in human nature to keep the eyes averted when the door slammed.

While living on thus quietly she heard the news that Henchard had caught cold and was confined to his room-possibly a result of standing about the meads in damp weather. She went off to his house at once. This time she was determined not to be denied admittance, and made her way upstairs. He was sitting up in the bed with a greatcoat round him, and at first resented her intrusion. "Go away-go away," he said. "I don't like to see 'ee!"

"But, father-"

"I don't like to see 'ee," he repeated.

However, the ice was broken, and she remained. She made the room more comfortable, gave directions to the people below, and by the time she went away had reconciled her stepfather to her visiting him.

The effect, either of her ministrations or of her mere presence, was a rapid recovery. He soon was well enough to go out; and now things seemed to wear a new colour in his eyes. He no longer thought of emigration, and thought more of Elizabeth. The having nothing to do made him more dreary than any other circumstance; and one day, with better views of Farfrae than he had held for some time, and a sense that honest work was not a thing to be ashamed of, he stoically went down to Farfrae's yard and asked to be taken on as a journeyman hay-trusser. He was engaged at once. This hiring of Henchard was done through a foreman, Farfrae feeling that it was undesirable to come personally in contact with the ex-corn-factor more than was absolutely necessary. While anxious to help him he was well aware by this time of his uncertain temper, and thought reserved relations best. For the same reason his orders to Henchard to proceed to this and that country farm trussing in the usual way were always given through a third person.

For a time these arrangements worked well, it being the custom to truss in the respective stack-yards, before bringing it away, the hay bought at the different farms about the neighbourhood; so that Henchard was often absent at such places the whole week long. When this was all done, and Henchard had become in a measure broken in, he came to work daily on the home premises like the rest. And thus the once flourishing merchant and Mayor and what not stood as a day-labourer in the barns and granaries he formerly had owned.

"I have worked as a journeyman before now, ha'n't I?" he would say in his defiant way; "and why shouldn't I do it again?" But he looked a far different journeyman from the one he had been in his earlier days. Then he had worn clean, suitable clothes, light and cheerful in hue; leggings yellow as marigolds, corduroys immaculate as new flax, and a neckerchief like a flower-garden. Now he wore the remains of an old blue cloth suit of his gentlemanly times, a rusty silk hat, and a once black satin stock, soiled and shabby. Clad thus he went to and fro, still comparatively an active man-for he was not much over forty-and saw with the other men in the yard Donald Farfrae going in and out the green door that led to the garden, and the big house, and Lucetta.

At the beginning of the winter it was rumoured about Casterbridge that Mr. Farfrae, already in the Town Council, was to be proposed for Mayor in a year or two.

"Yes, she was wise, she was wise in her generation!" said Henchard to himself when he heard of this one day on his way to Farfrae's hay-barn. He thought it over as he wimbled his bonds, and the piece of news acted as a reviviscent breath to that old view of his-of Donald Farfrae as his triumphant rival who rode rough-shod over him.

"A fellow of his age going to be Mayor, indeed!" he murmured with a corner-drawn smile on his mouth. "But 'tis her money that floats en upward. Ha-ha-how cust odd it is!

Here be I, his former master, working for him as man, and he the man standing as master, with my house and my furniture and my what-you-may-call wife all his own."

He repeated these things a hundred times a day. During the whole period of his acquaintance with Lucetta he had never wished to claim her as his own so desperately as he now regretted her loss. It was no mercenary hankering after her fortune that moved him, though that fortune had been the means of making her so much the more desired by giving her the air of independence and sauciness which attracts men of his composition. It had given her servants, house, and fine clothing-a setting that invested Lucetta with a startling novelty in the eyes of him who had known her in her narrow days.

He accordingly lapsed into moodiness, and at every allusion to the possibility of Farfrae's near election to the municipal chair his former hatred of the Scotchman returned. Concurrently with this he underwent a moral change. It resulted in his significantly saying every now and then, in tones of recklessness, "Only a fortnight more!"-"Only a dozen days!" and so forth, lessening his figures day by day.

"Why d'ye say only a dozen days?" asked Solomon Longways as he worked beside Henchard in the granary weighing oats.

"Because in twelve days I shall be released from my oath."

"What oath?"

"The oath to drink no spirituous liquid. In twelve days it will be twenty-one years since I swore it, and then I mean to enjoy myself, please God!"

Elizabeth-Jane sat at her window one Sunday, and while there she heard in the street below a conversation which introduced Henchard's name. She was wondering what was the matter, when a third person who was passing by asked the question in her mind. "Michael Henchard have busted out drinking after taking nothing for twenty-one years!" Elizabeth-Jane jumped up, put on her things, and went out.

Chapter 34

Next morning, accordingly, she rose at five o'clock and

went into the street. It was not yet light; a dense fog prevailed, and the town was as silent as it was dark, except that from the rectangular avenues which framed in the borough there came a chorus of tiny rappings, caused by the fall of water-drops condensed on the boughs; now it was wafted from the West Walk, now from the South Walk; and then from both quarters simultaneously. She moved on to the bottom of corn Street, and, knowing his time well, waited only a few minutes before she heard the familiar bang of his door, and then his quick walk towards her. She met him at the point where the last tree of the engirding avenue flanked the last house in the street.

He could hardly discern her till, glancing inquiringly, he said, "What-Miss Henchard-and are ye up so airly?"

She asked him to pardon her for waylaying him at such an unseemly time. "But I am anxious to mention something," she said. "And I wished not to alarm Mrs. Farfrae by calling."

"Yes?" said he, with the cheeriness of a superior. "And what may it be? It's very kind of ye, I'm sure."

She now felt the difficulty of conveying to his mind the exact aspect of possibilities in her own. But she somehow began, and introduced Henchard's name. "I sometimes fear," she said with an effort, "that he may be betrayed into some attempt to-insult you, sir.

"But we are the best of friends?"

"Or to play some practical joke upon you, sir. Remember that he has been hardly used."

"But we are quite friendly?"

"Or to do something-that would injure you-hurt you-wound you." Every word cost her twice its length of pain. And she could see that Farfrae was still incredulous. Henchard, a poor man in his employ, was not to Farfrae's view the Henchard who had ruled him. Yet he was not only the same man, but that man with his sinister qualities, formerly latent, quickened into life by his buffetings.

Farfrae, happy, and thinking no evil, persisted in making light of her fears. Thus they parted, and she went homeward, journeymen now being in the street, waggoners going to the harness-makers for articles left to be repaired, farm-horses going to the shoeing-smiths, and the sons of labour showing themselves generally on the move. Elizabeth entered her lodging unhappily, thinking she had done no good, and only made herself appear foolish by her weak note of warning.

But Donald Farfrae was one of those men upon whom an incident is never absolutely lost. He revised impressions from a subsequent point of view, and the impulsive judgment of the moment was not always his permanent one. The vision of Elizabeth's earnest face in the rimy dawn came back to him several times during the day. Knowing the solidity of her character he did not treat her hints altogether as idle sounds.

But he did not desist from a kindly scheme on Henchard's account that engaged him just then; and when he met Lawyer Joyce, the town-clerk, later in the day, he spoke of it as if nothing had occurred to damp it.

"About that little seedsman's shop," he said, "the shop overlooking the churchyard, which is to let. It is not for myself I want it, but for our unlucky fellow-townsman Henchard. It would be a new beginning for him, if a small one; and I have told the Council that I would head a private subscription among them to set him up in it-that I would be fifty pounds, if they would make up the other fifty among them."

"Yes, yes; so I've heard; and there's nothing to say against it for that matter," the town-clerk replied, in his plain, frank way. "But, Farfrae, others see what you don't. Henchard hates 'ee-ay, hates 'ee; and 'tis right that you should know it. To my knowledge he was at the Three Mariners last night, saying in public that about you which a man ought not to say about another."

"Is that so-ah, is that so?" said Farfrae, looking down. "Why should he do it?" added the young man bitterly; "what harm have I done him that he should try to wrong me?"

"God only knows," said Joyce, lifting his eyebrows. "It shows much long-suffering in you to put up with him, and keep him in your employ."

"But I cannet discharge a man who was once a good friend to me. How can I forget that when I came here 'twas he enabled me to make a footing for mysel'? No, no. As long as I've a day's work to offer he shall do it if he chooses. 'Tis not I who will deny him such a little as that. But I'll drop the idea of establishing him in a shop till I can think more about it."

It grieved Farfrae much to give up this scheme. But a damp having been thrown over it by these and other voices in the air, he went and countermanded his orders. The then occupier of the shop was in it when Farfrae spoke to him and feeling it necessary to give some explanation of his withdrawal from the negotiation Donald mentioned Henchard's name, and stated that the intentions of the Council had been changed.

The occupier was much disappointed, and straight-way informed Henchard, as soon as he saw him, that a scheme of the Council for setting him up in a shop had been knocked on the head by Farfrae. And thus out of error enmity grew.

When Farfrae got indoors that evening the tea-kettle was singing on the high hob of the semi-egg-shaped grate. Lucetta, light as a sylph, ran forward and seized his hands, whereupon Farfrae duly kissed her.

"Oh!" she cried playfully, turning to the window. "See-the blinds are not drawn down, and the people can look in-what a scandal!"

When the candles were lighted, the curtains drawn, and the twain sat at tea, she noticed that he looked serious. Without directly inquiring why she let her eyes linger solicitously on his face.

"Who has called?" he absently asked. "Any folk for me?"

"No," said Lucetta. "What's the matter, Donald?"

"Well-nothing worth talking of," he responded sadly.

"Then, never mind it. You will get through it, Scotchmen are always lucky."

"No-not always!" he said, shaking his head gloomily as he contemplated a crumb on the table. "I know many who have not been so! There was Sandy Macfarlane, who started to America to try his fortune, and he was drowned; and Archibald Leith, he was murdered! And poor Willie Dunbleeze and Maitland Macfreeze-they fell into bad courses, and went the way of all such!"

"Why-you old goosey-I was only speaking in a general

sense, of course! You are always so literal. Now when we have finished tea, sing me that funny song about high-heeled shoon and siller tags, and the one-and-forty wooers."

"No, no. I couldna sing to-night! It's Henchard-he hates me; so that I may not be his friend if I would. I would understand why there should be a wee bit of envy; but I cannet see a reason for the whole intensity of what he feels. Now, can you, Lucetta? It is more like old-fashioned rivalry in love than just a bit of rivalry in trade."

Lucetta had grown somewhat wan. "No," she replied.

"I give him employment-I cannet refuse it. But neither can I blind myself to the fact that with a man of passions such as his, there is no safeguard for conduct!"

"What have you heard-O Donald, dearest?" said Lucetta in alarm. The words on her lips were "anything about me?"-but she did not utter them. She could not, however, suppress her agitation, and her eyes filled with tears.

"No, no-it is not so serious as ye fancy," declared Farfrae soothingly; though he did not know its seriousness so well as she.

"I wish you would do what we have talked of," mournfully remarked Lucetta. "Give up business, and go away from here. We have plenty of money, and why should we stay?"

Farfrae seemed seriously disposed to discuss this move, and they talked thereon till a visitor was announced. Their neighbour Alderman Vatt came in.

"You've heard, I suppose of poor Doctor Chalkfield's death? Yes-died this afternoon at five," said Mr. Vatt Chalkfield was the Councilman who had succeeded to the Mayoralty in the preceding November.

Farfrae was sorry at the intelligence, and Mr. Vatt continued: "Well, we know he's been going some days, and as his family is well provided for we must take it all as it is. Now I have called to ask 'ee this-quite privately. If I should nominate 'ee to succeed him, and there should be no particular opposition, will 'ee accept the chair?"

"But there are folk whose turn is before mine; and I'm over

young, and may be thought pushing!" said Farfrae after a pause.

"Not at all. I don't speak for myself only, several have named it. You won't refuse?"

"We thought of going away," interposed Lucetta, looking at Farfrae anxiously.

"It was only a fancy," Farfrae murmured. "I wouldna refuse if it is the wish of a respectable majority in the Council."

"Very well, then, look upon yourself as elected. We have had older men long enough."

When he was gone Farfrae said musingly, "See now how it's ourselves that are ruled by the Powers above us! We plan this, but we do that. If they want to make me Mayor I will stay, and Henchard must rave as he will."

From this evening onward Lucetta was very uneasy. If she had not been imprudence incarnate she would not have acted as she did when she met Henchard by accident a day or two later. It was in the bustle of the market, when no one could readily notice their discourse.

"Michael," said she, "I must again ask you what I asked you months ago-to return me any letters or papers of mine that you may have-unless you have destroyed them? You must see how desirable it is that the time at Jersey should be blotted out, for the good of all parties."

"Why, bless the woman!-I packed up every scrap of your handwriting to give you in the coach-but you never appeared."

She explained how the death of her aunt had prevented her taking the journey on that day. "And what became of the parcel then?" she asked.

He could not say-he would consider. When she was gone he recollected that he had left a heap of useless papers in his former dining-room safe-built up in the wall of his old house-now occupied by Farfrae. The letters might have been amongst them.

A grotesque grin shaped itself on Henchard's face. Had that safe been opened?

On the very evening which followed this there was a great ringing of bells in Casterbridge, and the combined brass, wood, catgut, and leather bands played round the town with more prodigality of percussion-notes than ever. Farfrae was Mayor-the two-hundredth odd of a series forming an elective dynasty dating back to the days of Charles I-and the fair Lucetta was the courted of the town....But, Ah! the worm i' the bud-Henchard; what he could tell!

He, in the meantime, festering with indignation at some erroneous intelligence of Farfrae's opposition to the scheme for installing him in the little seed-shop, was greeted with the news of the municipal election (which, by reason of Farfrae's comparative youth and his Scottish nativity-a thing unprecedented in the case-had an interest far beyond the ordinary). The bell-ringing and the band-playing, loud as Tamerlane's trumpet, goaded the downfallen Henchard indescribably: the ousting now seemed to him to be complete.

The next morning he went to the corn-yard as usual, and about eleven o'clock Donald entered through the green door, with no trace of the worshipful about him. The yet more emphatic change of places between him and Henchard which this election had established renewed a slight embarrassment in the manner of the modest young man; but Henchard showed the front of one who had overlooked all this; and Farfrae met his amenities half-way at once.

"I was going to ask you," said Henchard, "about a packet that I may possibly have left in my old safe in the." He added particulars.

"If so, it is there now," said Farfrae. "I have never opened the safe at all as yet; for I keep ma papers at the bank, to sleep easy o' nights."

"It was not of much consequence-to me," said Henchard. "But I'll call for it this evening, if you don't mind?"

It was quite late when he fulfilled his promise. He had primed himself with grog, as he did very frequently now, and a curl of sardonic humour hung on his lip as he approached the house, as though he were contemplating some terrible form of amusement. Whatever it was, the incident of his entry did not diminish its force, this being his first visit to the house since he had lived there as owner. The ring of the bell spoke to him like the voice of a familiar drudge who had been bribed to forsake him; the movements of the doors were revivals of dead days.

Farfrae invited him into the dining-room, where he at once unlocked the iron safe built into the wall, HIS, Henchard's safe, made by an ingenious locksmith under his direction. Farfrae drew thence the parcel, ar d other papers, with apologies for not having returned them.

"Never mind," said Henchard drily. "The fact is they are letters mostly....Yes," he went on, sitting down and unfolding Lucetta's passionate bundle, "here they be. That ever I should see 'em again! I hope Mrs. Farfrae is well after her exertions of yesterday?"

"She has felt a bit weary; and has gone to bed airly on that account.

Henchard returned to the letters, sorting them over with interest, Farfrae being seated at the other end of the dining-table. "You don't forget, of course," he resumed, "that curious chapter in the history of my past which I told you of, and that you gave me some assistance in? These letters are, in fact, related to that unhappy business. Though, thank God, it is all over now."

"What became of the poor woman?" asked Farfrae.

"Luckily she married, and married well," said Henchard. "So that these reproaches she poured out on me do not now cause me any twinges, as they might otherwise have done....Just listen to what an angry woman will say!"

Farfrae, willing to humour Henchard, though quite uninterested, and bursting with yawns, gave well-mannered attention.

"'For me,'" Henchard read, "'there is practically no future. A creature too unconventionally devoted to you-who feels it impossible that she can be the wife of any other man; and who is yet no more to you than the first woman you meet in the street-such am I. I quite acquit you of any intention to wrong me, yet you are the door through which wrong has come to me. That in the event of your present wife's death you will place me in her position is a consolation so far as it goes-but how far does it go? Thus I sit here, forsaken by my few acquaintance, and forsaken by you!'"

"That's how she went on to me," said Henchard, "acres of words like that, when what had happened was what I could not cure."

"Yes," said Farfrae absently, "it is the way wi' women." But the fact was that he knew very little of the sex; yet detecting a sort of resemblance in style between the effusions of the woman he worshipped and those of the supposed stranger, he concluded that Aphrodite ever spoke thus, whosesoever the personality she assumed.

Henchard unfolded another letter, and read it through likewise, stopping at the subscription as before. "Her name I don't give," he said blandly. "As I didn't marry her, and another man did, I can scarcely do that in fairness to her."

"Tr-rue, tr-rue," said Farfrae. "But why didn't you marry her when your wife Susan died?" Farfrae asked this and the other questions in the comfortably indifferent tone of one whom the matter very remotely concerned.

"Ah-well you may ask that!" said Henchard, the new-grin adumbrating itself again upon his mouth. "In spite of all her protestations, when I came forward to do so, as in generosity bound, she was not the woman for me."

"She had already married another-maybe?"

Henchard seemed to think it would be sailing too near the wind to descend further into particulars, and he answered "Yes."

"The young lady must have had a heart that bore transplanting very readily!"

"She had, she had," said Henchard emphatically.

He opened a third and fourth letter, and read. This time he approached the conclusion as if the signature were indeed coming with the rest. But again he stopped short. The truth was that, as may be divined, he had quite intended to effect a grand catastrophe at the end of this drama by reading out the name, he had come to the house with no other thought. But sitting here in cold blood he could not do it. Such a wrecking of hearts appalled even him. His quality was such that he could have annihilated them both in the heat of action; but to accomplish the deed by oral poison was beyond the nerve of his enmity.

Chapter 36

Returning from her appointment Lucetta saw a man waiting by the lamp nearest to her own door. When she stopped to go in he came and spoke to her. It was Jopp.

He begged her pardon for addressing her. But he had heard that Mr. Farfrae had been applied to by a neighbouring to recommend a working partner; if so he wished to offer himself. He could give good security, and had stated as much to Mr. Farfrae in a letter; but he would feel much obliged if Lucetta would say a word in his favour to her husband.

"It is a thing I know nothing about," said Lucetta coldly.

"But you can testify to my trustworthiness better than anybody, ma'am," said Jopp. "I was in Jersey several years, and knew you there by sight."

"Indeed," she replied. "But I knew nothing of you."

"I think, ma'am, that a word or two from you would secure for me what I covet very much," he persisted.

She steadily refused to have anything to do with the affair, and cutting him short, because of her anxiety to get indoors before her husband should miss her, left him on the pavement.

He watched her till she had vanished, and then went home. When he got there he sat down in the fireless chimney corner looking at the iron dogs, and the wood laid across them for heating the morning kettle. A movement upstairs disturbed him, and Henchard came down from his bedroom, where he seemed to have been rummaging boxes.

"I wish," said Henchard, "you would do me a service, Jopp, now-to-night, I mean, if you can. Leave this at Mrs. Farfrae's for her. I should take it myself, of course, but I don't wish to be seen there." He handed a package in brown paper, sealed. Henchard had been as good as his word. Immediately on coming indoors he had searched over his few belongings, and every scrap of Lucetta's writing that he possessed was here. Jopp indifferently expressed his willingness.

"Well, how have ye got on to-day?" his lodger asked. "Any prospect of an opening?"

"I am afraid not," said Jopp, who had not told the other of his application to Farfrae.

"There never will be in Casterbridge," declared Henchard decisively. "You must roam further afield." He said to Jopp, and returned to his own part of the house.

Jopp sat on till his eyes were attracted by the shadow of the candle-snuff on the wall, and looking at the original he found that it had formed itself into a head like a red-hot cauliflower. Henchard's packet next met his gaze. He knew there had been something of the nature of wooing between Henchard and the now Mrs. Farfrae; and his vague ideas on the subject narrowed themselves down to these: Henchard had a parcel belonging to Mrs. Farfrae, and he had reasons for not returning that parcel to her in person. What could be inside it? So he went on and on till, animated by resentment at Lucetta's haughtiness, as he thought it, and curiosity to learn if there were any weak sides to this transaction with Henchard, he examined the package. The pen and all its relations being awkward tools in Henchard's hands he had affixed the seals without an impression, it never occurring to him that the efficacy of such a fastening depended on this. Jopp was far less of a tyro; he lifted one of the seals with his penknife, peeped in at the end thus opened, saw that the bundle consisted of letters; and, having satisfied himself thus far, sealed up the end again by simply softening the wax with the candle, and went off with the parcel as requested.

His path was by the river-side at the foot of the town. Coming into the light at the bridge which stood at the end of High Street he beheld lounging thereon Mother Cuxsom and Nance Mockridge.

"We be just going down Mixen Lane way, to look into Peter's finger afore creeping to bed," said Mrs. Cuxsom. "There's a fiddle and tambourine going on there. Lord, what's all the world-do ye come along too, Jopp-'twon't hinder ye five minutes."

Jopp had mostly kept himself out of this company, but

present circumstances made him somewhat more reckless than usual, and without many words he decided to go to his destination that way. Though the upper part of Durnover was mainly composed of a curious congeries of barns and farm-steads, there was a less picturesque side to the parish. This was Mixen Lane, now in great part pulled down.

Mixen Lane was the Adullam of all the surrounding villages. It was the hiding-place of those who were in distress, and in debt, and trouble of every kind. Farm-labourers and other peasants, who combined a little poaching with their farming, and a little brawling and bibbing with their poaching, found themselves sooner or later in Mixen Lane. Rural mechanics too idle to mechanize, rural servants too rebellious to serve, drifted or were forced into Mixen Lane.

The lane and its surrounding thicket of thatched cottages stretched out like a spit into the moist and misty lowland. Much that was sad, much that was low, some things that were baneful, could be seen in Mixen Lane. Vice ran freely in and out certain of the doors in the neighbourhood; recklessness dwelt under the roof with the crooked chimney; shame in some bow-windows; theft (in times of privation) in the thatched and mud-walled houses by the sallows. Even slaughter had not been altogether unknown here. In a block of cottages up an alley there might have been erected an altar to disease in years gone by. Such was Mixen Lane in the times when Henchard and Farfrae were Mayors.

Yet this mildewed leaf in the sturdy and flourishing Casterbridge plant lay close to the open country; not a hundred yards from a row of noble elms, and commanding a view across the moor of airy uplands and corn-fields, and mansions of the great. A brook divided the moor from the tenements, and to outward view there was no way across it-no way to the houses but round about by the road. But under every householder's stairs there was kept a mysterious plank nine inches wide; which plank was a secret bridge.

If you, as one of those refugee householders, came in from business after dark-and this was the business time here-you stealthily crossed the moor, approached the border of the aforesaid brook, and whistled opposite the house to which you belonged. A shape thereupon made its appearance on the other side bearing the bridge on end against the sky; it was lowered; you crossed, and a hand helped you to land yourself, together with the pheasants and hares gathered from neighbouring manors. You sold them slily the next morning, and the day after you stood before the magistrates with the eyes of all your sympathizing neighbours concentrated on your back. You disappeared for a time; then you were again found quietly living in Mixen Lane.

Walking along the lane at dusk the stranger was struck by two or three peculiar features therein. One was an intermittent rumbling from the back premises of the inn half-way up; this meant a skittle alley. Another was the extensive prevalence of whistling in the various domiciles-a piped note of some kind coming from nearly every open door. Another was the frequency of white aprons over dingy gowns among the women around the doorways. A white apron is a suspicious vesture in situations where spotlessness is difficult; moreover, the industry and cleanliness which the white apron expressed were belied by the postures and gaits of the women who wore it-their knuckles being mostly on their hips (an attitude which lent them the aspect of two-handled mugs), and their shoulders against door-posts; while there was a curious alacrity in the turn of each honest woman's head upon her neck-and in the twirl of her honest eyes, at any noise resembling a masculine footfall along the lane.

Yet amid so much that was bad needy respectability also found a home. Under some of the roofs abode pure and virtuous souls whose presence there was due to the iron hand of necessity, and to that alone. Families from decayed villages-families of that once bulky, but now nearly extinct, section of village society called "liviers," or lifeholders-copyholders and others, whose roof-trees had fallen for some reason or other, compelling them to quit the rural spot that had been their home for generations-came here, unless they chose to lie under a hedge by the wayside.

The inn called Peter's finger was the church of Mixen Lane.

It was centrally situate, as such places should be, and bore about the same social relation to the Three Mariners as the latter bore to the King's Arms. At first sight the inn was so respectable as to be puzzling. The front door was kept shut, and the step was so clean that evidently but few persons entered over its sanded surface. But at the corner of the public-house was an alley, a mere slit, dividing it from the next building. Half-way up the alley was a narrow door, shiny and paintless from the rub of infinite hands and shoulders. This was the actual entrance to the inn.

A pedestrian would be seen abstractedly passing along Mixen Lane; and then, in a moment, he would vanish, causing the gazer to blink like Ashton at the disappearance of Ravenswood. That abstracted pedestrian had edged into the slit by the adroit fillip of his person sideways; from the slit he edged into the tavern by a similar exercise of skill.

The company at the Three Mariners were persons of quality in comparison with the company which gathered here; though it must be admitted that the lowest fringe of the Mariner's party touched the crest of Peter's at points. Waifs and strays of all sorts loitered about here. The landlady was a virtuous woman who years ago had been unjustly sent to gaol as an accessory to something or other after the fact. She underwent her twelvemonth, and had worn a martyr's countenance ever since, except at times of meeting the constable who apprehended her, when she winked her eye.

To this house Jopp and his acquaintances had arrived. The settles on which they sat down were thin and tall, their tops being guyed by pieces of twine to hooks in the ceiling; for when the guests grew boisterous the settles would rock and overturn without some such security. The thunder of bowls echoed from the backyard; swingels hung behind the blower of the chimney; and ex-poachers and ex-gamekeepers, whom squires had persecuted without a cause, sat elbowing each other-men who in past times had met in fights under the moon, till lapse of sentences on the one part, and loss of favour and expulsion from service on the other, brought them here together to a common level, where they sat calmly discussing old times.

"Dost mind how you could jerk a trout ashore with a bramble, and not ruffle the stream, Charl?" a deposed keeper was saying. "'Twas at that I caught 'ee once, if you can mind?"

"That I can. But the worst larry for me was that pheasant business at Yalbury Wood. Your wife swore false that time, Joe-O, by Gad, she did-there's no denying it."

"How was that?" asked Jopp.

"Why-Joe closed wi' me, and we rolled down together, close to his garden hedge. Hearing the noise, out ran his wife with the oven pyle, and it being dark under the trees she couldn't see which was uppermost. 'Where beest thee, Joe, under or top?' she screeched. 'O-under, by Gad!' says he. She then began to rap down upon my skull, back, and ribs with the pyle till we'd roll over again. 'Where beest now, dear Joe, under or top?' she'd scream again. By George, 'twas through her I was took! And then when we got up in hall she sware that the cock pheasant was one of her rearing, when 'twas not your bird at all, Joe; 'twas Squire Brown's bird-that's whose 'twas-one that we'd picked off as we passed his wood, an hour afore. It did hurt my feelings to be so wronged!...Ah well-'tis over now."

"I might have had 'ee days afore that," said the keeper. "I was within a few yards of 'ee dozens of times, with a sight more of birds than that poor one."

"Yes-'tis not our greatest doings that the world gets wind of," said the furmity-woman, who, lately settled in this purlieu, sat among the rest. Having travelled a great deal in her time she spoke with cosmopolitan largeness of idea. It was she who presently asked Jopp what was the parcel he kept so snugly under his arm.

"Ah, therein lies a grand secret," said Jopp. "It is the passion of love. To think that a woman should love one man so well, and hate another so unmercifully."

"Who's the object of your meditation, sir?"

"One that stands high in this town. I'd like to shame her! Upon my life, 'twould be as good as a play to read her, the proud piece of silk and wax-work! For 'tis her love-letters that I've got here."

"Love letters? then let's hear 'em, good soul," said Mother Cuxsom. "Lord, do ye mind, Richard, what fools we used to be when we were younger? Getting a schoolboy to write ours for us; and giving him a penny, do ye mind, not to tell other folks what he'd put inside, do ye mind?"

By this time Jopp had pushed his finger under the seals, and unfastened the letters, tumbling them over and picking up one here and there at random, which he read aloud. These passages soon began to uncover the secret which Lucetta had so earnestly hoped to keep buried, though the epistles, being allusive only, did not make it altogether plain.

"Mrs. Farfrae wrote that!" said Nance Mockridge. "'Tis a humbling thing for us, as respectable women, that one of the same sex could do it. And now she's avowed herself to another man!"

"So much the better for her," said the aged furmity-woman. "Ah, I saved her from a real bad marriage, and she's never been the one to thank me." "I say, what a good foundation for a skimmity-ride," said Nance.

"True," said Mrs. Cuxsom, reflecting. "'Tis as good a ground for a skimmity-ride as ever I knowed; and it ought not to be wasted. The last one seen in Casterbridge must have been ten years ago, if a day."

At this moment there was a shrill whistle, and the landlady said to the man who had been called Charl, "'Tis Jim coming in. Would ye go and let down the bridge for me?"

Without replying Charl and his comrade Joe rose, and receiving a lantern from her went out at the back door and down the garden-path, which ended abruptly at the edge of the stream already mentioned. Beyond the stream was the open moor, from which a clammy breeze smote upon their faces as they advanced. Taking up the board that had lain in readiness one of them lowered it across the water, and the instant its further end touched the ground footsteps entered upon it, and there appeared from the shade a stalwart man with straps round his knees, a double-barrelled gun under his arm and some birds slung up behind him. They asked him if he had had much luck.

"Not much," he said indifferently. "All safe inside?"

Receiving a reply in the affirmative he went on inwards, the others withdrawing the bridge and beginning to retreat in his rear. Before, however, they had entered the house a cry of "Ahoy" from the moor led them to pause.

The cry was repeated. They pushed the lantern into an outhouse, and went back to the brink of the stream.

"Ahoy-is this the way to Casterbridge?" said some one from the other side.

"Not in particular," said Charl. "There's a river afore 'ee."

"I don't care-here's for through it!" said the man in the moor. "I've had travelling enough for to-day."

"Stop a minute, then," said Charl, finding that the man was no enemy. "Joe, bring the plank and lantern; here's somebody that's lost his way. You should have kept along the turnpike road, friend, and not have strook across here."

"I should-as I see now. But I saw a light here, and says I to myself, that's an outlying house, depend on't."

The plank was now lowered; and the stranger's form shaped itself from the darkness. He was a middle-aged man, with hair and whiskers prematurely grey, and a broad and genial face. He had crossed on the plank without hesitation, and seemed to see nothing odd in the transit. He thanked them, and walked between them up the garden. "What place is this?" he asked, when they reached the door.

"A public-house."

"Ah, perhaps it will suit me to put up at. Now then, come in and wet your whistle at my expense for the lift over you have given me."

They followed him into the inn, where the increased light exhibited him as one who would stand higher in an estimate by the eye than in one by the ear. He was dressed with a certain clumsy richness-his coat being furred, and his head covered by a cap of seal-skin, which, though the nights were chilly, must have been warm for the daytime, spring being somewhat advanced. In his hand he carried a small mahogany case, strapped, and clamped with brass.

Apparently surprised at the kind of company which

confronted him through the kitchen door, he at once abandoned his idea of putting up at the house; but taking the situation lightly, he called for glasses of the best, paid for them as he stood in the passage, and turned to proceed on his way by the front door. This was barred, and while the landlady was unfastening it the conversation about the skimmington was continued in the sitting-room, and reached his ears.

"What do they mean by a 'skimmity-ride'?" he asked.

"O, sir!" said the landlady, swinging her long earrings with deprecating modesty; "'tis a' old foolish thing they do in these parts when a man's wife is-well, not too particularly his own. But as a respectable householder I don't encourage it.

"Still, are they going to do it shortly? It is a good sight to see, I suppose?"

"Well, sir!" she simpered. And then, bursting into naturalness, and glancing from the corner of her eye, "'Tis the funniest thing under the sun! And it costs money."

"Ah! I remember hearing of some such thing. Now I shall be in Casterbridge for two or three weeks to come, and should not mind seeing the performance. Wait a moment." He turned back, entered the sitting-room, and said, "Here, good folks; I should like to see the old custom you are talking of, and I don't mind being something towards it-take that." He threw a sovereign on the table and returned to the landlady at the door, of whom, having inquired the way into the town, he took his leave.

"There were more where that one came from," said Charl when the sovereign had been taken up and handed to the landlady for safe keeping. "By George! we ought to have got a few more while we had him here."

"No, no," answered the landlady. "This is a respectable house, thank God! And I'll have nothing done but what's honourable."

"Well," said Jopp; "now we'll consider the business begun, and will soon get it in train."

"We will!" said Nance. "A good laugh warms my heart more than a cordial, and that's the truth on't."

Jopp gathered up the letters, and it being now somewhat

late he did not attempt to call at Farfrae's with them that night. He reached home, sealed them up as before, and delivered the parcel at its address next morning. Within an hour its contents were reduced to ashes by Lucetta, who, poor soul! was inclined to fall down on her knees in thankfulness that at last no evidence remained of the unlucky episode with Henchard in her past. For though hers had been rather the laxity of inadvertence than of intention, that episode, if known, was not the less likely to operate fatally between herself and her husband.

Chapter 38

The proceedings had been brief-too brief-to Lucetta whom an intoxicating Weltlust had fairly mastered; but they had brought her a great triumph nevertheless. The shake of the Royal hand still lingered in her fingers; and the she had overheard, that her husband might possibly receive the honour of knighthood, though idle to a degree, seemed not the wildest vision; stranger things had occurred to men so good and captivating as her Scotchman was.

After the collision with the Mayor, Henchard had withdrawn behind the ladies' stand; and there he stood, regarding with a stare of abstraction the spot on the lapel of his coat where Farfrae's hand had seized it. He put his own hand there, as if he could hardly realize such an outrage from one whom it had once been his wont to treat with ardent generosity. While pausing in this half-stupefied state the conversation of Lucetta with the other ladies reached his ears; and he distinctly heard her deny him-deny that he had assisted Donald, that he was anything more than a common journeyman.

He moved on homeward, and met Jopp in the archway to the Bull Stake. "So you've had a snub," said Jopp.

"And what if I have?" answered Henchard sternly.

"Why, I've had one too, so we are both under the same cold shade." He briefly related his attempt to win Lucetta's intercession.

Henchard merely heard his story, without taking it deeply

in. His own relation to Farfrae and Lucetta overshadowed all kindred ones. He went on saying brokenly to himself, "She has supplicated to me in her time; and now her tongue won't own me nor her eyes see me!...And he-how angry he looked. He drove me back as if I were a bull breaking fence....I took it like a lamb, for I saw it could not be settled there. He can rub brine on a green wound!...But he shall pay for it, and she shall be sorry. It must come to a tussle-face to face; and then we'll see how a coxcomb can front a man!"

Without further reflection the fallen merchant, bent on some wild purpose, ate a hasty dinner and went forth to find Farfrae. After being injured by him as a rival, and snubbed by him as a journeyman, the crowning degradation had been reserved for this day-that he should be shaken at the collar by him as a vagabond in the face of the whole town.

The crowds had dispersed. But for the green arches which still stood as they were erected Casterbridge life had resumed its ordinary shape. Henchard went down corn Street till he came to Farfrae's house, where he knocked, and left a message that he would be glad to see his employer at the granaries as soon as he conveniently could come there. Having done this he proceeded round to the back and entered the yard.

Nobody was present, for, as he had been aware, the labourers and carters were enjoying a half-holiday on account of the events of the morning-though the carters would have to return for a short time later on, to feed and litter down the horses. He had reached the granary steps and was about to ascend, when he said to himself aloud, "I'm stronger than he."

Henchard returned to a shed, where he selected a short piece of rope from several pieces that were lying about; hitching one end of this to a nail, he took the other in his right hand and turned himself bodily round, while keeping his arm against his side; by this contrivance he pinioned the arm effectively. He now went up the ladders to the top floor of the corn-stores.

It was empty except of a few sacks, and at the further end was the door often mentioned, opening under the cathead and chain that hoisted the sacks. He fixed the door open and looked over the sill. There was a depth of thirty or forty feet to the ground; here was the spot on which he had been standing with Farfrae when Elizabeth-Jane had seen him lift his arm, with many misgivings as to what the movement portended.

He retired a few steps into the loft and waited. From this elevated perch his eyes could sweep the roofs round about, the upper parts of the luxurious chestnut trees, now delicate in leaves of a week's age, and the drooping boughs of the lines; Farfrae's garden and the green door leading therefrom. In course of time-he could not say how long-that green door opened and Farfrae came through. He was dressed as if for a journey. The low light of the nearing evening caught his head and face when he emerged from the shadow of the wall, warming them to a complexion of. Henchard watched him with his mouth firmly set the squareness of his jaw and the verticality of his profile being unduly marked.

Farfrae came on with one hand in his pocket, and humming a tune in a way which told that the words were most in his mind. They were those of the song he had sung when he arrived years before at the Three Mariners, a poor young man, adventuring for life and fortune, and scarcely knowing witherward:-

"And here's a hand, my trusty fiere,
And gie's a hand o' thine."

Nothing moved Henchard like an old melody. He sank back. "No; I can't do it!" he gasped. "Why does the infernal fool begin that now!"

At length Farfrae was silent, and Henchard looked out of the loft door. "Will ye come up here?" he said.

"Ay, man," said Farfrae. "I couldn't see ye. What's wrang?"

A minute later Henchard heard his feet on the lowest ladder. He heard him land on the first floor, ascend and land on the second, begin the ascent to the third. And then his head rose through the trap behind.

"What are you doing up here at this time?" he asked, coming forward. "Why didn't ye take your holiday like the rest of the men?" He spoke in a tone which had just severity enough in it to show that he remembered the untoward event of the forenoon, and his conviction that Henchard had been drinking.

Henchard said nothing; but going back he closed the stair hatchway, and stamped upon it so that it went tight into its frame; he next turned to the wondering young man, who by this time observed that one of Henchard's arms was bound to his side.

"Now," said Henchard quietly, "we stand face to face-man and man. Your money and your fine wife no longer lift 'ee above me as they did but now, and my poverty does not press me down."

"What does it all mean?" asked Farfrae simply.

"Wait a bit, my lad. You should ha' thought twice before you affronted to extremes a man who had nothing to lose. I've stood your rivalry, which ruined me, and your snubbing, which humbled me; but your hustling, that disgraced me, I won't stand!"

Farfrae warmed a little at this. "Ye'd no business there," he said.

"As much as any one among ye! What, you forward stripling, tell a man of my age he'd no business there!" The anger-vein swelled in his forehead as he spoke.

"You insulted Royalty, Henchard; and 'twas my duty, as the chief magistrate, to stop you."

"Royalty be damned," said Henchard. "I am as loyal as you, come to that!"

"I am not here to argue. Wait till you cool doon, wait till you cool; and you will see things the same way as I do."

"You may be the one to cool first," said Henchard grimly. "Now this is the case. Here be we, in this four-square loft, to finish out that little wrestle you began this morning. There's the door, forty foot above ground. One of us two puts the other out by that door-the master stays inside. If he likes he may go down afterwards and give the alarm that the other has fallen out by accident-or he may tell the truth-that's his business. As the strongest man I've tied one arm to take no advantage of 'ee. D'ye understand? Then here's at 'ee!"

There was no time for Farfrae to do aught but one thing,

to close with Henchard, for the latter had come on at once. It was a wrestling match, the object of each being to give his antagonist a back fall; and on Henchard's part, unquestionably, that it should be through the door.

At the outset Henchard's hold by his only free hand, the right, was on the left side of Farfrae's collar, which he firmly grappled, the latter holding Henchard by his collar with the contrary hand. With his right he endeavoured to get hold of his antagonist's left arm, which, however, he could not do, so adroitly did Henchard keep it in the rear as he gazed upon the lowered eyes of his fair and slim antagonist.

Henchard planted the first toe forward, Farfrae crossing him with his; and thus far the struggle had very much the appearance of the ordinary wrestling of those parts. Several minutes were passed by them in this attitude, the pair rocking and writhing like trees in a gale, both preserving an absolute silence. By this time their breathing could be heard. Then Farfrae tried to get hold of the other side of Henchard's collar, which was resisted by the larger man exerting all his force in a wrenching movement, and this part of the struggle ended by his forcing Farfrae down on his knees by sheer pressure of one of his muscular arms. Hampered as he was, however, he could not keep him there, and Farfrae finding his feet again the struggle proceeded as before.

By a whirl Henchard brought Donald dangerously near the precipice; seeing his position the Scotchman for the first time locked himself to his adversary, and all the efforts of that infuriated Prince of Darkness-as he might have been called from his appearance just now-were inadequate to lift or loosen Farfrae for a time. By an extraordinary effort he succeeded at last, though not until they had got far back again from the fatal door. In doing so Henchard contrived to turn Farfrae a complete somersault. Had Henchard's other arm been free it would have been all over with Farfrae then. But again he regained his feet, wrenching Henchard's arm considerably, and causing him sharp pain, as could be seen from the twitching of his face. He instantly delivered the younger man an annihilating turn by the left fore-hip, as it used to be expressed, and following up his advantage thrust him towards the door, never loosening his hold till Farfrae's fair head was hanging over the window-sill, and his arm dangling down outside the wall. "Now," said Henchard between his gasps, "this is the end of what you began this morning. Your life is in my hands."

"Then take it, take it!" said Farfrae. "Ye've wished to long enough!"

Henchard looked down upon him in silence, and their eyes met. "O Farfrae!-that's not true!" he said bitterly. "God is my witness that no man ever loved another as I did thee at one time....And now-though I came here to kill 'ee, I cannot hurt thee! Go and give me in charge-do what you will-I care nothing for what comes of me!"

He withdrew to the back part of the loft, loosened his arm, and flung himself in a corner upon some sacks, in the abandonment of remorse. Farfrae regarded him in silence; then went to the hatch and descended through it. Henchard would fain have recalled him, but his tongue failed in its task, and the young man's steps died on his ear.

Henchard took his full measure of shame and self-reproach. The scenes of his first acquaintance with Farfrae rushed back upon him-that time when the curious mixture of romance and thrift in the young man's composition so commanded his heart that Farfrae could play upon him as on an instrument. So thoroughly subdued was he that he remained on the sacks in a crouching attitude, unusual for a man, and for such a man. Its womanliness sat tragically on the figure of so stern a piece of virility. He heard a conversation below, the opening of the coach-house door, and the putting in of a horse, but took no notice.

Here he stayed till the thin shades thickened to opaque obscurity, and the loft-door became an oblong of gray light-the only visible shape around. At length he arose, shook the dust from his clothes wearily, felt his way to the hatch, and gropingly descended the steps till he stood in the yard.

"He thought highly of me once," he murmured. "Now he'll hate me and despise me for ever!" He became possessed by an overpowering wish to see Farfrae again that night, and by some desperate pleading to attempt the well-nigh impossible task of winning pardon for his late mad attack. But as he walked towards Farfrae's door he recalled the unheeded doings in the yard while he had lain above in a sort of stupor. Farfrae he remembered had gone to the stable and put the horse into the gig; while doing so Whittle had brought him a letter; Farfrae had then said that he would not go towards Budmouth as he had intended-that he was unexpectedly summoned to Weatherbury, and meant to call at Mellstock on his way thither, that place lying but one or two miles out of his course. He must have come prepared for a journey when he first arrived in the yard, unsuspecting enmity; and he must have driven off (though in a changed direction) without saying a word to any one on what had occurred between themselves. It would therefore be useless to call at Farfrae's house till very late.

There was no help for it but to wait till his return, though waiting was almost torture to his restless and self-accusing soul. He walked about the streets and outskirts of the town, lingering here and there till he reached the stone bridge of which mention has been made, an accustomed halting-place with him now. Here he spent a long time, the purl of waters through the weirs meeting his ear, and the Casterbridge lights glimmering at no great distance off.

While leaning thus upon the parapet his listless attention was awakened by sounds of an unaccustomed kind from the town quarter. They were a confusion of rhythmical noises, to which the streets added yet more confusion by encumbering them with echoes. His first incurious thought that the clangour arose from the town band, engaged in an attempt to round off a memorable day in a burst of evening harmony, was contradicted by certain peculiarities of reverberation. But inexplicability did not rouse him to more than a cursory heed; his sense of degradation was too strong for the admission of foreign ideas; and he leant against the parapet as before.

Chapter 40

Long before this time Henchard, weary of his ruminations on the bridge, had repaired towards the town. When he stood at the bottom of the street a procession burst upon his view, in the act of turning out of an alley just above him. The lanterns, horns, and multitude startled him; he saw the mounted images, and knew what it all meant.

They crossed the way, entered another street, and disappeared. He turned back a few steps and was lost in grave reflection, finally wending his way homeward by the obscure river-side path. Unable to rest there he went to his step-daughter's lodging, and was told that had gone to Mr. Farfrae's. Like one acting in obedience to a charm, and with a nameless apprehension, he followed in the same direction in the hope of meeting her, the roysterers having vanished. Disappointed in this he gave the gentlest of pulls to the door-bell, and then learnt particulars of what had occurred, together with the doctor's imperative orders that Farfrae should be brought home, and how they had set out to meet him on the Budmouth Road.

"But he has gone to Mellstock and Weatherbury!" exclaimed Henchard, now unspeakably grieved. "Not Budmouth way at all."

But, alas! for Henchard; he had lost his good name. They would not believe him, taking his words but as the frothy utterances of recklessness. Though Lucetta's life seemed at that moment to depend upon her husband's return (she being in great mental agony lest he should never know the unexaggerated truth of her past relations with Henchard), no messenger was despatched towards Weatherbury. Henchard, in a state of bitter anxiety and contrition, determined to seek Farfrae himself.

To this end he hastened down the town, ran along the eastern road over Durnover Moor, up the hill beyond, and thus onward in the moderate darkness of this spring night till he had reached a second and almost a third hill about three miles distant. In Yalbury Bottom, or Plain, at the foot of the hill, he listened. At first nothing, beyond his own, was to be heard but the slow wind making its moan among the masses of spruce and larch of Yalbury Wood which clothed the heights on either hand; but presently there came the sound of light wheels whetting their felloes against the newly stoned patches of road, accompanied by the distant glimmer of lights.

He knew it was Farfrae's gig descending the hill from an indescribable personality in its noise, the vehicle having been his own till bought by the Scotchman at the sale of his effects. Henchard thereupon retraced his steps along Yalbury Plain, the gig coming up with him as its driver slackened speed between two plantations.

It was a point in the highway near which the road to Mellstock branched off from the homeward direction. By diverging to that village, as he had intended to do, Farfrae might probably delay his return by a couple of hours. It soon appeared that his intention was to do so still, the light swerving towards Cuckoo Lane, the by-road aforesaid. Farfrae's off gig-lamp flashed in Henchard's face. At the same time Farfrae discerned his late antagonist.

"Farfrae-Mr. Farfrae!" cried the breathless Henchard, holding up his hand.

Farfrae allowed the horse to turn several steps into the branch lane before he pulled up. He then drew rein, and said "Yes?" over his shoulder, as one would towards a pronounced enemy.

"Come back to Casterbridge at once!" Henchard said. "There's something wrong at your house-requiring your return. I've run all the way here on purpose to tell ye."

Farfrae was silent, and at his silence Henchard's soul sank within him. Why had he not, before this, thought of what was only too obvious? He who, four hours earlier, had enticed Farfrae into a deadly wrestle stood now in the darkness of late night-time on a lonely road, inviting him to come a particular way, where an assailant might have confederates, instead of going his purposed way, where there might be a better opportunity of guarding himself from attack. Henchard could almost feel this view of things in course of passage through Farfrae's mind.

"I have to go to Mellstock," said Farfrae coldly, as he loosened his reins to move on.

"But," implored Henchard, "the matter is more serious

than your business at Mellstock. It is-your wife! She is ill. I can tell you particulars as we go along."

The very agitation and abruptness of Henchard increased Farfrae's suspicion that this was a ruse to decoy him on to the next wood, where might be effectually compassed what, from policy or want of nerve, Henchard had failed to do earlier in the day. He started the horse.

"I know what you think," deprecated Henchard running after, almost bowed down with despair as he perceived the image of unscrupulous villainy that he assumed in his former friend's eyes. "But I am not what you think!" he cried hoarsely. "Believe me, Farfrae; I have come entirely on your own and your wife's account. She is in danger. I know no more; and they want you to come. Your man has gone the other way in a mistake. O Farfrae! don't mistrust me-I am a wretched man; but my heart is true to you still!"

Farfrae, however, did distrust him utterly. He knew his wife was with child, but he had left her not long ago in perfect health; and Henchard's treachery was more credible than his story. He had in his time heard bitter ironies from Henchard's lips, and there might be ironies now. He quickened the horse's pace, and had soon risen into the high country lying between there and Mellstock, Henchard's spasmodic run after him lending yet more substance to his thought of evil purposes.

The gig and its driver lessened against the sky in Henchard's eyes; his exertions for Farfrae's good had been in vain. Over this repentant sinner, at least, there was to be no joy in heaven. He cursed himself like a less scrupulous Job, as a vehement man will do when he loses self-respect, the last mental prop under poverty. To this he had come after a time of emotional darkness of which the adjoining woodland shade afforded inadequate illustration. Presently he began to walk back again along the way by which he had arrived. Farfrae should at all events have no reason for delay upon the road by seeing him there when he took his journey homeward later on.

Arriving at Casterbridge Henchard went again to Farfrae's house to make inquiries. As soon as the door opened anxious faces confronted his from the staircase, hall, and landing; and they all said in grievous disappointment, "O-it is not he!" The manservant, finding his mistake, had long since returned, and all hopes had centred upon Henchard.

"But haven't you found him?" said the doctor.

"Yes....I cannot tell 'ee!" Henchard replied as he sank down on a chair within the entrance. "He can't be home for two hours."

"H'm," said the surgeon, returning upstairs.

"How is she?" asked Henchard of Elizabeth, who formed one of the group.

"In great danger, father. Her anxiety to see her husband makes her fearfully restless. Poor woman-I fear they have killed her!"

Henchard regarded the sympathetic speaker for a few instants as if she struck him in a new light, then, without further remark, went out of the door and onward to his lonely cottage. So much for man's rivalry, he thought. Death was to have the oyster, and Farfrae and himself the shells. But about Elizabeth-lane; in the midst of his gloom she seemed to him as a pin-point of light. He had liked the look on her face as she answered him from the stairs. There had been affection in it, and above all things what he desired now was affection from anything that was good and pure. She was not his own, yet, for the first time, he had a faint dream that he might get to like her as his own,-if she would only continue to love him.

Jopp was just going to bed when Henchard got home. As the latter entered the door Jopp said, "This is rather bad about Mrs. Farfrae's illness."

"Yes," said Henchard shortly, though little dreaming of Jopp s complicity in the night's harlequinade, and raising his eyes just sufficiently to observe that Jopp's face was lined with anxiety. "Somebody has called for you," continued Jopp, when Henchard was shutting himself into his own apartment. "A kind of traveller, or sea-captain of some sort."

"Oh?-who could he be?"

"He seemed a well-be-doing man-had grey hair and a broadish face; but he gave no name, and no message."

"Nor do I gi'e him any attention." And, saying this, Henchard closed his door.

The divergence to Mellstock delayed Farfrae's return very nearly the two hours of Henchard's estimate. Among the other urgent reasons for his presence had been the need of his authority to send to Budmouth for a second physician; and when at length Farfrae did come back he was in a state bordering on distraction at his misconception of Henchard's motives. A messenger was despatched to Budmouth, late as it had grown; the night wore on, and the other doctor came in the small hours. Lucetta had been much soothed by Donald's arrival; he seldom or never left her side; and when, immediately after his entry, she had tried to lisp out to him the secret which so oppressed her, he checked her feeble words, lest talking should be dangerous, assuring her there was plenty of time to tell him everything.

Up to this time he knew nothing of the skimmington-ride. The dangerous illness and miscarriage of Mrs. Farfrae was soon rumoured through the town, and an apprehensive guess having been given as to its cause by the leaders in the exploit, compunction and fear threw a dead silence over all particulars of their orgie; while those immediately around Lucetta would not venture to add to her husband's distress by alluding to the subject.

What, and how much, Farfrae's wife ultimately explained to him of her past entanglement with Henchard, when they were alone in the solitude of that sad night, cannot be told. That she informed him of the bare facts of her peculiar intimacy with the corn-merchant became plain from Farfrae's own statements. But in respect of her subsequent conduct-her motive in coming to Casterbridge to unite herself with Henchard-her assumed justification in abandoning him when she discovered reasons for fearing him (though in truth her inconsequent passion for another man at first sight had most to do with that abandonment)-her method of reconciling to her conscience a marriage with the second when she was in a measure committed to the first: to what extent she spoke of these things remained Farfrae's secret alone.

Besides the watchman who called the hours and weather in Casterbridge that night there walked a figure up and down corn Street hardly less frequently. It was Henchard's, whose retiring to rest had proved itself a futility as soon as attempted; and he gave it up to go hither and thither, and make inquiries about the patient every now and then. He called as much on Farfrae's account as on Lucetta's, and on Elizabeth-Jane's even more than on either's. Shorn one by one of all other interests, his life seemed centring on the personality of the stepdaughter whose presence but recently he could not endure. To see her on each occasion of his inquiry at Lucetta's was a comfort to him. The last of his calls was made about four o'clock in the morning, in the steely light of dawn. Lucifer was fading into day across Durnover Moor, the sparrows were just alighting into the street, and the hens had begun to cackle from the outhouses. When within a few yards of Farfrae's he saw the door gently opened, and a servant raise her hand to the knocker, to untie the piece of cloth which had muffled it. He went across, the sparrows in his way scarcely flying up from the road-litter, so little did they believe in human aggression at so early a time.

"Why do you take off that?" said Henchard.

She turned in some surprise at his presence, and did not answer for an instant or two. Recognizing him, she said, "Because they may knock as loud as they will; she will never hear it any more."

Chapter 42

But the emotional conviction that he was in Somebody's hand began to die out of Henchard's breast as time slowly removed into distance the event which had given that feeling birth. The apparition of Newson haunted him. He would surely return.

Yet Newson did not arrive. Lucetta had been borne along the churchyard path; Casterbridge had for the last time turned its regard upon her, before proceeding to its work as if she had never lived. But Elizabeth remained undisturbed in the belief of her relationship to Henchard, and now shared his home. Perhaps, after all, Newson was gone for ever. In due time the bereaved Farfrae had learnt the, at least, proximate cause of Lucetta's illness and death, and his first impulse was naturally enough to wreak vengeance in the name of the law upon the perpetrators of the mischief.

He resolved to wait till the funeral was over ere he moved in the matter. The time having come he reflected. Disastrous as the result had been, it was obviously in no way foreseen or intended by the thoughtless crew who arranged the motley procession. The tempting prospect of putting to the blush people who stand at the head of affairs—that supreme and piquant enjoyment of those who writhe under the heel of the same—had alone animated them, so far as he could see; for he knew nothing of Jopp's incitements. Other considerations were also involved. Lucetta had confessed everything to him before her death, and it was not altogether desirable to make much ado about her history, alike for her sake, for Henchard's, and for his own. To regard the event as an untoward accident seemed, to Farfrae, truest consideration for the dead one's memory, as well as best philosophy.

Henchard and himself mutually forbore to meet. For Elizabeth's sake the former had fettered his pride sufficiently to accept the small seed and root business which some of the Town Council, headed by Farfrae, had purchased to afford him a new opening. Had he been only personally concerned Henchard, without doubt, would have declined assistance even remotely brought about by the man whom he had so fiercely assailed. But the sympathy of the girl seemed necessary to his very existence; and on her account pride itself wore the garments of humility.

Here they settled themselves; and on each day of their lives Henchard anticipated her every wish with a watchfulness in which paternal regard was heightened by a burning jealous dread of rivalry. Yet that Newson would ever now return to Casterbridge to claim her as a daughter there was little reason to suppose. He was a wanderer and a stranger, almost an alien; he had not seen his daughter for several years; his affection for her could not in the nature of things be keen; other interests would probably soon obscure his recollections of her, and prevent any such renewal of inquiry into the past as would lead to a discovery that she was still a creature of the present. To satisfy his conscience somewhat Henchard repeated to himself that the lie which had retained for him the coveted treasure had not been deliberately told to that end, but had come from him as the last defiant word of a despair which took no thought of consequences. Furthermore he pleaded within himself that no Newson could love her as he loved her, or would tend her to his life's extremity as he was prepared to do cheerfully.

Thus they lived on in the shop overlooking the churchyard, and nothing occurred to mark their days during the remainder of the year. Going out but seldom, and never on a, they saw Donald Farfrae only at rarest intervals, and then mostly as a transitory object in the distance of the street. Yet he was pursuing his ordinary avocations, smiling mechanically to fellow-tradesmen, and arguing with bargainers—as bereaved men do after a while.

Time, "in his own grey style," taught Farfrae how to estimate his experience of Lucetta—all that it was, and all that it was not. There are men whose hearts insist upon a dogged fidelity to some image or cause thrown by chance into their keeping, long after their judgment has pronounced it no rarity—even the reverse, indeed, and without them the band of the worthy is incomplete. But Farfrae was not of those. It was inevitable that the insight, briskness, and rapidity of his nature should take him out of the dead blank which his loss threw about him. He could not but perceive that by the death of Lucetta he had exchanged a looming misery for a simple sorrow. After that revelation of her history, which must have come sooner or later in any circumstances, it was hard to believe that life with her would have been productive of further happiness.

But as a memory, nothwithstanding such conditions, Lucetta's image still lived on with him, her weaknesses provoking only the gentlest criticism, and her sufferings attenuating wrath at her concealments to a momentary spark now and then. By the end of a year Henchard's little retail seed and grain shop, not much larger than a cupboard, had developed its trade considerably, and the stepfather and daughter enjoyed much serenity in the pleasant, sunny corner in which it stood. The quiet bearing of one who brimmed with an inner activity characterized Elizabeth-Jane at this period. She took long walks into the country two or three times a week, mostly in the direction of Budmouth. Sometimes it occurred to him that when she sat with him in the evening after those invigorating walks she was civil rather than affectionate; and he was troubled; one more bitter regret being added to those he had already experienced at having, by his severe censorship, frozen up her precious affection when originally offered.

She had her own way in everything now. In going and coming, in buying and selling, her word was law.

"You have got a new muff, Elizabeth," he said to her one day quite humbly.

"Yes; I bought it," she said.

He looked at it again as it lay on an adjoining table. The fur was of a glossy brown, and, though he was no judge of such articles, he thought it seemed an unusually good one for her to possess.

"Rather costly, I suppose, my dear, was it not?" he hazarded.

"It was rather above my figure," she said quietly. "But it is not showy."

"O no," said the netted lion, anxious not to pique her in the least.

Some little time after, when the year had advanced into another spring, he paused opposite her empty bedroom in passing it. He thought of the time when she had cleared out of his then large and handsome house in corn Street, in consequence of his dislike and harshness, and he had looked into her chamber in just the same way. The present room was much humbler, but what struck him about it was the abundance of books lying everywhere. Their number and quality made the meagre furniture that supported them seem absurdly disproportionate. Some, indeed many, must have been recently purchased; and though he encouraged her to buy in reason, he had no notion that she indulged her innate passion so extensively in proportion to the narrowness of their income. For the first time he felt a little hurt by what he thought her extravagance, and resolved to say a word to her about it. But, before he had found the courage to speak an event happened which set his thoughts flying in quite another direction.

The busy time of the seed trade was over, and the quiet weeks that preceded the hay-season had come—setting their special stamp upon Casterbridge by thronging the market with wood rakes, new waggons in yellow, green, and red, formidable scythes, and pitchforks of prong sufficient to skewer up a small family. Henchard, contrary to his wont, went out one Saturday afternoon towards the market-place from a curious feeling that he would like to pass a few minutes on the spot of his former triumphs. Farfrae, to whom he was still a comparative stranger, stood a few steps below the Corn Exchange door—a usual position with him at this hour—and he appeared lost in thought about something he was looking at a little way off.

Henchard's eyes followed Farfrae's, and he saw that the object of his gaze was no sample-showing farmer, but his own stepdaughter, who had just come out of a shop over the way. She, on her part, was quite unconscious of his attention, and in this was less fortunate than those young women whose very plumes, like those of Juno's bird, are set with Argus eyes whenever possible admirers are within ken.

Henchard went away, thinking that perhaps there was nothing significant after all in Farfrae's look at Elizabeth-Jane at that juncture. Yet he could not forget that the Scotchman had once shown a tender interest in her, of a fleeting kind. Thereupon promptly came to the surface that idiosyncrasy of Henchard's which had ruled his courses from the beginning and had mainly made him what he was. Instead of thinking that a union between his cherished step-daughter and the energetic thriving Donald was a thing to be desired for her good and his own, he hated the very possibility.

Time had been when such instinctive opposition would have taken shape in action. But he was not now the Henchard of former days. He schooled himself to accept her will, in this as in other matters, as absolute and unquestionable. He dreaded lest an antagonistic word should lose for him such regard as he had regained from her by his devotion, feeling that to retain this under separation was better than to incur her dislike by keeping her near.

But the mere thought of such separation fevered his spirit much, and in the evening he said, with the stillness of suspense: "Have you seen Mr. Farfrae to-day, Elizabeth?"

Elizabeth-Jane started at the question; and it was with some confusion that she replied "No."

"Oh—that's right—that's right....It was only that I saw him in the street when we both were there." He was wondering if her embarrassment justified him in a new suspicion—that the long walks which she had latterly been taking, that the new books which had so surprised him, had anything to do with the young man. She did not enlighten him, and lest silence should allow her to shape thoughts unfavourable to their present friendly relations, he diverted the discourse into another channel.

Henchard was, by original make, the last man to act stealthily, for good or for evil. But the solicitus timor of his love—the dependence upon Elizabeth's regard into which he had declined (or, in another sense, to which he had advanced)—denaturalized him. He would often weigh and consider for hours together the meaning of such and such a deed or phrase of hers, when a blunt settling question would formerly have been his first instinct. And now, uneasy at the thought of a passion for Farfrae which should entirely displace her mild filial sympathy with himself, he observed her going and coming more narrowly.

There was nothing secret in Elizabeth-Jane's movements beyond what habitual reserve induced, and it may at once be owned on her account that she was guilty of occasional conversations with Donald when they chanced to meet. Whatever the origin of her walks on the Budmouth Road, her return from those walks was often coincident with Farfrae's emergence from corn Street for a twenty minutes' blow on that rather windy highway—just to winnow the seeds and chaff out of him before sitting down to tea, as he said. Henchard became aware of this by going to the Ring, and, screened by its enclosure, keeping his eye upon the road till he saw them meet. His face assumed an expression of extreme anguish.

"Of her, too, he means to rob me!" he whispered. "But he has the right. I do not wish to interfere."

The meeting, in truth, was of a very innocent kind, and matters were by no means so far advanced between the young people as Henchard's jealous grief inferred. Could he have heard such conversation as passed he would have been enlightened thus much:—

HE.—"You like walking this way, Miss Henchard—and is it not so?" (uttered in his undulatory accents, and with an appraising, pondering gaze at her).

SHE.—"O yes. I have chosen this road latterly. I have no great reason for it."

HE.—"But that may make a reason for others."

SHE (reddening).—"I don't know that. My reason, however, such as it is, is that I wish to get a glimpse of the sea every day.

HE.—"Is it a secret why?"

SHE (reluctantly).—"Yes."

HE (with the pathos of one of his native ballads).—"Ah, I doubt there will be any good in secrets! A secret cast a deep shadow over my life. And well you know what it was."

Elizabeth admitted that she did, but she refrained from confessing why the sea attracted her. She could not herself account for it fully, not knowing the secret possibly to be that, in addition to early marine associations, her blood was a sailor's.

"Thank you for those new books, Mr. Farfrae," she added shyly. "I wonder if I ought to accept so many!"

"Ay! why not? It gives me more pleasure to get them for you, than you to have them!"

"It cannot."

They proceeded along the road together till they reached the town, and their paths diverged.

Henchard vowed that he would leave them to their own devices, put nothing in the way of their courses, whatever they might mean. If he were doomed to be bereft of her, so it must be. In the situation which their marriage would create he could see no locus standi for himself at all. Farfrae would never recognize him more than superciliously; his poverty ensured that, no less than his past conduct. And so Elizabeth would grow to be a stranger to him, and the end of his life would be friendless solitude.

With such a possibility impending he could not help watchfulness. Indeed, within certain lines, he had the right to keep an eye upon her as his charge. The meetings seemed to become matters of course with them on special days of the week.

At last full proof was given him. He was standing behind a wall close to the place at which Farfrae encountered her. He heard the young man address her as "Dearest," and then kiss her, the girl looking quickly round to assure herself that nobody was near.

When they were gone their way Henchard came out from the wall, and mournfully followed them to Casterbridge. The chief looming trouble in this engagement had not decreased. Both Farfrae and Elizabeth-Jane, unlike the rest of the people, must suppose Elizabeth to be his actual daughter, from his own assertion while he himself had the same belief; and though Farfrae must have so far forgiven him as to have no objection to own him as a father-in-law, intimate they could never be. Thus would the girl, who was his only friend, be withdrawn from him by degrees through her husband's influence, and learn to despise him.

Had she lost her heart to any other man in the world than the one he had rivalled, cursed, wrestled with for life in days before his spirit was broken, Henchard would have said, "I am content." But content with the prospect as now depicted was hard to acquire.

There is an outer chamber of the brain in which thoughts

unowned, unsolicited, and of noxious kind, are sometimes allowed to wander for a moment prior to being sent off whence they came. One of these thoughts sailed into Henchard's ken now. Suppose he were to communicate to Farfrae the fact that his betrothed was not the child of Michael Henchard at all—legally, nobody's child; how would that correct and leading townsman receive the information?

He might possibly forsake Elizabeth-Jane, and then she would be her step-sire's own again. Henchard shuddered, and exclaimed, "God forbid such a thing! Why should I still be subject to these visitations of the devil, when I try so hard to keep him away?"

Chapter 45

It was about a month after the day which closed as in the last chapter. Elizabeth-Jane had grown accustomed to the novelty of her situation, and the only difference between Donald's movements now and formerly was that he hastened indoors rather more quickly after business hours than he had been in the habit of doing for some time.

Newson had stayed in Casterbridge three days after the wedding party (whose gaiety, as might have been surmised, was of his making rather than of the married couple's), and was stared at and honoured as became the returned Crusoe of the hour. But whether or not because Casterbridge was difficult to excite by dramatic returns and disappearances through having been for centuries an assize town, in which sensational exits from the world, antipodean absences, and such like, were half-yearly occurrences, the inhabitants did not altogether lose their equanimity on his account.

On the fourth morning he was discovered disconsolately climbing a hill, in his craving to get a glimpse of the sea from somewhere or other. The contiguity of salt water proved to be such a necessity of his existence that he preferred Budmouth as a place of residence, notwithstanding the society of his daughter in the other town. Thither he went, and settled in lodgings in a green-shuttered cottage which had a bow-window, jutting out sufficiently to afford glimpses of a vertical strip of blue sea to any one opening the sash, and leaning forward far enough to look through a narrow lane of tall intervening houses.

Elizabeth-Jane was standing in the middle of her upstairs parlour, critically surveying some re-arrangement of articles with her head to one side, when the housemaid came in with the announcement, "Oh, please ma'am, we know now how that bird-cage came there."

In exploring her new domain during the first week of residence, gazing with critical satisfaction on this cheerful room and that, penetrating cautiously into dark cellars, sallying forth with gingerly tread to the garden, now leaf-strewn by autumn winds, and thus, like a wise field-marshal, estimating the capabilities of the site whereon she was about to open her housekeeping campaign-Mrs. Donald Farfrae had discovered in a screened corner a new bird-cage, shrouded in newspaper, and at the bottom of the cage a little ball of feathers-the dead body of a goldfinch. Nobody could tell her how the bird and cage had come there, though that the poor little songster had been starved to death was evident. The sadness of the incident had made an impression on her. She had not been able to forget it for days, despite Farfrae's tender banter; and now when the matter had been nearly forgotten it was again revived.

"Oh, please ma'am, we know how the bird-cage came there. That farmer's man who called on the evening of the wedding-he was seen wi' it in his hand as he came up the street; and 'tis thoughted that he put it down while he came in with his message, and then went away forgetting where he had left it." This was enough to set Elizabeth thinking, and in thinking she seized hold of the idea, at one feminine bound, that the caged bird had been brought by Henchard for her as a wedding gift and token of repentance. He had not expressed to her any regrets or excuses for what he had done in the past; but it was a part of his nature to extenuate nothing, and live on as one of his own worst accusers. She went out, looked at the cage, buried the starved little singer, and from that hour her heart softened towards the self-alienated man.

When her husband came in she told him her solution of the bird-cage mystery; and begged Donald to help her in finding out, as soon as possible, whither Henchard had banished himself, that she might make her peace with him; try to do something to render his life less that of an outcast, and more tolerable to him. Although Farfrae had never so passionately liked Henchard as Henchard had liked him, he had, on the other hand, never so passionately hated in the same direction as his former friend had done, and he was therefore not the least indisposed to assist Elizabeth-Jane in her laudable plan.

But it was by no means easy to set about discovering Henchard. He had apparently sunk into the earth on leaving Mr. and Mrs. Farfrae's door. Elizabeth-Jane remembered what he had once attempted; and trembled.

But though she did not know it Henchard had become a changed man since then-as far, that is, as change of emotional basis can justify such a radical phrase; and she needed not to fear. In a few days Farfrae's inquiries elicited that Henchard had been seen by one who knew him walking steadily along the Melchester highway eastward, at twelve o'clock at night-in other words, retracing his steps on the road by which he had come.

This was enough; and the next morning Farfrae might have been discovered driving his gig out of Casterbridge in that direction, Elizabeth-Jane sitting beside him, wrapped in a thick flat fur-the victorine of the period-her complexion somewhat richer than formerly, and an incipient matronly dignity, which the serene Minerva-eyes of one "whose gestures beamed with mind" made becoming, settling on her face. Having herself arrived at a promising haven from at least the grosser troubles of her life, her object was to place Henchard in some similar quietude before he should sink into that lower stage of existence which was only too possible to him now.

After driving along the highway for a few miles they made further inquiries, and learnt of a road-mender, who had been working thereabouts for weeks, that he had observed such a man at the time mentioned; he had left the Melchester coachroad at Weatherbury by a forking highway which skirted the north of Egdon Heath. Into this road they directed the horse's head, and soon were bowling across that ancient country whose surface never had been stirred to a finger's depth, save by the scratchings of rabbits, since brushed by the feet of the earliest tribes. The tumuli these had left behind, dun and shagged with heather, jutted roundly into the sky from the uplands, as though they were the full breasts of Diana Multimammia supinely extended there.

They searched Egdon, but found no Henchard. Farfrae drove onward, and by the afternoon reached the neighbourhood of some extension of the heath to the north of Anglebury, a prominent feature of which, in the form of a blasted clump of firs on a summit of a hill, they soon passed under. That the road they were following had, up to this point, been Henchard's track on foot they were pretty certain; but the ramifications which now began to reveal themselves in the route made further progress in the right direction a matter of pure guess-work, and Donald strongly advised his wife to give up the search in person, and trust to other means for obtaining news of her stepfather. They were now a score of miles at least from home, but, by resting the horse for a couple of hours at a village they had just traversed, it would be possible to get back to Casterbridge that same day, while to go much further afield would reduce them to the necessity of camping out for the night, "and that will make a hole in a sovereign," said Farfrae. She pondered the position, and agreed with him.

He accordingly drew rein, but before reversing their direction paused a moment and looked vaguely round upon the wide country which the elevated position disclosed. While they looked a solitary human form came from under the clump of trees, and crossed ahead of them. The person was some labourer; his gait was shambling, his regard fixed in front of him as absolutely as if he wore blinkers; and in his hand he carried a few sticks. Having crossed the road he descended into a ravine, where a cottage revealed itself, which he entered.

"If it were not so far away from Casterbridge I should say that must be poor Whittle. 'Tis just like him," observed

Elizabeth-Jane. "And it may be Whittle, for he's never been to the yard these three weeks, going away without saying any word at all; and I owing him for two days' work, without knowing who to pay it to."

The possibility led them to alight, and at least make an inquiry at the cottage. Farfrae hitched the reins to the gate-post, and they approached what was of humble dwellings surely the humblest. The walls, built of kneaded clay originally faced with a trowel, had been worn by years of rain-washings to a lumpy crumbling surface, channelled and sunken from its plane, its gray rents held together here and there by a leafy strap of ivy which could scarcely find substance enough for the purpose. The rafters were sunken, and the thatch of the roof in ragged holes. Leaves from the fence had been blown into the corners of the doorway, and lay there undisturbed. The door was ajar; Farfrae knocked; and he who stood before them was Whittle, as they had conjectured.

His face showed marks of deep sadness, his eyes lighting on them with an unfocused gaze; and he still held in his hand the few sticks he had been out to gather. As soon as he recognized them he started.

"What, Abel Whittle; is it that ye are heere?" said Farfrae.

"Ay, yes sir! You see he was kind-like to mother when she wer here below, though 'a was rough to me."

"Who are you talking of?"

"O sir-Mr. Henchet! Didn't ye know it? He's just gone-about half-an-hour ago, by the sun; for I've got no watch to my name."

"Not-dead?" faltered Elizabeth-Jane.

"Yes, ma'am, he's gone! He was kind-like to mother when she wer here below, sending her the best ship-coal, and hardly any ashes from it at all; and taties, and such-like that were very needful to her. I seed en go down street on the night of your worshipful's wedding to the lady at yer side, and I thought he looked low and faltering. And I followed en over Grey's Bridge, and he turned and zeed me, and said, 'You go back!' But I followed, and he turned again, and said, 'Do you hear, sir? Go back!' But I zeed that he was low, and I followed on still. Then 'a said, 'Whittle, what do ye follow me for when I've told ye to go back all these times?' And I said, 'Because, sir, I see things be bad with 'ee, and ye wer kind-like to mother if ye wer rough to me, and I would fain be kind-like to you.' Then he walked on, and I followed; and he never complained at me no more. We walked on like that all night; and in the blue o' the morning, when 'twas hardly day, I looked ahead o' me, and I zeed that he wambled, and could hardly drag along. By the time we had got past here, but I had seen that this house was empty as I went by, and I got him to come back; and I took down the boards from the windows, and helped him inside. 'What, Whittle,' he said, 'and can ye really be such a poor fond fool as to care for such a wretch as I!' Then I went on further, and some neighbourly woodmen lent me a bed, and a chair, and a few other traps, and we brought 'em here, and made him as comfortable as we could. But he didn't gain strength, for you see, ma'am, he couldn't eat-no appetite at all-and he got weaker; and to-day he died. One of the neighbours have gone to get a man to measure him."

"Dear me-is that so!" said Farfrae.

As for Elizabeth, she said nothing.

"Upon the head of his bed he pinned a piece of paper, with some writing upon it," continued Abel Whittle. "But not being a man o' letters, I can't read writing; so I don't know what it is. I can get it and show ye."

They stood in silence while he ran into the cottage; returning in a moment with a crumpled scrap of paper. On it there was pencilled as follows:-

Michael Henchard's Will: "That Elizabeth-Jane Farfrae be not told of my death, or made to grieve on account of me. "and that I be not bury'd in consecrated ground. "and that no sexton be asked to toll the bell. "and that nobody is wished to see my dead body. "and that no murners walk behind me at my funeral. "and that no flours be planted on my grave, "and that no man remember me. "To this I put my name.

Michael Henchard: "What are we to do?" said Donald, when he had handed the paper to her.

She could not answer distinctly. "O Donald!" she cried at

last through her tears, "what bitterness lies there! O I would not have minded so much if it had not been for my unkindness at that last parting!...But there's no altering-so it must be."

What Henchard had written in the anguish of his dying was respected as far as practicable by Elizabeth-Jane, though less from a sense of the sacredness of last words, as such, than from her independent knowledge that the man who wrote them meant what he said. She knew the directions to be a piece of the same stuff that his whole life was made of, and hence were not to be tampered with to give herself a mournful pleasure, or her husband credit for.

All was over at last, even her regrets for having misunderstood him on his last visit, for not having searched him out sooner, though these were deep and sharp for a good while. From this time forward Elizabeth-Jane found herself in a latitude of calm weather, kindly and grateful in itself, and doubly so after the Capharnaum in which some of her preceding years had been spent. As the lively and sparkling emotions of her early married live cohered into an equable serenity, the finer movements of her nature found scope in discovering to the narrow-lived ones around her the secret (as she had once learnt it) of making limited opportunities endurable; which she deemed to consist in the cunning enlargement, by a species of microscopic treatment, of those minute forms of satisfaction that offer themselves to everybody not in positive pain; which, thus handled, have much of the same inspiring effect upon life as wider interests cursorily embraced.

Her teaching had a reflex action upon herself, insomuch that she thought she could perceive no great personal difference between being respected in the nether parts of Casterbridge and glorified at the uppermost end of the social world. Her position was, indeed, to a marked degree one that, in the common phrase, afforded much to be thankful for. That she was not demonstratively thankful was no fault of hers. Her experience had been of a kind to teach her, rightly or wrongly, that the doubtful honour of a brief transmit through a sorry world hardly called for effusiveness, even when the path was suddenly irradiated at some half-way point by daybeams rich as hers. But her strong sense that neither she nor any human being deserved less than was given, did not blind her to the fact that there were others receiving less who had deserved much more. And in being forced to class herself among the fortunate she did not cease to wonder at the persistence of the unforeseen, when the one to whom such unbroken tranquility had been accorded in the adult stage was she whose youth had seemed to teach that happiness was but the occasional episode in a general drama of pain.

Chapter 9

Study Questions

Q. What kind of person auctions off their wife and baby? Discuss with reference to The Mayor of Casterbridge.

Or

Q. Discuss the social standards in The Mayor of Casterbridge.

In The Mayor of Casterbridge, Thomas Hardy explores the personality of a man, Michael Henchard, who hands his family off to a stranger, Richard Newsom, for a mere five guineas. Oblivious to the consequences of such an act, Michael Henchard, intoxicated, lets go of his wife, Susan, and daughter, Elizabeth-Jane, who remain silent and unsure of what lies ahead. Just beginning his struggle in accepting standards of society, Michael Henchard realizes the disastrous effects of alcohol and promises to never drink again for twenty-one years. In his novel, Thomas Hardy examines the standards of society in Casterbridge at the turn of the twentieth century while detailing Michael Henchard's responses to these standards.

In addition to not tolerating alcoholics, people did not permit adultery. A couple stayed together a while before committing to marriage. Marriage lasted until death. People sought to keep their families together, and families existed as the basis of society. The husband worked to provide food, clothing, and shelter for his family, while the wife raised the children and kept busy with household chores. In order to gain respect, people composed themselves in a positive manner when in the workplace and all around. Political figures reflected the utmost dignity and honesty. People avoided working for and buying from people who lacked the respect of others in society. The wealthy helped the poor and people in society worked together to make their lives the best they could be.

In contrast to the many people who obeyed society's rules and aspired to follow these standards, Michael Henchard suffered dreadful consequences for failing to accept society's standards. First, he did not comprehend his actions at the auction. He could not explain the location or status of his wife and child. Not only did he not know if they were in good health, he did not even know if they were alive. Ashamed, he moved away to put the event behind him, hoping it would remain a secret. Working in the corn trade, Henchard became well-known, ran for mayor, and served as mayor, still wondering about his family and regretting that day at the fair. At the same time, recovering from the loss of her husband and Elizabeth-Jane's father, Richard Newsom, Susan told Elizabeth-Jane of her relation to Henchard by marriage. As a result of Elizabeth-Jane's curiosities, the two women decided to go and see him only to satisfy Elizabeth-Jane. At the meeting, relief struck him and he insisted they come and live with him and later proposed to Susan.

However, since society would not accept such an immediate ceremony, they waited an appropriate amount of time, keeping Susan and Elizabeth-Jane hidden in a cottage outside of town. Unfortunately, possibly because of the emergence of his family into his life, Michael Henchard lost sight of his business in the corn trade and cleared the path for his employee, Donald Farfrae, to take control of the corn trade in the area. This could have been prevented, though, if Henchard had treated his employees well. People noticed Henchard's indifference and negativity to other people. This affected Henchard in that

he lost his popularity. Elected to the mayoral office because of his energy and prospects in the town council, Henchard could not please members of society. When the auction secret broke out, it revealed Henchard's dishonesty to society in serving a public office. With this overall decline in respect came a decrease in the money Henchard earned. Henchard's life had taken a turn for the worst. His wife, Susan, died, and he thought it the time to tell Elizabeth-Jane the truth that he was her father. After informing her of this news, he found a letter addressed to him from Susan. It read that Elizabeth-Jane's father was Richard Newsom because their daughter had died at three months old and she named their new daughter Elizabeth-Jane to fill the void her deceased daughter had left in her heart.

So, Henchard went against society's standards again, failing to tell Elizabeth-Jane of her true father. Henchard found himself childless, unmarried, unloved, and poverty-stricken. Then, to everyone's surprise, Richard Newsom had not been dead all along. He returns, looking for his daughter and Henchard lies and says that she died. The lies dug him deeper and deeper into the ground. Not accepting the standards of society, he lost Elizabeth-Jane.

If Michael Henchard had followed the standards of society, he may have led a happy life. Instead, he gave away his happiness, his family, and his wealth. He had many chances, too. He could have gone back for his family after the auction. Instead he hoped the problems would go away. He began treating people poorly, and lost respect from the people of the town. Then he lied and could not stop the lies. His personality consisted of many different sides--both good and evil. He didn't have the ability to take control of his life. When he saw his happiness go away, he did not grab hold of it. He reverted to revenge, envy, and lies. In turn, he lost all he had.

Q. Discuss the Family-Systems Theory, Addiction, and Thomas Hardy's The Mayor of Casterbridge.

When we look beyond the Brontës to the rest of Victorian fiction, we find other novels in which alcoholism is prominent and many others in which the dependencies are more subtle. The Mayor of Casterbridge, for example, revolves around chemical dependence. Like Arthur, Helen, and little Arthur, the main characters of this novel-Henchard, his wife Susan, and daughter Elizabeth-display almost all the features associated with the classic alcoholic family. Henchard, the alcoholic, suffers from many of the accompanying afflictions: "self-will run riot," low self-esteem, shame, guilt, self-castigation, self-punishment, loneliness, a death wish, and a tendency to depression. In his interactions with people he is often impulsive, unprincipled, quarrelsome, blaming, controlling, and verbally and emotionally abusive. Susan, like Helen, emerges as a classic coalcoholic or codependent, but with more severe pathology and less hope.

She agrees to drink with him, resigns herself to her fate, tunes out his verbal abuse at first and later makes only mild protests and timid threats. She accepts being auctioned off in order to escape from him, but returns and puts herself entirely in his hands for the sake of her daughter. A family systems critic can explore the psychosomatic reactions she experiences when she sees her husband, her irresolution when he challenges her, and her repression of her emotions.

A student of coalcoholism is not surprised to discover that instead of rejoicing when she finds that he has sobered up, she is "Overpowered," "Down," and wants to die, because the only life she knows is blaming and being the victim. She feels better when he admits his shame, but still refuses to forgive him. She has an even stronger death wish than Henchard does, and, like him, she suffers from low self esteem, loneliness, humorlessness, and sadness. Some readers identify more with Elizabeth Jane, a classic child of an alcoholic, who also suffers from low self-esteem. A family systems critic can reveal why she too is "sober " and humorless, and why her desire to see, to hear, and to understand is "repressed."

When this family first appears it is characterized by loneliness and silence. Both parents are obsessed with secrecy, the standard rule of many if not most family systems. Their meeting site is secret and they agree that secrecy is necessary to protect their shame. Henchard insists on keeping the secret of her parentage from Elizabeth even though his friend Farfrae recommends that he tell the truth.

Also unable to tell her daughter the truth, Susan lies to Henchard and constantly worries about being discovered. At first Elizabeth is unsuspicious but eventually becomes aware (as many readers did) of the presence of secrets in the system and becomes troubled by them. What is most remarkable about this novel from the point of view of the family systems approach to chemical dependency is that when Henchard sobers up some of his actions foreshadow those to be recommended by Alcoholics Anonymous, Al-Anon, and many other twelve-step groups in the next century. What is most surprising in a Hardy novel, the protagonist briefly experiences faith in a higher power, the equivalent of steps two and three: "Elizabeth-Jane heard him say, 'Who is such a reprobate as I! And yet it seems that even I be in Somebody's hand!'" When Henchard tells all to Farfrae it is very much like a fifth step.

He then proceeds to what would be the eighth and ninth steps: making amends. He feels genuine remorse, is kind to Elizabeth-Jane and Susan, apologizes to Susan, and determines to make amends to her.

Like many A. A. members to come after him, Henchard renounces secrets and adopts a stance of rigorous honesty. He scrupulously reveals his debts and admits to the whole town that he auctioned off his wife. He even gives up some measure of control. For example, he initially attempts to control the choice of a last name for Elizabeth but he catches himself, backs off, and tells her not to agree with his choice just to please him. Even when Elizabeth chooses Farfrae as her lover (whom he almost killed) "Henchard vowed that he would leave them to their own devices, put nothing in the way of their courses, whatever they might mean."

However, Henchard remains isolated in the novel, conspicuously without ready access to a higher power and the support of a group such as A. A. Hence his efforts alone are not enough to save the family, and he returns to drinking and starves himself to death. Nevertheless, as in Wuthering Heights, the second generation, Elizabeth-Jane and Farfrae, seems more functional.

Q. Discuss the Sensation Novel Elements in The London Graphic's Twenty-Part Serialisation of Hardy's The Mayor of Casterbridge.

Or

Q. F.B. Pinion in "The Effect of Serialization on the Narrative" states that Hardy "removed one or two of the less convincing situations when he revised the serial version for the more critical readers who were likely to read the novel when it appeared in book form." Discuss

Bryn Caless notes that for the volume edition "Hardy excised various of the superfluous incidents"--the most important being "a meeting between Susan and Lucetta in the marketplace, Susan being unaware of Lucetta's identity, and the whole scene witnessed by an agonized Henchard." Caless evidently considers Farfrae's delivery of Henchard's letter to Lucetta at Budmouth harbour to be less important, although with its multiple coincidences this scene epitomizes the gross sorts of improbabilities that seem to have appealed to serial readers. In The Graphic's serial version of the novel, Henchard's motive for exiling himself from Casterbridge is merely jealousy at the prospect of Elizabeth's marriage. It is revealed after his departure that she has been meeting Newson secretly at Farfrae's house for some months.

These and other changes from serial to volume, as Purdy notes in his bibliographical study, "are not, as in the case of several subsequent novels, simply a return to an original unbowdlerized version." Hardy himself had been worried about the demands of weekly publication "with the need to force an incident into each instalment, [which] would strain the credulity of the reader of the novel as a whole,"according to Frederick R. Karl. Joseph W. Beach in "Bowdlerized Versions of Hardy" observes that in both The Well-Beloved and The Mayor of Casterbridge Hardy "made special provision for the sensibilities of the magazine reader" by substituting "a regular marriage for the illicit love affair which [each] story calls for."Beach adds that this alteration in The Mayor of Casterbridge "was made at a great expense of plausibility and art". However, as Hardy wrote to Leslie Stephen, then editor of The Cornhill, probably in regard to the part-publication of Far From The Madding Crowd (then being run in that magazine) he was

always willing, and indeed anxious, to give up any points

which may be desirable in a story when read as a whole, for the sake of others which shall please those who read it in numbers. Perhaps I may have higher aims some day, and be a great stickler for the proper artistic balance of the completed work, but for the present circumstances lead me to wish merely to be considered a good hand at a serial.

Beach explains the apparent discrepancy between Hardy's positive attitude towards serialisation in 1874 and his railing against the "literary compromises" it entailed in an 1890 contribution to a symposium on "Candour in English Fiction" by noting that such changing attitudes and a "drift towards greater frankness and bolder realism" were shared by many other late Victorians. William Rutland notes that the manuscript for the 1886 novel shows "the manipulations necessary to appease editors... subsequently done in different coloured ink" Perhaps, as would be the case with the Tess of the D'Urbervillesmanuscript, the different-coloured ink signals Hardy's intention to delete for the text to be published in volume certain passages he was putting in expressly to satisfy "the proprieties demanded by the conventions of the time, which were becoming increasingly irksome to Hardy".

In her chapter on The Mayor of Casterbridge in Thomas Hardy from Serial to Novel (1927), Marv Ellen Chase mentions that the novel finished its serial run on 15 May, 1886, in The Graphic, leaving "plenty of time for revision before book publication...." 8 However, the novel's part-publication preceded its appearance in volume form only if one excepts the last number, for Smith, Elder brought out the two-volume edition on 10 May, 1886. According to Richard Little Purdy in his bibliographical study of Hardy's writings, the last page of the novel was actually written on 17 April, 1885. Thus, Hardy would have had a year rather than months in which to conduct his manuscript revisions for Smith, Elder, but even in volume form The Mayor of Casterbridge betrays its 'commercial' and Sensation Novel origins: "weekly serialization no doubt helps to account for the high proportion of dramatic and sensational incident in this novel, some of it contrived and inessential."

Caless notes that some material excised after part-publication was restored in 1895; in particular, Hardy put back the illicit, sexual nature of Lucetta and Henchard's relationship on Jersey. "In 1886 Hardy cut nearly all of the chapter relating to Henchard's return to Casterbridge on Elizabeth's wedding-day, but he was persuaded to restore the chapter in 1895 by an American friend", identified by Carl J. Webber in "The Restoration of Hardy's Starved Goldfinch" as either Rebekah or Catherine Owen of New York City.

In a more general way, Hardy later sought to improve the diction of The Mayor of Casterbridge as he had done in revising The Return of the Native (1878); "there are also sentences which have been obviously reconstructed for greater coherence or emphasis". In addition, as Chase remarks, Hardy strengthened his delineation of the characters of Farfrae and Elizabeth Jane during the 1886 revision. Of twenty-six principal incidents in the plot, Chase states that Hardy altered eight after the story's serial run in The Graphic; these she designates as 5, 8, 14, 16, 17, 18, 24, and 25.

Chase feels that, "in spite of the author's announcement in his preface [of 1895], which would surely lead one to expect few alterations, the changes from serial to book, in incident and plot alone, are many and significant". The changes in character are negligible, however, with the exception of Lucetta. In Chapter 12, Henchard's narration and subsequent relationship with Lucetta on Jersey is somewhat changed in the volume from the serial.

A. From a boating accident the previous summer in which he had struck his head and nearly drowned (but for the timely intervention of Lucetta, who dove in to rescue him) in the serial, Henchard merely "fell quite ill, and... sank into one of those gloomy fits" of his in the book. Chase rightly describes the serial's version of Henchard's narrative as "far more sensational." "Surely to fall out of a boat in the harbour, to strike one's head in falling, and to be saved by a woman from drowning afford greater dramatic effect", although such specifics do lend the serial's inset narrative a certain verisimilitude.

B. Whereas in the volume version the young lady who

nurses Henchard is merely staying at the same boarding house (and, despite her breeding and education, is described as "the daughter of some harum-scarum military officer who had got into difficulties"), in the serial Lucetta had already "had a foolish liking for [Henchard] for more than five years"; She is the daughter of a merchant with whom Henchard has dealt.

C.. Whereas in the volume version the woman and Henchard, becoming "intimate," caused a local scandal that damaged her reputation, in the serial Henchard "did marry her at St. Heliers a fortnight" prior to Susan's return; No sooner has Susan returned to life than Henchard's bride is due to arrive "by the packet to-morrow night"; Henchard had regretted his new marriage (even before he learned that Susan was still alive" because he "felt [he] did not care for this young woman, much as she might like [him]". Chase speculates that "either Hardy, or [M. E. Braddon, a Sensation novelist in her own right, and] the editor of the London Graphic, or both, thought it was wiser to depict the conventional love affair, rather than the unconventional, for their Victorian readers".

As a consequence of his having already married Lucetta in the serial, Henchard asks Farfrae to ride down to Budmouth to deliver a letter and a cheque to the young woman at the quay as soon as the packet-boat lands. Conveniently, the lady--now identified as "Mrs. Henchard'!--is first described as being in a disarranged state owing to the breezy passage...". Thus, admitted to the entrance of the sole female passenger's cabin, Farfrae sees only "a white hand and arm... stretched out from behind a red curtain," but again--conveniently--he hears her pronounce only a single word in answer to his query as to whether she is his employer's wife. Half-an-hour later, when he returns to the boat to assist her to board a vessel returning to Jersey, she has already disembarked and caught the return packet-boat.

Improbable as this incident sounds in summary, Hardy has used it artistically, first to describe the change from an interior to a maritime countryside-

About half way he passed the top of a ridge which formed a kind of girdle enclosing the rural districts of the country from those shoreward. A marine sentiment in the landscape followed; there was a change in the smell of the air from field and fruit cosiness of the inland country had gone--and then to reveal Farfrae's discomfort at having to under take so delicate a mission: Farfrae, to tell the truth, though pitying her [i. e., Henchard's bride of a few weeks] was somewhat relieved that the letter had done its work so smoothly and promptly that circumstances had relieved him of the responsibility of having to assist her in starting her return journey after she has received such distressing news (namely that the long-lost wife of the man whom she has just married has reappeared).

Despite these fine touches, however, Hardy's manoevering so as to prevent a face-to-face meeting between Farfrae and Lucetta here is reminiscent of Mrs. Wood's plot manipulations in East Lynne (1861). The series of improbable coincidences in the serial's twelfth chapter also recalls those in such sensation novels as Wilkie Collins's No Name (1862) and Armadale(1866) and Hardy's own Desperate Remedies (1871). Chase considers that such sensational touches were

probably not unpleasing to the magazine public. The Hardy reader is, however, quite conscious of the sacrifice of the author's usual conciseness in the handling of incident by the intrusion of so many more or less ill-chosen details..

In fact, as the above quotations from The Graphicillustrate, it is not the "details" but the construction of the plot itself that is ill-fashioned. There are simply too many complications and improbable coincidences involved in Henchard's having already married Lucetta and now having to keep her away from Casterbridge--and his first wife.

Hardy's machinations in the twelfth chapter of the serial can be appreciated fully when one arrives at Farfrae's courting and marrying Lucetta. Setting aside the impropriety of Henchard's and Lucetta's indulging in what Chase terms "intimacy without marriage"--such unintentional bigamy being a feature of both East Lynneand Lady Audley's Secret which "effectively enabled a man and women to enjoy the sweets of adultery"--one recognizes that Hardy's original conception (restored in the volume version) is far less complicated and far more believable. There is no reason why Farfrae should be sent to meet Lucetta, other than to prevent her arrival in Casterbridge and spare his employer the embarrassment of having to meet her himself. The elimination of the St. Heliers marriage also solves the problem of Lucetta's imminent arrival; therefore, Henchard can deal with his Jersey mesalliance by mail.

In an April, 1863, Quarterly Review article condemning contemporary sensation novels, H. L. Manse castigates the kind of readers who patronize "periodicals, circulating libraries, and railway bookstalls" as having little "discrimination" and "a diseased appetite" for "excitement alone... ." In particular, Manse notes the tendency of early sensation novels to utilize bigamy as part of the plot (by accident rather than design, Henchard's St. Heliers marriage is bigamous): "Indeed, so popular has this crime become, as to give rise to an entire sub-class in this branch of literature, which may be distinguished as that of Bigamy Novels".

Another feature common to both Hardy's novels and the Sensation Novels is the misdirected letter. Chase feels that the biggest difference between serial and volume forms of The Mayor of Casterbridge lies in the author's handling of Lucetta's request for and receipt of her love letters. Hardy's original conception of the Henchard/Lucetta relationship renders Jopp's later treatment of these letters more credible since intimacies between persons not merely informally engaged but actually married would hold greater titillation for the crowd at Peter's Finger. Knowing nothing of Henchard's already being married to Susan, the crowd would assume that Lucetta was in law Henchard's wife when she married Farfrae. The chief differences in the plot surrounding the letters are the meeting of Susan and Lucetta ("a decidedly ironical situation to the serial reader," as Chase remarks since both are Mrs. Henchard) and Henchard's entrusting the letters to a coach guard through Elizabeth Jane and Farfrae. That the guard should fail to deliver them "suggests a desire on the part of the author of the serial to give an added emphasis to the vicissitudes through which Lucetta's unfortunate letters must pass". As an experienced serial writer, Hardy knew exactly how to toy with his reader: once again, he holds out then cancels the prospect of a meeting between Farfrae and Lucetta, thereby hinting at the importance to the plot of their future relationship. Such authorial manoeuvering, too, suggests an emphasis of the machinations of plot rather than on the mainsprings of character, the latter being Hardy's clear preference in the volume version.

The "Paisley shawl with a red centre" that identifies Lucetta to Henchard generates considerable anxiety for the Mayor when he sees "a veiled young woman" talking to Susan in the serial. The meeting, as Chase suggests, tends "to excite suspense at the possibility of something happening" only if there is a danger of Henchard's having married Lucetta coming out. The suspense-getting value of such a meeting is much reduced in the pre-serial version, and would strain credibility for no real reason since Henchard has written to his fiancee on Jersey explaining why he cannot go through with the marriage. Once Hardy had determined to cancel the serial's secret marriage, there was simply no cat to let out of the bag.

Curiously, in the serial version Lucetta is travelling to Bristol by coach under the name "Miss St. Helier," rather than either "La Sueur" or "Templeman," the latter being the name she adopts in accord with the wishes of her benefactress, her Aunt Templeman. The additional alias in the serial was perhaps intended to heighten the atmosphere of secretiveness and deception surrounding Lucetta, in accord with the practice of sensation novels, in which false identity and disguise are usually central features of the plot. The second alias is further evidence of what H. L. Manse termed the "commercial atmosphere" of the sensation novel pervading the serialised version of The Mayor of Casterbridge.

Similarly, that Hardy in the serial devotes nearly three times the amount of space it occupies in the book to the incident with the bull (in the March 27th instalment) suggests Hardy's recognition of the necessity for suspense and excitement in part-publication. The effect of the material later cut is to prolong the bull's pursuit of the two women. More subtly, the excised material shows Elizabeth Jane to advantage, for Hardy describes her as "much the cooler as well as the stronger" as she directs her companion to safety while actively trying to outwit their adversary, "by a combination of dexterity and courage... seiz[ing] the staff affixed to the bull.." Lucetta appears quite the reverse, rendering her self an easy target for the charging bull rather than climbing the cloverstack, as Elizabeth has suggested.

Her addle-headed confusion lowers her character in the reader's estimation. On the other hand, Hardy emphasizes her craftiness as she prepares to entreat Henchard for the return of her correspondence. In the revised work, Lucetta hopes that "tears and pleadings" will move her former lover, but in the serial (the April 17th instalment) to these she adds "artifice" and "hypocrisy" by cosmetically ageing and "disfiguring" her features through two hours' application: The chemist up the street, who eked out a meagre drug trade by scented soaps, cosmetics, and disfiguring ointments of various kinds, was three or four times requisitioned for this proceeding. By the time she had sicklied herself to her mind the hour [for meeting Henchard at the Ring] had arrived.

A further piece of melodrama cut for volume publication is Farfrae's detecting a "female figure"--in fact, his wife Lucetta--emerging from the Ring in company with Henchard. Ironically, Farfrae has "no suspicion as to the personality of his [Henchard's] companion" because she is wearing unfamiliar clothing. Credibility is further strained by Farfrae's sketching in for Henchard his plans for the seedshop while Lucetta walks on the other side of Henchard: "They had walked on together through the gloom, Henchard drawing Lucetta's arm through his own to lend a delusive aspect to the rendezvous he had been surprised in, and keeping her on the outside." Wisely Hardy chose to remove this highly awkward scene from the volume, but in doing so also eliminated the line uttered by Donald after Lucetta has surreptitiously crept back into the house and "restored herself to her natural hues...." When she encounters her husband in the dining-room, he cheerfully retails to her the news that Henchard is again wooing: "Well, Lucetta, I've a bit of news for ye," he said gaily. "I think poor Henchard is going to console himself by speculating in a wife once more. I met him courting just now."

Although the irony must have been delicious to Hardy, the whole incident for the sake of probability had to go. This paragraph, which closes the serial version of Chapter XXXV, is the basis for the April 27th number's illustration by Robert Barnes, a picture of Lucetta and Farfrae rendered almost meaningless to the modern reader deprived of these deleted plot machinations worthy of the author of Desperate Remedies.

"The incident of Henchard's discovery of Newson on the Budmouth Road" in Chapter 41, important in the volume form because it motivates Henchard's decision to leave Casterbridge, "is entirely omitted in the serial"Chase 41). Instead, Hardy offers as the motivational factor Henchard's discovery of Elizabeth's clandestine love-affair with his enemy Farfrae. In the serial we do not learn until the end of Chapter 43 that Elizabeth Jane has known for some time (weeks or even months) that Newson is in Budmouth, for she has been meeting her natural father "two or three times a week" on the Budmouth Road. In protracting this situation Hardy has gained suspense at "a sacrifice of plausibility".

Not restored in English editions until 1912 was, as the author himself remarked in the 1912 preface, "nearly a chapter which... was printed in the serial issue"; Chase concludes that Hardy was referring to Henchard's returning to town in Chapter 44 for Elizabeth Jane's wedding day. Chase speculates that in revising the story for volume publication Hardy wished to attenuate "the sensational and melodramatic in his finished product," but that he also far misinterpreted the effect of Henchard's return... as to sacrifice... the culminating episode which so fittingly brings his great tragedy to a close".

The effect of serialisation on characterization is even more significant than its effect on plot. Despite Henchard's telling a long story at the public dinner in Chapter 5, Henchard's character is much the same in the volume, although "the magazine reader might have gathered that he was more loquacious". As has been noted, the serial version makes

Lucetta seem stupid in the bull incident, but crafty when preparing herself for her interview with Henchard regarding the return of her letters. Where Hardy made changes from the serial to the volume is in the characters of Elizabeth and Farfrae.

The blue-eyed Elizabeth Jane of the serial is characterized by such adjectives as "sensible" and "unselfish," ~simple~ and ~sober", her black-eyed counterpart of the book is never described as sensible and unselfish, she is "studious" instead of "simple," and "quiet" instead of "sober." She of the serial is, moreover, not particularly pleasing to look upon.... In the serial she is "ignorant" and "uninstructed"; in the book, only "unfinished" and "unsophisticated."

In Farfrae's case, Chase has identified "eighteen distinct changes, either in spelling or in phraseology, to suggest a more pronounced Scotch accent". In addition, she notes that after the publication of the first and second volume editions (Smith, Elder in 1886 and Sampson Low, Marston Searle and Rivington in 1887), the "professor of the tongue in question" (whom R. L. Purdy in Thomas Hardy: A Bibliographical Study [1954] identifies as Sir George Douglas) "suggested the seven distinct changes" evident in the 1912 fifth volume of Macmillan's "Wessex Edition." In the 1912 version "the Wessex atmosphere is unmistakably stressed and strengthened" by the addition of "Wessex" at the opening of the first chapter and at the close of the second chapter, by making the river specifically "the river Froom," a "hill" "Yalbury Hill," the "White Hart Vale" The Vale of Blackmoor," and "Stickleford" "Kingsbere" (the last having associations with Tess of the D'Urbervilles, not written until five years after The Mayor of Casterbridge). Chase identifies passages which have become markedly more dialectal in the 1912 version, notably "saw" to "zeed" and "zilver zix-pence" for "silver sixpence," and "zang" for "sang." The total effect of these changes is to heighten the realism of The Mayor of Casterbridge's setting and characters, thereby muting any improbabilities in plot while, like its sensation forebears,"throw[ing] ironical light on the theme of irrationality in human affairs." 13 In a sense, Hardy's revision subsequent to the serial run suggests what Terry terms "detailism"--the Sensation practice of rendering the improbabilities of suspense, melodrama, and behavioural extremes in "commonly shared experience" and bourgeois actuality, or, as Terry puts it, "photographic reality of character and background".

Although in The Mayor of Casterbridge, as Rutland notes, Hardy did not make "the slightest concession" to "public taste so far as to concoct a 'happy ending'," the novelist did pander to that general taste for suspense, melodrama, and extremes of behaviour in both serial and volume forms. However, in neither does he adopt wholly the standard Sensation Novel "apparatus of ruined heiresses, impossible wills, damning letters, skeletons in cupboards and the like... ". Early in his career as a writer, Hardy fell under the spell of the Sensation Novel, thanks in part to his first publisher, William Tinsley, who brought out the works of Braddon, Wood, Sala, Black, Ouida, and Payn, as well as Hardy's first published novel, Desperate Remedies [March, 1871), which clearly falls within this genre. (A Pair of Blue Eyes ran in Tinsley's Magazine from September, 1872, to July, 1873, before that same publisher's bringing it out as a triple-decker; furthermore, Tinsley paid Hardy forty pounds for the British and continental rights to Under The Greenwood Treein the spring of 1872.) Hardy's Collected Letters document the nature of his friendships with Sensation Novelists James Payn and William Black--as well as his working for Mary Elizabeth Braddon, who was not only editor of Belgravia but also the author of the best-selling Lady Audley's Secret (1862). Throughout Hardy's works, but perhaps nowhere else so graphically as in Desperate Remedies and the serial text of The Mayor of Casterbridge the features of the Sensation Novel are much in evidence: excitement, suspense, surprises, mysteries, instalment closings known as "curtains," strongly delineated characters, numerous coincidences, disguises, misdirected letters, overheard conversations, bigamous or secret marriages, and illegitimacy. However, The Mayor of Casterbridge in volume form is distinguished from its Sensation Novel kin by its treatment of nature, its careful motivation of character, and its lack of what Manse terms "some demon in human shape". Hardy won his place of prominence in Mudie's 1888 catalogue, tieing George Meredith with eleven titles listed, by producing not Sensation but Art out of the bourgeois issues of money, ambition, and social status, to say nothing of the irrational, unpredictable nature of human affairs.

Q. Discuss the subtitle of The Mayor of Casterbridge.

Or

Q. The book's main focus is "the spiritual and material career of Micheal Henchard, whose governing inclinations are tragically at war with each other" Do you agree.

The Mayor of Casterbridge, which was subtitled The Life and Death of a Man of Character, was written by Thomas Hardy. Henchard, in a fit of drunkenness, has decided to sell his wife and daughter at a fair. Afterwards, Henchard becomes a wealthy man and the mayor of the town Casterbridge. His wife and child seek him out years later. In the end, it is neither his supposed child, Elizebeth-Jane, nor his wife, Susan, who ruins him but his own self-destructive nature.

The novel was published serially in the Graphic and in Harper's Weekly. The Graphic was the English version and Harper's Weekly was the American version. They ran concurrently over the nineteen-week period from January second to May fifteenth in the year of 1886. There were no major differences between the serial versions "except that for reasons of space Harper's Weekly omitted some passages which were restored in later editions" (Norton Critical Edition, xiii). There were three hundred changes from the manuscript. Essentially, they were only minor "local" improvements. For example, in the Graphic the slang words "damn it" become "hang it". It appears that the American Harper's Weekly was not so worried about the novel's usage of "inappropriate" language.

There were various cancelled plotlines for The Mayor of Casterbridge. The "notes or plans Hardy had made for the novel before he began writing have not survived" (Norton

Critical Edition, xiii). Therefore, there is a great interest in the manuscript as "evidence" of these ever-changing plotlines. The Norton Critical Editon of the novel says that through the various plotlines they deducted that "as Hardy began writing, large areas of the action were still to be decided: at one stage there were two be two daughters, one staying with Henchard, the other going with Susan and Newson" (xiii). Furthermore, "the Elizebeth-Jane of the opening chapters was not to die, so the figure we meet in the body of the novel was to be Henchard's real daughter" (xiii). Hardy's reasoning for the many plot changes was to "distribute the interest of the novel more evenly" (xiii).

More interesting in this novel is the town of Casterbridge itself. When one reads The Mayor of Casterbridge they have a feeling that this place actually may exist when in fact it does not. In 1895, Hardy explained in his preface to Far From the Maddening Crowd "that he had "disinterred" the name Wessex-used for the first time in chapter fifty of that novel-because he thought some such "territorial definition" would lend unity to a series of novels with a mainly local character". The usage of such a fictional map gave Thomas Hardy a "brand name". Hardy became well known as the "Wessex Novelist". Although the Wessex map is fictional, Hardy explained that the territory was "a partly real, partly dream-country". The Mayor of Casterbridge, in particular, has a "high degree of correspondence between fiction and actuality". For example, "Richard Hutton, writing for the Spectator, had no difficulty in recognizing Casterbridge as Dorchester, and neither did most other readers".

The Mayor of Casterbridge did not get good receptions for its time period. The Athenaeum stressed that the "language of the peasants again is a point on which we have an old quarrel with Mr. Hardy. It is neither one thing nor the other-neither dialect exactly reproduced nor a thorough rendering into educated English" (The Athenaeum, May 29, 1886). Most of the contemporary reception is hell-bent on the problems of Hardy's grammer and his usage of peasant dialect. The Atheneaum also made comments about the novels "old faults, chiefly of style" (Norton Critical Edition, 315). Furthermore, they said that Hardy had a tendency to use "far-fetched and unpleasant similes and epithets". George Saintsbury of the Saturday Review said, "The Mayor of Casterbridge is a disappointment. The story which is very slight and singularly devoid of interest, is, at the same time, too improbable" (Norton Critical Edition, 316).

It is apparent that the critics of this novel have problems with Thomas Hardy's approaches to realism. The critics are less concerned with the morals and psychology of the story that Hardy tried to convey. Rather, these contemporary critics focused more on the dialect of the peasants and the comparison to other novels prior to The Mayor of Casterbridge's publication.

Q Give an Introduction to Hardy's Novels: Intended Audience and Serial Structure

Qr

Q. Discuss the Structure, Physical Setting and Chronological Setting in the novels of Thomas Hardy.

Addressing himself initially to magazine readers rather than the book-buying public and the memberships of lending libraries, Hardy is writing outside the traditions of London society and university education. The somewhat headstrong but virtuous female protagonist and the villainous man of education and substance seem to be derived more from the conventions of the contemporary theatre rather than from the Victorian novel prior to 1870, although one sees affinities between Hardy's characters and those of Wilkie Collins. Although a voracious reader and consumer of ideas, Hardy was still very much a countryman when his first critical success, Far From the Madding Crowd, was published in the pages of London's respectable Cornhill Magazine, edited by a man of letters, in 1874.

Hardy, wanting desperately to give up architecture and become a professional writer, desired, as he told his editor, "to be a good hand at a serial." Thus, each monthly 'part' (anything from three to five chapters, but of roughly the same number of pages) moved towards a climax and a cliff-hanger, the "curtain" (ending of one instalment and opening of the next) both implicitly posing and answering a question of suspense in the reader's mind. For example, at the close of Part One of Far From the Madding Crowd, one is left wondering what will become of Gabriel Oak after the younger of his dogs has destroyed his flock and bankrupted him. This implicit question Hardy immediately addresses at the start of Part Two (Chapters 6 through 8): what question does he similarly pose then answer at the close of Part Two and the opening of Part Three ?

Physical Setting

Hardy's handling of physical setting is unparalled in English fiction, although in the verse of the Lake Poets and Robert Burns one has a similar sense of a specific topography and landscape. But, when Hardy is at his best, as in The Return of the Native, the natural backdrop becomes another person in the picture, so to speak. Egdon Heath is not described sop frequently and in such detail merely for the sake of "local colour." Indeed, such rural settings were outside the range of experience of the primarily urban readership that purchased the periodicals such as Belgravia in which Hardy originally published his "Novels of Character and Environment." How does Hardy convey the numinous, atavistic sense that pervades the glade where Tess encounters the dying pheasants, for instance? Egdon in The Return of the Native is an objective correlative for the forces of tradition and environment that condition the actions of its denizens, and ultimately destroy the lives of the outsiders Eustacia Vye and Damon Wildeve.

How is the tragic ending of Tess of the D'Urbervilles, then, both similar to that of The Return of the Native and yet a departure? Prior to The Return of the Native,in such lesser novels as Under the Greenwood Tree and The Hand of Ethelberta Hardy brought his stories to closure by marrying off his heroines. Although one might argue that Ethelberta's being outsmarted by Lord Mountclere represents a dimunition of the feminine principle, it is hardly as extreme as the execution that brings Tess of the D'Urbervilles to a close. Had only Alec died, the book might well be categorised as a Victorian melodrama translated from the stage to the page: what motivated Hardy to kill off a heroine he genuinely admired? And why does he have Angel marry Tess's younger sister, Liza Lu, when in Far From the Madding Crowd he is content to dispose of Gabriel's rivals in a single shot, leaving Bathsheba free to marry the self-taught, resilient rustic who has stood by the quixotic heroine through thick and thin?

Chronological Setting

Unless Hardy gives the reader specific clues such as "before the nineteenth century had run one-third of its span" at the beginning of The Mayor of Casterbridge, the reader should presume that the chronological setting is roughly contemporaneous with the year of publication. But Hardy is not always direct in his presentation of chronological setting; for example, only by certain internal references and a conspicuous lack of railway travel is one to deduce that The Return of the Native, published serially in 1878, is set thirty years earlier. Life in rural Dorset and the surrounding counties that make up Thomas Hardy's "Wessex of the novels and poems" moved more slowly than in metropolis of London or the industrial north, so that a novel such as Under The Greenwood Tree may seem to be set much earlier than it actually is. To a certain extent, the world of Hardy's peasantry is timeless, their lives determined by the natural rhythms of planting and harvest rather than by clocks and railway timetables, so that the movement of most Hardy narratives is through seasons rather than through months. Hardy's Wessex is generally pre-industrial and agricultural, its society close-knit and traditional.

Figures such as Donald Farfrae in The Mayor of Casterbridge and the Baron in The Romantic Adventures of a Milkmaid who are associated with technological progress (the seed drill and the steam yacht, respectively)and "the ache of modernity" are outsiders, marked by their clothing and speech as contrary to the traditional usages of the Wessex folk. It is not difficult, therefore, to spot these interlopers, whose arrival often bodes trouble for the story's principals--Sergeant Troy in Far From the Madding Crowd (1874) and William Dare in A Laodicean pose a threat to the security of the society, the stability of industrial employment and the traditional servant-master relationship; hence, their symbols and past-times are sordid, violent, and disruptive. What activities and symbolic objects represent Dare and mark him out as "modern"? How is Troy's sword indicative of his role as a womanizer and seducer? How are Alec D'Urberville's smoking, dressing fashionably, and racing about in a dog-cart intended to comment upon his "outlandish" (and morally out-of-bounds) nature?

Narrative Voice

If Hardy's handling of the plot mechanisms seems derived from the pot-boiler and Sensation Novel, his handling of narrative voice is highly sophisticated in diction, allusion, syntax, and tone, largely as a result of his modelling his narrative voice on that of the mid-Victorian Sage, George Eliot. A modern reader unused to the lengthy, carefully subordinated sentence that is the hallmark of Hardy's prose style may encounter some difficulty in comprehending the overall effect and meaning of the sentence.

For example, the opening sentence of Far From the Madding Crowd requires that the reader distinguish the principal clauses from the subordinate elements in order to focus on the subject and the narrative intention (the revelation of Farmer Oak's character): "When Farmer Oak smiled, the corners of his mouth spread till they were within an unimportant distance of his ears, his eyes were reduced to mere chinks, and divergent wrinkles appeared round them, extending upon his countenance like the rays in a rudimentary sketch of the rising sun." Wisely, editor Stephen has formatted this complex sentence as a paragraph by itself. After the initial subordinate clause, the sentence rushes by, the principal clause being a mere six words (the corners...spread),the remainder being the consequent effects of that smile. The closing of the sentence, actually a simple simile ("like the rays...sun"), identifies the force and vigour of Farmer Oak's genial nature with that of the morning sun, the source of the cornland's strength and fecundity. The tone behind the sentence suggests satire rather than straight exposition, an impression that the remainder of his physical description reinforces, for as a farmer he is unfortable and awakward in his Sunday best. The narrative voice is, in fact, working two ways at once, mildly satirizing Gabriel Oak inn his best clothes and yet praising him as "a young man of sound judgment" on "working" days.

To the urban Victorian reader, the sort of person who purchased The Cornhill Magazine month by month, such a protagonist would have been a conundrum, for he is not clearly middle-class, andcertainly not professional. Gabriel is a rustic, often a figure of fun on the London stage, but he is also the single character with whom Hardy wishes us to identify ourselves now and throughout the novel. Despite the complexities of the syntax, the narrator through direct analysis leaves us with an impression of congeniality, physical strength, massive size, diligence, and developing intellect. On the other hand, instead of presenting the heroine, Bathsheba Everdene, directly, Hardy has others (Gabriel and the toll-booth operator) comment upon her and has the reader judge her from her actions and from others' responses to her. Thus, the narrator does not commit himself to unqualified approval of the heroine. Even though the undoubtedly amused, tolerant masculine narrator enjoys her beauty and vigour, he does not entirely approve of her willful nature.

Q Comparing Imagery in Conrad and Hardy

Or

Q. Discuss the Tartarean Imagery in The Return of Native by Thomas Hardy.

Writing shortly after the death of Joseph Conrad, Richard Aldington credited the impressionistic novelist with both a "brooding poetic fire" and "powers of evocation" greater than those of another senior British novelist, Thomas Hardy. Aldington's casual dismissal of Hardy as merely a regional novelist (recording characters and customs fast becoming extinct, but unable to tell a good story) seems somewhat surprising from a late twentieth-century perspective. However, since Conrad began to publish fiction at the very time that Hardy ceased, Aldington was doubtless responding to the biases of his own generation against the tastes of the previous generation. Aldington finds Hardy's chief defect to be his style, which he pronounces "never particularly beautiful and... sometimes almost clumsy". In contrast, he feels that Conrad's prose is of a higher quality-'wondrous' and 'mysterious'-because of its power to make the reader visualise the scene described. In other words, he evaluates Conrad's imagery as being of a higher denotative as well as a higher connotative quality than Hardy's.

While Aldington's essay may be categorized as something between an appreciation or eulogy for Conrad and a depreciation of Hardy, Aldington's method is largely anecdotal; he makes little rational justification for what amounts to a purely personal preference. In contrast, in the next decade Richard Gordon Lillard addressed himself to the question of "Irony in Hardy and Conrad" more analytically, concluding that "Hardy's irony is more objective, more systematic, more dramatic, Conrad's more introspective, more reflective, more psychological." Lillard observes that Hardy works from a formal, logical, almost architectonic plan, Conrad from feeling and connotation. Put another way, Hardy was by nature a story-teller and observer of human nature; "Conrad's vision," as Arthur Kay remarks, "was instinctively symbolic."

In their applications of the techniques of symbolism and imagery Hardy and Conrad are likewise different. Hardy enriches his descriptions and narrative commentary with allusions to great deeds, thoughts, and persons, to music, art, philosophy, and mythology to create a sense of the eternal lurking behind the aspirations and passions of his Wessex characters, whose significance as individuals Time works to diminish. Conrad's method is quite different, more recognizably Romantic and less Classical than Hardy's. For the most part, Conrad couples the general symbol with a straightforward simile: his symbolic patterns draw their energy from the very nature of things, from the ancient elements of earth, air, fire, and water, from darkness and light and all the colours in between, from the great chain of being itself, connecting the lowliest beast and tormented devil to the noblest man and the enigmatic creator of all. Whereas Hardy is overt in his use of images and symbols, Conrad in his speaks what Shakespeare terms "a kind Of excellent dumb discourse." In his novels, Hardy attempts to state a meaning through his symbols; in his novels, Conrad is content to imply rather than define. Hardy's symbolism is neither so elemental nor so readily apprehensible as Conrad's; often Hardy's symbols are oblique, shrouded in garments which only informed readers may see through, a legacy in narrative technique that Hardy received from his reading the works of the erudite George Eliot.

Like Conrad, Hardy attempts to produce impressions through an orchestrated pattern of allusions, similes, metaphors, and images, investing certain characters, objects, and elements with powers not inherently their own. A case in point is the Tartarean imagery of The Return of the Native (1878) and The Nigger of the 'Narcissus' (1897).

Whereas Hardy builds his symbols upon associations with Egdon Heath, its inhabitants, and vegetation, Conrad works with connotations from the sea, its ships, and its men. Hardy confines his stage to the Heath, which, like the Rainbarrow that approximates its centre, is a accretion of generations of humanity, animals, and plants, age piled upon age....all things merge in one another--good into evil, generosity into justice, religion into politics, the year into the ages, the world into the universe. With this in view the evolution of species seems but a minute and obvious process in the same movement.

In Hardy's terms, the action of the first five books of The Return of the Native occurs not in a year and a day, but in a fraction of the time that humanity has inhabited the planet. As Dale Kramer remarks, Hardy dwells upon the "contrast between the profound permanence of Egdon Heath and the transitory importance of its human inhabitants [, and thus] points to an analogous correlation between nature's and man's notions of time." Like his persona of the Heath, Hardy views human actions in a continuum, so that future and past are connected immediately in the present.

The Hardyan paradox that what is past and dead still impinges upon the present and the living is well illustrated by his poem "The Moth Signal," in which the lovers' passions are doomed to the brief existence of the insect that in the novel Wildeve employs to signal Eustacia. While Hardy's characters egocentrically believe that their emotions are important and that their works will endure, they themselves are as easily "burnt and broken" as the moth in the poem. The grinning Ancient Briton, serving a chorus and commentator from one side of the stage foregrounded with the business of the living, applies a second narrative perspective as he points out that the human condition is immutable, that people love "In these days as in mine!". In the novel the moth signal must be appreciated in the context of the fire imagery, which, as John Paterson notes in "The 'Poetics' of 'The Return of the Native'," is "by inference Promethean." For Paterson the novel's furtive lovers, Eustacia and Wildeve, are "Consumed in the flames of their own passion and in effect by their own aggressive humanity", drawn by their overweening desires and a fatal attraction analogous to the that of a moth for a flame.

The fires that illuminate the darkened form of the "Titanic" Egdon Heath at the opening of the novel are at first associated with the life force, the "Festival fires to Thor and Woden" that demonstrate humanity's eternal rebellion against the dark. At the opening of the story the heath-dwellers light bonfires which "are rather the lineal descendants from the jumbled Druidical rites and Saxon ceremonies than the invention of popular feeling about Gunpowder Plot". Egdon joins with the menacing darkness to become representative of "the eternal natural forces which control the destiny of man" and the standard by which the reader is to judge the struggles, desires, and passions of both the individual and the human species: though different in temperament and life-span, the Heath and humanity are alike in their changeless natures. Where once Celts constructed a burial pyre for a chief, now Grandfer Cantle and his cronies dance around a blaze of furze. The dead are trampled under foot; their monuments and works, the Rainbarrow and the Roman via, are neither venerated nor understood. Man is as unknowing, as insentient as nature. The barrow is "but as a wart on [the Heath's] Atlantean brow", and a human being is as of little consequence relative to the whole universe. As the Romans conquered and subdued the ancient Britons, so too does the Heath overwhelm their puny works; where once, as Hardy remarks in the lyric "The Roman Road," "Helmed legionaries" marched, a mother and her child now walk, oblivious to the road's origins and significance. The Heath becomes, then, both change agent and symbol, the sum total of decay and rebirth, of past, present, and future, affecting humanity but apparently unaffected by it.

The Nigger of the 'Narcissus' demonstrates how differently Conrad uses symbolism from Thomas Hardy. Conrad constructs his symbols not on this tension of past and present, but on that of binary opposites such as day and night, life and death, dream and reality. His symbol is the poetic equivalent of a Hegelian concept: thesis plus antithesis equals synthesis. In this early Conrad novel visible reality is a juxtaposition of opposites-the crew, for example, contains both Singleton, devoted to his craft, and Donkin the shirker. Oxymoron abounds:

"Life seemed an indestructible thing.... It was bright like the twisted flare of lightning, and more full of surprises than the dark night," and "the sky [was] like a triumphal arch of eternal light, thrown over the dark pathway of the earth". In both the instances cited Conrad utilizes the light-dark dichotomy to suggest that all experience is a fusion of diametrically-opposed opposites: "white, symbolizing the pure abstract virtue and ideality, and black, symbol of material reality and evil."

While time in Hardy moves forward through seasonal cycles and human epochs, Conrad redefines time as a stream whose currents wash images up on the shores of human consciousness. As no two people perceive the world in the same way, so in Conrad no two persons' conceptions of time's passing can be identical. What is and what seems to be exist in the same proportion as the visible and unseen parts of an iceberg....man's participation in Ideality may be far more "real" to him than his participation in the material world; and so the [Conrad] novel works extensively with the paradox that the real is unreal and dead, whereas the unreal is alone real and alive.

Such an apprehension of material reality as unreality is a reflection of the fundamental pessimism of the latter part of the nineteenth century. This Arnoldian frame of mind, which Conrad and Hardy share, is apparent in their choice of symbols, and in the relationships they establish between these symbols and their characters. Acccording to Paterson's Making of "The Return of the Native", Hardy "persistently identifie[s]" Egdon Heath "with the Tartarean underworld of the ancients" to reinforce Eustacia's conception of the Heath: "Egdon was her Hades". Whereas the female protagonist in Hardy's novel has arrived in Hell prior to the story's opening, in Conrad's novel the 'Narcissus' is a vessel bound thither.

Through an accumulation of images Conrad renders the voyage from Bombay to London as a Dantesque, Virgillian, or Homeric descent. As they complete their initial muster in Bombay harbour the crew are confronted by James Wait, emerging from the darkness beyond the ship; gradually for his fellows he becomes "a symbol, not of death but of fear of death" to which each member of the crew must reconcile himself. James Wait is significant only insofar as he influences his fellows and they perceive him. "He is merely as Conrad put it, the centre of the psychology and action". In this voyage of inner exploration the elements through which the 'Narcissus' passes reflect the conflicting emotions and ephemeral moods of the crew: "As with the sea, so with the universe; and so with ourselves". Conrad's crew constitute a "minute world", a microcosm of humanity that carries within itself visions of hell and heaven, visions that are ever-present in each man's mind and therefore more real to him than the ship's physical destination. Thus, Conrad renders the experience of the crew of the 'Narcissus' Tartarean through a series of images that play upon the reader's subconscious rather than, in the manner of

Hardy, through specific, 'learned' allusions. As in Lord Jim and Heart of Darkness, Conrad here imparts a nebulous glow to elements of his setting and his characters in order to develop his symbolic patterns. Conversely, through clearly-defined similes and metaphors Hardy works from the outset to endow the inanimate Heath with superhuman attributes, breathing poetic life into "its Titantic form" through classical allusions and images. It is intended from the first to remind the reader of that region where in Virgil's Aeneid "the breed of Titans, who / Were hirled down by Jove's lightning writhe" because they refused to acknowledge Jupiter's supremacy over the universe. Hardy associates the Heath with the classical underworld as a whole rather than with any particular set of occupants.

It is "the home of strange phantoms" where with "Promethean rebelliousness" the denizens, "fettered gods of earth", light bonfires to dispel the anarchic gloom of night. Both Homer and Virgil mention the suffering in the outer darkness of the Titan Tityos, and the earlier poet Hesiod recounts how a vengeful Zeus punished Prometheus for having stolen fire to comfort his creatures, shivering humanity. Although Hesiod places the chained Titan on a rock upon Mt. Caucasus, his Prometheus suffers the same torture as that which Zeus imposed upon Tityos.

Since later Greek poets tended to confuse the rebellious giants with the warring Titans, the same figure is likely the subject of all three poets from classical antiquity: "He lay more than nine measures long / And two vultures, perched on both sides, rent at his liver / Plunging into the caul." The giant's perpetual torment is analogous to Eustacia's on Egdon, the liver being held to be (appropriately enough) the source of sexual and reproductive energies. In that Prometheus has come to represent a pagan Christ, suffering in order to redeem feckless humanity, Eustacia's sufferings are hardly Promethean since they are the direct consequence of her egocentricity. However, in his image of the heath-dwellers as shackled Titans at the opening of the novel Hardy is attempting to demonstrate the futility of humanity's age-old struggle against the natural, environmental forces arrayed against it. The denizens of the heath are the product of ages of natural selection: like their ancestors, they have survived on the heath because they have adapted to it rather than, as is Eustacia's case, struggled against it. Consequently, her suffering is not totally unmerited since, by refusing to adjust her ambitions and desires to her environment, she wilfully brings her suffering upon herself. "Like Oedipus," as Charles E. May observes, "Eustacia meets the destiny she unknowingly created in the very process of trying to escape that destiny."

Like Oedipus' father Laius in his attempt to cheat the Delphic Oracle and the divine ordinances, Eustacia's vying with circumstance in an attempt to escape it leads ironically to her destruction. However, since it is her character and not unknown deities who shape her fate, Eustacia is responsible for her own downfall in a way that Sophocles' Oedipus is not: through her determination not to adapt to life on the heath through her willing herself to be unhappy and unfulfilled on Egdon, she suffers, schemes, rebels against social norms, and drowns.

Chapter 10

Critical Essays

INTRODUCTION TO THOMAS HARDY-NOVELIST OR POET?

Thomas Hardy: Novelist or Poet?, a title which Bill Morgan has quite justly termed "unfortunate," is nonetheless a fascinating book. It is at once rich and thin, expert and amateurish, informed and ignorant. Privately printed in Philadelphia in 1929, the book is clearly a labor of love: large format, hard covers with cloth spine and glassine wrapper, 19 pages of text and 23 pages of reproductions of Hardy's letters. Although its author at one point refers to it as an "essay," it is something more--and less.

The author was not a critic, but a bibliophile, A Edward Newton of Philadelphia. He owned an electrical business in Philadelphia, but spent most of his adult life collecting first editions, manuscripts, and ephemera. Newton built a huge library of 10,000 volumes, called "Oak Knoll"; after his death in 1940, "his famous 'Oak Knoll' library in Pennsylvania was auctioned and for that purpose an elaborate catalogue of three volumes was printed."One of his possessions, as he describes in the text, was the manuscript of Far From the Madding Crowd.

Newton was more than a collector, however. He was the founder of the Trollope Society and the president of the Johnson Society--positions which explain references to both of these authors in his book. In 1935-36 he was the Rosenback Lecture Fellow in bibliography at the University of Pennsylvania. Finally, he published several books on book collecting, and was a frequent contributor to The Atlantic Monthly.

For all his bibliographical experience, Newton does not seem endowed with a particularly sophisticated literary palate. Reading Thomas Hardy--Novelist or Poet?, one is struck by his tastes. He was clearly put off by Hardy's tragic muse. Tess barely makes his list of Hardy's top five novels; on some days Two on a Tower beats out The Mayor for number six; and of Jude, "personally I dislike it exceedingly." Indeed, Newton's eponymous question becomes no question at all when he remarks, "Now the bald fact is that gloom and pessimism, relieved only here and there by flashes of sardonic humour, is not the stuff out of which the finest poetry is made."

Given all his reservations, it is fair to ask why Newton admires Hardy as much as he clearly does. Some of the attraction is probably related to Hardy's stature as "the grand old man" of English letters in the first quarter of the twentieth century. Anyone with any pretension to catholic biblophilia would have to make much of the chronicler of Wessex. Another reason may lie in Newton's affection for Trollope and his explicit comparison to Wessex and Barsetshire. Both Hardy and Trollope "peopled [an 'imaginary county'] with characters which are as real to [their] readers... as any people of their acquaintance." Certainly this is a logical connection. Hardy corresponded with Trollope, asking advice on matters of the writer's business, and Michael Millgate suggests that he may have modeled his use of the Wessex locale on Trollope's series.

Bibliography

Alden, H.M., Review of *The Mayor of Casterbridge*, in *Harper's New Monthly Magazine*, November 1886, pp. 961–62.

Guerard, Albert J., *Thomas Hardy: The Novels and Stories*, Harvard University Press, 1949.

Seymour-Smith, Martin, Introduction, in *The Mayor of Casterbridge*, Penguin Books, 1978, p. 21.

Bloom, Harold, ed. *Modern Critical Interpretations: Thomas Hardy's* The Mayor of Casterbridge. New York: Chelsea House Publishers, 1988.

Casagrande, Peter J. *Unity in Hardy's Novels: Repetitive Symmetries*. Lawrence: University Press of Kansas, 1982.

Daleski, H.M. *Thomas Hardy and the Paradoxes of Love*. Columbia: University of Missouri Press, 1997.

Edwards, Duane D. "*The Mayor of Casterbridge* as Aeschylean Tragedy," *Studies in the Novel*. 4 (1972): 608–618.

Guerard, Albert J. *Thomas Hardy: The Novels and Stories*. Cambridge, Massachusetts: Harvard University Press, 1949.

Howe, Irving. *Thomas Hardy*. New York: Macmillan Publishing Co., 1966.

Kramer, Dale. "Character and the Cycle of Change in *The Mayor of Casterbridge*," in *Tennessee Studies in Literature*, vol. 16 (Knoxville: University of Tennessee Press, 1971). 111–120.

Lerner, Laurence. *Thomas Hardy's The Mayor of Casterbridge: Tragedy or Social History*. London: Sussex University Press, 1975.

Mickelson, Anne Z. *Thomas Hardy's Women and Men: The Defeat of Nature*. Metuchen, New Jersey: Scarecrow, 1976.